WITHIN THE IVORY TOWER

RL Smith

Best Wishes
Reck
2024

For all the faculty, staff, and administrators of colleges and universities everywhere who make an academic career so interesting and enriching.

CONTENTS

WITHIN THE IVORY TOWER

The Ivory Tower:

A state of privileged seclusion
from the facts and practicalities
of the real world.

(Oxford Languages)

An impractical often escapist
attitude marked by aloof lack of
concern with or interest in practical
matters or urgent problems.

(Miriam-Webster)

CAST OF CHARACTERS

The Department of Economics

Prof. Robert Hill (Bob): A tenured full professor of economics currently serving as Department Chair.

Prof. Lawrence Faquhir (Larry): A tenured full professor of economics interested in political economy.

Prof. Rearden Koopman: A very senior tenured full professor of economics who is near retirement.

Prof. Mark Nikolaidis: A highly technical tenured full professor of economics.

Prof. Daniel Edwards (Dan): A tenured professor of economics, educated in the U.K, and a macroeconomics champion.

Prof. James Noach (Jamie): A tenured professor economics. An Israeli who is a microeconomics champion.

Prof. Kristina Novikova (Krista): A tenured professor of finance and a champion of the finance and accounting areas.

Prof. Nicole Stewart (Niki): A tenured professor of economics.

Prof. Nadir Kaur: A tenured associate professor of accounting.

Prof. Cory Sarks: A contentious full professor of economics.

Prof. Kyle Phillips: An assistant professor of economics being considered for tenure this year, male and Black.

Prof. Sean Lopez: An assistant professor of finance being considered for tenure this year, male and Caucasian.

Prof. Lin Chang: An assistant professor of accounting being considered for tenure this year, female and Asian.

Prof. Trevor Butler (TB): A recently hired assistant professor of economics.

Prof. Abby Rhodes: A recently hired assistant professor of economics.

Other Faculty

Prof. Jennifer Morris (Jen): A professor of mathematics, spouse of Joseph Gardner.

Prof. Joseph Gardner (Joey): A professor of physics, spouse of Jennifer Morris.

Prof. Andres Collings: A young professor of sociology.

Prof. Patricia Paulson: A professor of philosophy.

Professors Barron, Granville, Fabre, and Gordon: economics faculty prospects.

Professor Tullock: A member of the campus Academic Personnel Committee

The Administration

Thomas Hansen: A full professor of chemistry, hired four years ago as President of Baird.

Jacqueline Hansen (Jacqui): Spouse of President Hansen.

David Gomez: Vice President for Operations, a male.

Heather Martin: Vice President for Finance, CFO, ELT member.

David Knight (Dave): Vice President for Admission, ELT member.

John Cook: Director of Career Counseling.

Jonathan Richardson (Jack): Vice President for Advancement, ELT member.

Gloria Moreno: University General Counsel.

James May (Jim): Provost, a professor of chemistry, hired by Hansen, ELT member.

Bronwyn Warren: Dean of Students.

Others

George Jennings: An alum of the Economics Department, who has had a successful professional career as an oil wildcatter and donor to the School.

Sarah Hill: Daughter of Robert Hill.

Rebecca Prescott (Becca): Economics Ph.D. student.

Trevor Alexander: Chair of the Board of Trustees.

PART 1

***

Fall Term

***

PROLOGUE

Thomas Hansen shrugged into his academic regalia and surveyed his six-foot, three-inch frame, the three-day stubble beard over his richly tanned complexion and his distinctive salt-and-pepper hair in the mirror. Hansen was experiencing a sense of optimism that he'd rarely felt in recent months and that he knew would soon be forced aside by the daily onslaught of the demands and challenges of his position. The beginning of a new school year, it seemed to him, in a view that was not universally shared, was always an exciting time at Baird University. Ceremonial occasions like the one that day were a large part of what had drawn him from the ranks of the faculty into campus administration. Sure, the speeches would be largely ceremonial and mostly trite. His own would be much like the one he'd given last year and the year before. But, of course, this year's entering students wouldn't know the difference.

Strutting across campus toward his destination, regalia open and flowing in the morning breeze, President Hansen's thoughts centered on the day ahead. Most of the first-year students had arrived on campus at the beginning of the week. Now, having finished their trips to Walmart in search of the homey items that might help their students personalize their dorm rooms and lay claim to as much territory as possible, most of the parents -- at the urging of their teenage children, to be sure -- had departed. Most of the kitschy decorations parents had imposed on their offspring, would go untouched under dorm room beds or in closets, to be transported, at the end of the academic year, to the nearest dumpster.

Reflecting, as he strode through the main quad, on his own academic career as a professor of chemistry, Hansen knew that faculty members would have returned from their summer homes, conference travels, or vacations, and were probably consumed with catching up with colleagues, preparing for fall classes, and discovering what new "mischief" his administration had been able to accomplish during the summer - the only time during which the faculty were distracted and so as not to be effective contributors to the so-called shared governance of the University. Staff members, after a quiet summer, would, he suspected, be busy dealing with the petty complaints from certain prima-donna, but equally male, faculty members -- those who seldom deigned to acknowledge staff members unless they needed something -- those who thought themselves to be too important to take personal responsibility for such things as preparing materials for distribution to their classes, refilling the Keurig water tank, or upending a new bottle onto the water dispenser.

Just as at the start of every academic year during his short tenure at Baird University, the campus was in magnificent form -- at least it appeared to be. President Hansen took pride in the monolithic buildings he could see across the quad. As he'd explained many times, to, perhaps, hundreds of parents, these buildings were constructed in the mid-1800s of two shades of argillite stone that had been quarried from nearby formations. The path he followed today, and that he followed most days, sloped down from the town's main street and passed through the large and well-manicured campus green before beginning a gentle uphill slope. From his vantage, Baird presented a cathedral-like homage to the lofty pursuit of knowledge. As he had ordered, the grounds keeping staff had freshly planted many areas in the lawn, along the walks, and surrounding the with late-season flowers that were in full bloom. The pine, elm, and maple trees that were scattered throughout the green promised a spectacular fall. In discordant contrast to the pastoral setting, the lawn that spread before him was alive with students -- the first-years seeking out new friends, and the others renewing their acquaintances and romances after a summer of separation.

When he was on campus, President Hansen spent most of his time in the iconic buildings on the quad. These buildings housed mainly administrative functions... Admission of course, to put on the best possible face for prospective students and their families; Advancement, for alums and prospective donors; and the offices of the President and the Provost. The campus chapel, usually deserted -- except during campus tours offered to prospective students -- was also on the quad, its carillon proclaiming the passing hours throughout the day... a somewhat ominous reminder of the passage of time.... Another hour has passed. Did you accomplish anything?

Spreading beyond the quad, in the places where students would spend most of their time, Hansen was well aware that the architecture became more modern... more utilitarian. Since the 1930s, new construction at Baird had been "value-engineered" based on the evolving standards of the times. Asbestos was used, beginning in the 1940s, to improve the effectiveness of insulation, so that an open feel could be maintained, with pleasing views from office and classroom windows. In the 1960s, dual-pane windows had improved to the point where they were consistently being used in campus construction. By the 1980s, moving to the newer buildings that were farther from the quad, asbestos had been phased out and campus architects had turned to designs with fewer and smaller windows, white walls, and white roofs, all to reduce the impact of sun exposure. Along with this latest step in the architectural progression came the perception that by limiting outside distractions, windowless classrooms might be more conducive to learning, and being window-free also complemented the increasing use of technology in the classroom. If nothing more, Hansen reflected, this claim was, at least, an effective way to silence those who wished for more impressive... and more expensive... edifices. Except for the dorms, the newest construction on campus looked more like a modern industrial park. In an effort to counterbalance, Baird had modestly increased expenditures on landscaping and public art.

The campus physical plant spread over two low hills, separated by a small stream that was dry, except after rains. On the larger of the two were the academic buildings. On the smaller were the dormitories. In the valley between and to the south, were the athletic facilities, including the main sports fields. Beyond those, the stream that bisected the campus emptied into a creek that flowed year-round and defined the southern boundary of the campus. In the distance, as he passed from the quad, Hansen sought to distract himself from the utilitarian structures and surveyed the surrounding forested hills. Today, on the last day of orientation week, the convocation that would formally kick off the academic year was to take place on the soccer field.

Turning in that direction, the President ambled on. Unnoticed, at some point in his stroll through the quad, he'd stepped in a fresh dog dropping, left behind, no doubt, by the office companion of one of the faculty members who had joined the recent trend of bringing their dogs to work.

CHAPTER 1

CONVOCATION

As President Hansen neared the soccer field the walkway grew more congested with students, a few parents, and occasionally a faculty member, who, like he, was dressed in academic regalia, in some cases over denims and tennis shoes, or, sometimes among more senior faculty, sandals with white socks. Except for an occasional nod or wave, the faculty members took no special notice of Hansen. Parents and students took no notice at all.

Hansen, like members of the faculty, was navigating toward the south end of the field, where they and a few trustees would cluster to begin their formal procession to a makeshift dais that the athletics field grounds maintenance crew had erected at the north end. Once the group had properly assembled and prepared for their procession, Hansen could hear, in the distance, the glowering whine of bagpipes. For dramatic effect the bagpiper would make his way from a hundred or so yards farther south, through the flocked press of faculty, and then would lead the procession past the students and their parents to ascend the dais.

Keeping with Baird tradition, the bagpiper was playing *Scotland the Brave,* though someone long ago had altered the lyrics to ones more suitable for a small university whose mascot was a Highlander. President Hansen recognized that the origin of the school song, and of the Highlander mascot, was an allusion to the Scottish origin of the School's name. Baird, he knew, in addition to being the name of an important early donor whose bronze sculpture was still a focal point on the quad, was Gaelic for poet, which struck Hansen as an appropriate name for a university that had originated as a liberal arts college.

Personally, the President found the bagpipes to be depressing and pondered why the School seemed incapable of finding a more upbeat way to celebrate the new academic year. The School song, when played on bagpipes, reminded him of *Amazing Grace*, and called to mind a funeral. After hearing a bagpipe march, it took him days to get *Amazing Grace* out of his head.

As the bagpipe neared the soccer field and the wail grew more insistent, President Hansen could now see that it was being played by a history professor who had been at the University for much longer than he had. The bagpiper, Hansen knew, was a product of the University of Edinburgh and was purported to be an excellent teacher of Western European History. Supported by research grants in his early career, he had published enough to gain tenure. His interests, no longer grant supported, had become narrowly focused on the Jacobean era. He had developed his competency on the bagpipes to complement his research and teaching, and so that he could perform for his classes and at important campus events.

Today, the professor/piper led a procession, resembling a mostly stern-faced parade of high priests on their way to an altar, of about 80 faculty members. Each was dressed in the ceremonial academic regalia of the university from which they had earned their degree, and with hoods reflecting their terminal degrees. Most gowns were black, with velvet trim and deeply draping hoods in a variety of colors. Among the procession were a smattering of gowns in red, orange, light blue, and a few other colors. President Hansen felt that he stood out distinctively in his MIT regalia of gray with crimson velvet trim.

Along with several regalia-clad trustees, the University

Provost, the Dean of Students, and the Chair of the Faculty, President Hansen took his place on the platform. As the faculty filed in behind, Hansen noted with consternation that, as usual, more than half had decided their time was too valuable to attend the convocation. Apparently, the free breakfast that had been offered to faculty prior to the convocation was not enough of an inducement to boost their participation.

Standing before the group that had assembled on the dais, among the rows of seats on the turf, were roughly 850 first-year students. In bleachers to the left and right, were a sprinkling of parents and friends – parents who, notwithstanding the urgings of their progeny, were unready to relinquish the illusion of control. Over recent years, it was apparent to some of the longer-term faculty members that the numbers of parents who remained for the convocation had been on the rise, part of the continuing trend among parents, Hansen supposed, to try to manage their children's education from end to end and beyond.

As master of ceremony for the event, the elected Faculty Chair stepped to the lectern and invited the audience to take their seats. After a stodgy welcome to the students, their families, and friends, he introduced the President, the Provost, the Trustees, and the Dean of Students and invited President Hansen to the lectern.

Seconds before, the Chair of the Board of Trustees had nodded with a half-smirk toward the pungent mess on the President's left shoe. As he was being introduced, Hansen, with little success, was attempting to discretely scrape the sides of his shoe. Shaking off the distraction, he stepped to the podium. "Welcome Highlanders!" he cheered. "At the risk of sounding a bit trite, let me be among the first to congratulate each of you on your decision to attend this distinguished university.... I mean this with all sincerity.... Having chosen Baird University, you are among a very distinguished group. Over the years, our graduates have gone on to become doctors, lawyers, members of Congress, entrepreneurs, and corporate CEOs. Some have even gone on to pursue Ph.Ds. and have, themselves, become professors. Baird students have been educated by a world-renowned faculty that includes Nobel Laureates in the sciences, winners of distinguished literary awards, and recipients of important science grants. They are scholars working at the frontiers of academic research in the sciences and humanities. As you enter this exciting new stage of your life, on the path to becoming a well-educated adult, these are the faculty members who will help you learn to think critically… to write clearly… to speak with conviction in public forums… and to appreciate the fine arts. When you graduate, four years from now, you will carry the imprimatur of Baird University and will be prepared to make your mark on the world. You have made an excellent choice!"

This was largely the opening speech Hansen had made at each convocation since joining Baird four years ago as its President. In none of those years did he bother to point out the uncomfortable reality that most of the aforementioned awards had been achieved decades ago, and that, since then, recognitions of the School's faculty had been in decline in virtually all areas. Nor did he mention that the School's record of placing its graduates also had a disturbing negative trend. The new students would figure this out for themselves soon enough.

"In addition to educating the mind," he continued, "here at Baird University we are committed to nurturing the heart. We believe education must reinforce the importance of values including respect of others of all races and their different points of view, fairness, and personal responsibility. We seek to educate students to become lifetime learners and the best human beings possible."

"What hyperbolic nonsense," thought President Hansen as he spoke. He was well aware that the Baird reality was far from this aspiration. There was wide disagreement among the faculty and among some students as to what "being the best human beings" might mean. He knew that the curriculum of the University no longer provided a balanced exposure to diverse points of view and that there were concerted efforts by some, even among the faculty, to shut down expression of viewpoints with which they did not agree. He knew that many members of the faculty equated "fairness" with something like egalitarianism, whereas a few others, especially in economics, viewed "fairness" as equality of opportunity. Like other universities, Baird had drifted away from the notion of the university as a forum for exploring and seeking to understand diverse points of view. Even in the economics department, there was pressure to accentuate perceived negative aspects of markets and competition and to look to government for solutions to social problems. While Hansen himself ascribed generally to this position, he did wonder, to himself but not publicly, if Baird, like many other universities, was going too far in this direction. As with many other things at the University, he felt almost powerless to affect the drift.

Not being inclined to making long speeches, President Hansen continued for a few more minutes on the reimagined history and traditions of Baird.

"Now let me conclude by encouraging each of you to always challenge yourself. Try things you may not have considered before, take intellectual risks that may cause you to question your beliefs, past actions, and future directions. Above all, strive to keep an open mind. Let me leave you with this final thought, a thought that comes from a fortune cookie I once received. It read, simply, "If you want more, make yourself worth more." Not bad words to be guided by, I think." Unnoticed by him, this last remark led some members of the faculty seated behind him to shake their heads.

"I wish you all success in your time at Baird... and beyond."

As Professor Kristina Novikova listened, for what was now the fourth time, to the President's remarks, she struggled to resist a yawn. They sounded much like the special occasion remarks of other college and university presidents she had heard. Could there be some mysterious source that university presidents all shared... like a Toastmaster's guide to banal speeches for university presidents? As to his remarks on fairness and personal responsibility, and especially to his fortune-cookie philosophy, she was aware that, even in the few short years since Hansen's arrival at Baird, both faculty and student attitudes had drifted considerably, to the point where fairness was often heard as code for egalitarianism and personal responsibility was sometimes seen as a duty to aggressively promote change. More and more students, she felt, based on the experience from her own classes, rejected the notion of personal worth as threatening.

Novikova, the senior finance professor in the Economics Department, had come to Baird nearly a decade earlier, from her tenured position at a highly-ranked state university. Her move to Baird, at some cost to her research program, had been motivated by a desire for more exposure to diverse ways of thinking than she could find in a large department of finance in a public university. Like some of the other faculty members in attendance, Professor Novikova believed that, particularly at a private university, it was important for faculty members to be seen by students and their families at such events as convocations and commencements. So she always sought to do her part. But, for how many more years, she wondered, would Hansen be able to get away with his challenge to students to make themselves worth more?

After concluding his prepared remarks, President

Hansen continued, "Now, let me introduce Bronwyn Warren, your Dean of Students, who will tell you about some of the opportunities you'll have while you're here.... Dean Warren...."

***

Though feeling obligated to make an appearance, Professor Novikova felt no duty to listen to the rest of the program. Powering up her iPhone, she began to skim circumspectly through some of the blog posts to which she subscribed.

***

After also welcoming the new batch of students, and explaining her role, the Dean of Students turned to a few specifics.

"Let me expand on President Hansen's admonition that you seek to challenge yourself during your time here.... We, at Baird, expect that you will soon discover that some classes and co-curricular activities may touch on subjects or matters that could make you uncomfortable or angry. To help you meet such challenges, a couple of years ago we established a number of safe spaces for those of particular races, religions, or gender identities. Anytime you feel uncomfortable... or just want to get away for awhile, you can go to these rendezvous points to meet and interact with others who share your ethnicity, beliefs, or values. We don't want to interfere with useful discourse, but we don't believe discourse requires discomfort."

"This is a great time to be joining the Baird family," she continued. "We recognize that a proper education is not possible without a healthy body and that, along with their intellectual growth, our students need opportunities to work on their physical well-being. As one factor contributing to both your intellectual growth and physical well-being, we are delighted that this year we've been able to place all first-year students in our new, architectural-award-winning dormitories. These dorm rooms, you will find, are designed and engineered for your academic success. The dorms will enable students to study more effectively, and each dorm includes space for small group working meetings, a coffee bar and snack room, an exercise room, and a laundry facility."

As the Dean of Students spoke these words, President Hansen reflected on the many other priorities that had needed to be postponed or foregone so that Baird could keep up with competitive pressures for amenities that were being driven by better funded schools.

"To promote your physical well-being, I hope you will also take advantage of our new student fitness center and our many sports facilities, including baseball, basketball, tennis, pickleball, soccer, swimming, and more. We support a number of intermural sports and clubs. I encourage you to take advantage of them."

"Finally, I want to mention our international travel program. We've designed a number of our courses around tours of countries throughout the world. Because we believe international experiences are important to the understanding of diverse cultures, we want to make sure that these courses are accessible to all students. To accomplish this, the university covers the full cost of participation. We provide for the international travel cost, pay for lodging and meals, and cover all of the in-country incidentals. I sincerely hope that each of you will participate in at least one of these courses during your time at Baird."

As the Dean of Students talked through the long list of non-curricular and travel related opportunities, President Hansen, still working surreptitiously on his shoe, resisted telegraphing the anxiety he was feeling. The dorms and the other facilities, the clubs and activities, and the international travel program were all expensive and severely strained the School's resources. But he was sitting on a platform next to trustees who had supported and often promoted these initiatives and he knew that showing his anxiety could negatively impact their support for others he had in mind. He had argued to the more fiscally attuned trustees that the facilities and programs were essential for attracting the best students, and that the investments would pay off over time through enrollments of full-pay students and future donations. He hoped he was right, or at least would not be found to be wrong for a few more years.

A few of the faculty members on the dais were listening Dean Warren and looking over the audience. Others, like Novikova, were busily attending to their mobile phones, or were reading journal articles they'd brought along, concealed under their regalia during the processional. A few who were seated in the back row of the platform discovered that with a bit of maneuvering, they could slide under the curtain at the back and exit the stadium, presumably unnoticed.

Reardon Koopman, a very senior Professor from Economics, was one of those seated in the back row. Unlike some of the others, he felt it was his duty to attend and fully support these kinds of ceremonial events. In his more than 40 years at Baird, he had never missed a convocation. As had been typical in the more recent past, except for Novikova, Koopman was the only member of the Department faculty in attendance. This time, he found himself sitting next to a young female faculty member whom he did not recognize. As they'd taken their seats, she had turned to him and introduced herself simply as "Jade from Dance." He stammered out his own name and department in response.

***

"I could go on to mention the many other opportunities you will have as a Baird student," continued Dean Warren, "but I'm sure you'll discover them soon enough on your own. One more thing... please don't forget to study a bit now and then," she smiled stiffly and attempted a wink.

"Now let me yield the floor to the Chair of the Faculty, who will introduce our keynote speaker."

The Faculty Chair stepped up to the rostrum and, glancing at a notecard, began nervously and without preamble, "Each year, the faculty of Baird University votes to select one of their own to speak at the opening convocation. You can be sure that the person they select is an outstanding speaker with an important message. This year, the faculty have selected Professor Patricia Paulson. Doctor Paulson is a Distinguished Professor of Philosophy. She holds the Raelian Chair in Philosophy. I look forward to hearing what she has to say."

"Please join me in welcoming Professor Paulson."

To scattered applause, the convocation speaker came to the lectern…

***

As Professor Koopman settled in to hear the address, he noticed that somehow Jade had managed to produce a banana, which she cradled, left handed, in her lap, apex toward the podium and stem curving upward toward her abdomen. As the keynote speaker launched into her talk, Jade began to slowly glide her right thumb along an inside seam of the banana peel, running gently from the apex toward her waist. Slowly, she repeated this stroking motion, gradually increasing pressure until her thumbnail began to part the seam near the apex. Koopman, who had never seen a banana handled in this way, could not resist an occasional furtive glance. As Jade continued, the seam slowly parted wider, revealing an occasional whitish glimpse of banana flesh. Under Jade's continued motion, the peel continued to spread, and eventually the tip of the banana began to emerge. When she had competed this task, Jade turned to Koopman. "I noticed you watching. Would you care for a bite?" Koopman, blushing furiously, could only shake his head and turned away.

Around the same time as the peeling ritual came to an end, the speaker concluded her talk. What she had said had been abstruse, and had left many in the audience confused and struggling to understand her unexpected message.

After a polite but spotty round of applause for the speaker and a few final remarks, the Faculty Chair concluded the convocation, those on the dais exited to a bagpiped recessional after which the crowd began, unceremoniously, to disperse.

CHAPTER 2

THE EXECUTIVE LEADERSHIP TEAM (ELT)

The Convocation concluded at 11AM. At 3PM on the same day, President Hansen met with the four other members of the group he referred to as his "Executive Leadership Team."

The Provost, of course, was on the team, and was responsible for all academic programs. Except for the President, he was the only academic member of an even broader group of administrators that included a few other senior staff members. The Provost would fill in for the President whenever necessary. The Vice President for Admission, another member of the ELT, was a professional who had held his position for many years and was responsible for student recruitment as well as for undergraduate admission decisions. Graduate admission decisions were made by the faculty of the academic program to which the candidate was seeking admission. The Vice President for Finance was the University's Chief Financial Officer. She was a CPA who had been hired by a previous President. Her main responsibilities were to manage the annual budget and try to keep spending in line with available funds. She also supervised investment of the School endowment, but core investment decisions were made by the Investment Committee of the Board of Trustees. So, in that context, she mainly reported to and facilitated the work of that Committee. The Vice President for Advancement was responsible for gifts and donations and for alumni relations.

Although the team had met informally during the summer, several members, including the President and the Provost, had busy travel schedules. Accordingly, summer meetings were on an as-needed basis by conference call or Zoom, usually with single-item agendas in response to the latest calamity. Today's meeting was the first opportunity in several months for the full five-member ELT to meet in person. The main purpose of the meeting was to share perspectives on last year's somewhat worse-than-anticipated financial performance. President Hansen had not been looking forward to the discussion, but he knew it was necessary, since the discussion could affect decisions that would need to be made and actions that would need to be taken in the coming year. "Might as well put it behind us," he thought to himself.

The meeting took place in the walnut-paneled office of the President's residence, a University-owned facility adjacent to the campus. The floor of hand-scraped hickory was covered by an antique Kashan rug with red as the dominant color. A traditional walnut desk stood in front of one large window with a view that overlooked the campus. Across the room, near a window facing out to the President's garden, stood a conference table of highly polished reclaimed wood. Arrayed around the table were a half-dozen Herman Miller Aeron chairs. An Eames lounge chair facing the fireplace completed the room.

Against this authoritative background, to set a light tone for the meeting, the President had opened the office wet bar. Maybe a bit of alcohol would help relax everyone and soften the discussion, he thought. A couple of the team members, the Provost and the head of Advancement, had helped themselves to glasses of wine. The head of Admission and the President poured scotch or bourbon. Anticipating the need for a clear head, Heather Martin, the CFO, opted for bottled water. A few minutes of casual conversation ensued as the group members chatted and gazed out the windows.

"What the hell was that about?" asked David Knight, the VP for Admission, referring to the keynote speech they all had heard.

"Yeah, David," VP for Advancement, Jack Richardson, boomed, in a voice he had cultivated to command attention. "That has to have been the weirdest effing keynote I've ever heard.... All that talk about civilization having been launched on earth... by aliens claiming to be angels.... Probably scared the you-know-what out of the parents who were still hanging around," Richardson continued, his double scotch gripped in a hand that rested on the protruding belly he'd developed from too many lavish meals with prospective alumni donors. "Not so good for our fundraising either."

"I couldn't follow too much of it," conceded Provost Jim May. Still seeking to find a way to support the choice of Professor Paulson as keynote speaker, he somewhat defensively pressed ahead. "But I thought that maybe there were some good points... like the charge to students that they need to strive for world peace, sharing, and nonviolence." At 5 feet, 3 inches, even with lifts, May was known to throw out his chest and clench his fists in something like a fighting stance when challenged, and was doing so during this exchange.

"Yeah, right," Richardson smirked. "And while they're at it, maybe they can do something about global warming," he quipped.

"Well," began CFO Heather Martin, ignoring Richardson's diversion, "it didn't seem to me that the remarks about sex-positive feminism had much place in a keynote address aimed at students who'd just graduated from high school."

Hansen, feeling the need to offer a more positive spin, sought to defend the choice. "You all recall that a few years ago we decided we could save some money on events like the Convocation by featuring our own faculty instead of bringing in expensive marquee speakers. When we set this up, to get faculty buy-in, we had decided to leave the specific choice to the faculty. I know that this year there were few faculty members interested in providing the keynote. Professor Paulson was kind enough to agree to do it. I recognize that her talk was a bit confusing, so to speak, but maybe it helps to recognize that she holds the Raelian Chair in Philosophy. I don't understand it very well, but I think some of the ideas we heard today may have had underpinnings of Raelianism."

"Hold on a second.... It sounds like Raelianism is sort of a cult... like Scientology. How did we ever end up with such a chair?" asked Martin, her eyes focused, accusatively, on Richardson. "To me, it seems more like a religious cult than a branch of philosophy."

Deflecting from the challenge to Richardson, Hansen chose to respond, "Well, the short answer, Heather, is that we had a significant donor who insisted on it.... But let's not get into that now. We have a lot to cover before dinner, so I'd like to get started on our agenda."

After the five were seated around the conference table, speaking like the academic that he was, the President began, "As, I think you all know, we ran a bit over our budget last year. Much as I'd prefer not to start the year off on a negative tone, I think it's important for all of us to be brought up to speed on some of the details.... We'll need to figure out whether last year was an aberration... or if we should make some adjustments going forward. Beyond that, I have no specific program for today. Since we all have some catching up to do, I'd like for us to, maybe, take turns letting the team know what was important to you from last year, and also giving us a heads-up of any concerns you may have that could bear on the year ahead."

"I suppose maybe I should take the lead on this," Heather Martin smiled tensely, not looking forward to the blowback she was expecting, "since I think our financial condition is something each of us needs to take into account." As the University's CFO, on budgetary matters, Heather often found herself at loggerheads with the President or with certain Trustees, who seemed always eager to spend beyond the budget. Her no-nonsense posture demanded, in her view, a muted wardrobe of solid colors, black, navy, or gray, an all-business hairstyle, and minimal makeup. Today, she wore a tailored medium gray suit with slacks and color-coordinated low heels. She kept her hair in a mid-length bob, parted on the left. She shunned hair dyes, sanctioning the sprinkling of gray in her predominantly chestnut hair.

"Excellent, Heather, please do proceed." Despite his posturing words of encouragement, Hansen was not actually looking forward to hearing anything his CFO had to say. He fully expected that Martin's comments would be pessimistic and obstructive of his vision.... They almost always were. Moreover, though he was comfortable with the math of chemistry, he was truly uncomfortable with budgetary math. Too many numbers, too many ridiculous accounting rules, too much hand waiving and reliance on assumptions, and, more importantly, her "bad news" views were limiting his own ability to pursue the things he hoped to accomplish during his tenure. "But, Heather, this has been a nice sunny and upbeat day so far, so please try not to cast a gloom cloud over it." Hansen chided as he grimaced at the triteness of his own metaphor.

Steeling herself, Martin pushed back, "Well, I'm sorry to be the bearer of bad news, but, as they say, please don't shoot the messenger." Hansen grimaced imperceptibly again at Martin's equally trite retort. "Let me try to be as upbeat as I can... but still objective," she began. "When all the numbers were in from last year, we turned out to be more than just 'a bit over budget'." The others around the table, especially Hansen, postured with mock surprise.

"Is that what you think of as 'upbeat', Heather?" the Provost quipped.

As CFO, Heather was used to being in a contrary position to the others. And she had grown used to the obvious animus the President and the Provost held for her and for anything related to budget. Martin had previously joked with a close friend in the economics department that she always brought her purse and laptop to meetings with the President since she never knew if she'd be fired. But that was not going to keep her from giving an accurate and honest assessment. Dismissing the Provost and locking eyes with the President, she continued, "As you noted, Tom, we were aware last spring that we were going to run modestly over our operating budget. So that's not news. Unfortunately, however, the overrun turned out to be more than we thought might happen... and there were some other matters, as well. All things considered, we ended up overspending our endowment by about three percent... which, I believe, is still manageable.... So... I guess that's the upbeat part...."

Hearing that the shortfall was only three percent, the others in the group relaxed. The shortfall was trivial, they thought, and easily made up.

Richardson scoffed, "Only fucking three percent," he exclaimed. "I was expecting something serious.... Maybe we should just move on to something else."

Heather bristled at the attempted intimidation and responded with aggressive decorum, "I understand, Jack, that your focus is on fundraising. But it seems to me that you don't know jack about fiscal management.... Let me try to explain for the benefit of the others."

Recovering from a momentary near loss of self-control, she continued, "I think you all know... or all but you, Jack, apparently..." she joked tensely, trying to make light of the prior exchange, "that we try to operate mainly from tuition, grant support, and planned endowment spending. I want to focus on how the endowment feeds into our budgeting. I'll try to be brief."

"It's important for us all to recognize that Baird's endowment is comprised mainly of gifts from benefactors that the School has developed over many years," she continued, "and on the investment returns on those gifts.... We use part of the investment return to fund our operations and we reinvest the rest to grow the endowment. Generally, schools in our peer group allocate about five percent of their endowment each year to financial aid and current expenses."

"TMI, Heather, we do all know this, after all... even Jack..." Provost May interrupted, evoking perturbation from Martin and a smug nod from Richardson.

Except for the news about a bit of overspending, this was all old news to the team, mused May. He wondered why Martin troubled to review it. "Can't you just skip over the numbers and speed this along...? With due respect, Heather, I think I agree with Jack.... A three-percent shortfall seems trivial and not worth taking much of our time on." Like the President, the Provost was a Professor of Chemistry, a discipline that seemed to account for a disproportionate percentage of university administrators, perhaps because academic salaries in Chemistry were among the lowest, so that moving into administration was financially compelling, even if not intellectually so.

To avoid conflicts with existing faculty who might also have aspired to the position, May was hired as Provost through a national search and came from a liberal arts undergraduate background. In a transparently unsuccessful effort to hide the weight he had gained in his administrative role, May generally over-dressed. He usually wore sports jackets that varied in style from casual to more formal. The jacket *de jour* was a double-stitched, tightly woven black wool that he felt contrasted nicely with his silvering hair, but had to acknowledge, was straining the lower button to the point where his white shirt was protruding below.

"The idea," continued Martin, glaring at the Provost and not altering the pace of her presentation, "is that we try to keep endowment spending low enough so that the endowment will grow over time to keep up with inflation. Historically, if we spent about five percent of the endowment each year, we could accomplish that, and generally we did stay within the five percent limit. But, this past year, we spent over eight percent.... That's a big deal, I think.... Now, it's true, of course, that while we try not to spend more than five percent, we do have some flexibility since the university endowment is also designed to provide a year-to-year buffer."

"Obviously, Heather, I get it... that we ran over a bit," the Provost interrupted, shaking his head, "but, really... three percent overspending! That seems trivial... and you just told us that the endowment can operate as a buffer, smoothing out good and bad years. So it still seems to me that this just is not a big deal."

"Well... thanks so much for your perspective, Jim. I realize that a three percent shortfall may not seem like much to you and some of the others," reacted Martin unassumingly, as she tried to explain. "But because of past overspending, our endowment is smaller than it would have been with normal spending. The overspending last year is going to make it harder to close the gap this year... and the shortfall is more worrisome because we also had a large operating shortfall the year before. I think, Jim, that we're all going to have to recognize that these shortfalls seem to be symptomatic of a fundamental problem. I really do think we need to find a way to operate with the resources we have.... And," glancing quickly at Hansen, "that includes more disciplined adherence to our endowment spending target."

"Well, I don't know if I agree with you, Heather," countered May, recognizing that he might have over-argued his position but being unwilling to abandon it. "I'm sure we could operate for quite a few years with shortfalls of this magnitude, so it seems to me that we have plenty of time to adjust... if we even need to.... Can we just move along now?"

Hansen, annoyed by Martin's last remark, was pleased to see his Provost acting as a good lieutenant and pushing back against pressure to rein in spending, even if ineffectively doing so. Martin was tough, and he much preferred to have May trying to fight on her turf than to do so himself. There were too many important things that he was planning to do before his tenure as President was up, and, for that, he needed to keep May on point and Martin in line. Moreover, he expected some similar arguments from a few members of the Board of Trustees, even without prodding from Martin. Certain members could become irate when the School did not operate within its budget, even if the budget was unrealistic and there were good reasons for overspending. It was good to see that May would be making some of his arguments for him and taking some of the flack.

"I'm afraid the problem might be upon us sooner than you think," Martin pushed back against the Provost's latest remark, "especially if we lose our competitiveness. I'm actually quite concerned that we may be nearing a tipping point after which things could get much worse very rapidly.... Let me explain."

"If you can do so quickly, Heather," Hansen responded, hoping for a speedy end to the budget discussion.

Martin went on to compare the Baird endowment to those of some selected set top schools and those that the ELT group considered to be peers. She pointed out that the top colleges and universities had much higher endowment dollars per student than did Baird. "If they wanted to," she pointed out, "these top schools could fully fund student tuition from endowment and students could attend for free."

"With due respect," May commented, sarcastically, having spotted a new vulnerability. "I think you're being an alarmist... and I don't really see the point of spending any of our time today discussing schools that are not at our level."

"Come on, Jim," Martin rejoined, feeling a bit thrown off stride by the continuing challenges, "of course we don't compete head on with Harvard, Yale, or Princeton, but those schools are trendsetters. Eventually, whatever they do to make themselves more attractive to prospective students puts pressure on us... and on everyone else like us... to increase spending in an effort not to fall too far behind. After all, isn't that why we built the new dorms and the athletic center, neither of which we could really afford...? So, let me continue... if you can just be patient for a few minutes."

In a comparison to peer liberal arts colleges, Martin explained that while Baird was trying to compete on rankings, it was doing so with a much lower level of endowment dollars per student, only about two-third of what the peers were reported to have.

"I suppose I'm with Jim, Heather," hazarded David Knight, who did not normally engage in quarrelsome discussions. "Doesn't most of our operating revenue come from tuition, fees, and grants?" As VP for Admissions, Knight often met with parents of prospective students and he felt it was important to dress in his image of how an ivy league professor should look, meaning, in his mind, a brown tweed jacket. Today's choice even included chocolate suede elbow patches. Knight, who had directed Admissions for a number of years, took great pride in always being able to meet or exceed admission/enrollment targets.

"Yes, of course it does, David," fumed Martin, as she turned to face the VP for Admissions, "but maybe my point still isn't coming across. Let me try to spell it out more clearly for you... and the others.... With normal spending, our endowment would throw off spendable funds equal to about 20% of gross tuition. That's gross tuition, not net tuition... so about $10 thousand per student. Yet our student aid expenditures, as you, in particular, must know, David... since this *is* your area... are around $25 thousand per student.... That's almost half of gross tuition. And, of course, most of that aid comes from tuition discounting, not from some imaginary pot of money we have stashed away somewhere. What's troubling to me is that we now are discounting tuition to a greater extent than are our peer schools. Along with the outlays for new facilities, tuition discounting is a large part of what caused us to overspend from the endowment last year. In simple terms, on average we lose money on every student we admit."

"With our actual rate of spending from the endowment being so high last year, we're falling behind our peers at the exact time when we need to be catching up.... I'm very concerned.... If we don't turn this around, our rankings could fall, and if that happens our applications will probably decline and the need to use tuition discounts to attract students will probably increase. If our reputation declines, I think it'll also be harder to attract good faculty, harder to secure national research grants, and harder to borrow money for new capital projects.... In short, I think our enterprise is much more fragile than you might guess. So the overspending problem is not just a short-run aberration. It's much more serious than the smallness of the percentage might suggest."

"That's an interesting story," muttered the Provost as he sought to stifle a yawn, "but even if we accept your story in full, isn't the solution obvious? We just need to bring in more gifts from donors. If we spend three percent more than we budget, that's no big deal if you ask me. Don't we just need to grow the endowment three percent faster through gifts? All we need is for our donors to do a bit more."

"Not so fast, Jim," interjected the VP for Advancement.

He did not want to see the group's focus shift to his area of responsibility. Jonathan Richardson had been recently promoted from his position as Assistant VP for Alumni Relations. The promotion occurred shortly after the resignation of the previous VP for Advancement. The President and the Trustees had become disenchanted with the chronic failure of the previous VP to meet the giving targets the Board had established, targets the previous VP had argued were unrealistic to begin with. When he saw that his termination was inevitable, the former head of Advancement had accepted a new position at a nearby school. The Baird Administration countered by promoting Richardson, the only member of the Advancement staff they perceived to be worth keeping, and now the youngest and fittest member of the ELT. Comporting with his role, he believed, it was important that he always dress formally in a suit and tie.

"I know I'm new to the role of VP for Advancement," Richardson sought to shield himself from attack, "but I've worked in advancement for more than a decade. Based on that experience, I can tell you that it's a bit dangerous to rely on trying to offset spending with an aspirational increase in gifts.... Now, I haven't been in this job long enough to know exactly how our giving history relates to our endowment size, but I do know that, overall, for private schools, it's pretty much like Heather says. New gifts add only about two percent per year to endowment. With three percent overspending, just maintaining our competitive position would take new gifts totaling about five percent of the endowment.... That's huge! It's more than double the normal level of giving to universities. So, bottom line... I don't think we can rely on more giving. We need to look at what we can do on the cost side or find ways to reduce financial aid and increase grant funding."

"That's a good point, Jon," interposed Hansen, who could see that the Provost was preparing to dispute it, since the point about grant funding hit close to home. As

President, Hansen spent much of his time on fundraising and was not optimistic about making up for overspending with increased gifts. He, like Richardson, was not happy to have the discussion focus on efforts to increase gifts. At the same time, he'd grown tired of Martin's budget negativity and felt he would need to do something about it soon, before she became too vocal with others or tried to speak directly to members of the Board. For now, he'd just try to tone down the rhetoric. "Heather, I guess you should tell us a bit more about what was behind what you are calling overspending?"

"Well, I don't know all of the details, but I can give you an overview," Martin responded more calmly after the confrontation with May. "In total, we overspent our operating budget by about $14 million last year. I understand, partly from speaking with Dave Gomez, that several factors contributed to the operating shortfall."

The others around the table were dreading the esoteric and jargon-filled monologue they suspected was about to follow. But none saw a way out. Martin launched into a long explanation, describing operating performance in terms of what she called an "efficiency ratio," and how expenses exceeded revenues by about $14 million. She pointed out that the level of spending per student was in line with peer schools but above budget. Heather conceded that she did not know the specific reasons expenses had run over budget and indicated that Gomez, the School's VP for Operations, should have some details and that perhaps Jim May could provide some insight about the higher-than-budgeted faculty salaries.

At that point, May, who was sensitive about the criticism of overspending on academic programs and faculty, was no longer willing to make eye contact with Heather. He refrained from responding and turned his attention to the gardeners who were working outside, on the President's flower garden.

"Now, in addition to our expenses being over budget," Martin continued, "our net revenues were below what we had projected." She looked pointedly at Knight. "Those two, together... low revenues and high expenses... are what resulted in an operating shortfall."

"Going to the next level, I think it's clear that the two main causes of the revenue shortfall were the tuition discounting, which we've already discussed, and low grant income. It appears that, in an effort to maintain our target student population at about 4000, we ended up providing more financial aid that we'd planned. We had budgeted $20 thousand per student in institutional aid, what I've been referring to as tuition discounting. That works out to about 45 percent of gross tuition. We actually ended up with discounting closer to 48 percent. That probably sounds small but it's actually a very large percentage increase when you consider that it's mainly driven by the roughly one-fourth of students who are starting here this year.... So, the net tuition from first-year students was more like 36 percent of gross tuition. That's way below the targeted 55 percent. So, you see my point? Because of that discounting, instead of $88 million in net tuition revenue, we netted only about $83 million. Maybe David can help us to understand the reasons for such a big increase in tuition discounting."

Knight, who had been slumping in his chair, trying to read email on an iPhone he was holding below the table, straightened and tried to recall the gist of Martin's latest remarks. Given his success at meeting enrollment targets, he was unused to being under scrutiny. Hoping to deflect, he responded somewhat sarcastically, "So, $5 million out of $14... is that it, Heather...? Way too many numbers for me to follow. But at least it's good to hear that what you're calling the tuition shortfall was much less than half of the total shortfall," he said sarcastically.

"Yes, that's true," responded Martin, who had not picked

up on Knight's sarcasm. "Revenue from government grants was the other important contributor to the decline in net revenue. Our grant revenue was about $2 million lower than the $33 million we'd projected. Here, again, maybe Jim can give some perspective."

"Not at this time," May deflected, still looking out at the gardeners. "Grant revenues are under increasing pressure nationally due to government funding cuts. Perhaps..." He shrugged but left the conclusion unstated.

Knight, having successfully avoided a more fulsome discussion of overspending on financial aid, returned attention to his email.

"In any case," Martin continued, picking up her thread, "we had to fund the operating shortfall by drawing down our endowment more than we'd planned."

"Now maybe an operating deficit of $14 million doesn't sound like much, given the size of our endowment and our annual budget of about $200 million, but remember that we also had a shortfall the year before.... So, is this just an unusual period...?" she asked, rhetorically, and paused for emphasis, "Or is the shortfall part of a fundamental shift in the economics of private universities at our level...? I suspect it may be some of both, and that's worrisome to me."

At this point, the President's office phone rang on the line from his administrative assistant. Hansen took the call and learned from her that there was an urgent matter that his AA felt he should be aware of, "in case any parents call or anything serious happens." She indicated she was forwarding a message that had just been mass-emailed to the entire campus.

After disconnecting the call, Hansen spoke to the assembled group. "I'm sorry to interrupt you, Heather, but something's come up. Why don't we take a brief comfort break? Feel free to refresh your drinks or grab a coffee from the

Nespresso, and we'll resume in ten minutes or so."

He then walked over to his desktop computer and opened an email message from the Office of Emergency Preparedness with "Campus Bee Alert" in the subject line. He read,

Dear Baird Community,

This afternoon, the Bee Wranglers have been on site to remove a large beehive from an oak tree near the Humanities Building. The hive, which was discovered this morning, was collected from a branch of a nearly 40-foot high tree. The bees (including the queen) will be relocated to a nearby forest.

To protect our community from the aftereffects of the hive removal, we are closing the outdoor seating area near the Humanities Building and will be re-routing traffic on the sidewalks in that general area for the next week. Please avoid the seating area except to pass through to the building. You may notice ongoing bee activity in the area, with bees crawling on the ground and/or flying in the area.

If you notice any increased activity, please contact Cheryl Mase, Emergency Preparedness and Safety Manager immediately at X11911 or cmase@baird.edu. Outside of normal business hours (8 a.m. - 4:30 p.m.) contact Campus Safety at X74000 to report hazardous bee activity. The Student Health Center is also available as a resource if a student is stung and needs medical attention. Additionally, report any bee stings to your supervisor, faculty, or the Dean of Students office to complete an accident/incident/injury report.

Thank you for your cooperation.

Cheryl Mase

SAFETY ABOVE ALL!!

Emergency Preparedness & Safety Manager

The President could not help but laugh at the overzealousness of some members of the campus staff. He spoke briefly with his AA and rolled his eyes at something he heard, after which he called the group back to the table. "False alarm," he said, "I suppose some of you have already found an email message on your iPhones from the Office of Emergency Preparedness, since apparently the message went to virtually everyone with a baird.edu email address, including alums, retired faculty and staff... and, unfortunately, the Trustees. It seems that over the summer a bee swarm moved onto campus and established a hive near the Wilson Humanities Building. Apparently, someone in Emergency Preparedness felt that the risk of getting a bee sting was high enough to warn everyone and close down part of the campus for a week."

"But that's not quite the end of it," continued the President. "It turns out that one of our entomology professors who studies pollinators was upset by our relocating the hive. He's organizing a group of students to protest the hive removal. I suppose, if that's the worst thing that happens this week, we'll be off to a good start."

Over scattered smiles and soft laughter, he refocused the group. "Unfortunately, I think I should talk to the professor before things get too out of hand. So let's see if we can get quickly to a good stopping point. That will leave me a few minutes to get in touch with him before our spouses begin to arrive for dinner. We'll have to continue the meeting at another time to cover the rest of our business."

Martin found no humor in the occurrence and somewhat resented the interruption of her review for something so pointless, as well as over the pressure to get through her remaining remarks quickly. "Let me try to get back on track.... I'll be brief. I was just concluding that last year we ran over our operating budget by $14 million and I'd explained why this happened and why it's a cause for concern. Now let me turn back to the endowment, where we have some additional problems."

"There were a couple of things that affected the endowment directly. One was cost overruns associated with constructing the new dorms. That also had to come out of endowment. Here, again, maybe David Gomez has some perspective, so we can follow up with him. The other was that we had an unplanned expenditure for campus beautification. That happened because one of our Trustees..., whom I will not name, reached out to the key donor on the dorm project and convinced him to redirect $1 million of his gift to a large fountain and sculpture garden instead of more basic landscaping that would mostly still be needed to complete the project. So, that was roughly another $1 million in cost overruns. Putting it all together, we ran a deficit this year of about $18 million – about three percent of the endowment."

"Well, that's a good, albeit painful, summary. You've given us much to think about, Heather," said Hansen, who had lost track of the numbers after the first mention of a $14 million shortfall. "I suppose this is why the ideal donor is a dead one... in my experience, it's harder for them to change their minds...."

After some polite laughter, Hansen concluded. "Ok," he summarized. "We're close to our five o'clock ending time. It was helpful to have this recap.... I'm sorry we ran out of time to hear more directly from the rest of you. Based on today's discussion, I'll be meeting separately with a few other senior staff members, and we can schedule another meeting of our group in the next few weeks. In preparation for that meeting, I'd ask that each of you give some thought to steps we can take to help close the projected budget gap for this year. Also, in the meantime, I'll be meeting with the Chair of the Board of Trustees to brief him on our discussion today."

"How about the four of you adjourn to the patio bar while I finish up about the bees. I understand that some of our spouses have already arrived and that others are on their way. Dinner will start at around six. The meal of lobster tails and filet mignon is being catered by Chez Gourmet. So it should be good." Whereupon the group members stood and, eager to get their minds off the tensions some of the remarks in the meeting had surfaced, headed for the bar.

All except Heather Martin, who was disturbed that the President seemed unable to comprehend the gravity of the budget situation. How could he, in the face of these problems, host a catered profligate dinner of steak and lobster? Why did university presidents so often seem to see themselves as removed from campus budgetary considerations? Perhaps a good Pinot Noir would help her to see things in a better light, she thought as she headed for the open bar.

***

While Hansen's AA was greeting spouses at the door, his wife, Jacqueline, in her role as hostess, was busily steering people toward the bar and doing what she could to encourage cordial conversation among the ELT members, some of whom were still simmering over having been singled out during parts of the meeting. She was doing what she could to bring spouses into the conversations and make them comfortable in the business-like environment, something she'd come to learn was not easy with some of the more stand-offish of them. Maybe after a glass or two of wine, she mused, they would relax a bit.

Among the scattered conversations, no one, she noticed without surprise, was speaking with Heather Martin, who, with drink in hand, was typing into her iPhone and gazing at the flower garden. Heather seemed to be anxiously waiting for her husband to arrive.

Martin was actually reflecting on the meeting. She was disappointed, but not surprised, that she had been unable to gain more support for her concern about the School's financial condition. But, as usual, it seemed that the others were so much more concerned about their own areas of responsibility and deflecting potential criticism that they seemed not to be able to coordinate a plan of action to address overspending.

"How was your summer, Heather?" Jacqueline asked. "Did you find time to do anything interesting?"

"Well," Martin began, shifting gears in response to the patronizing overture and shutting down her iPhone and storing it in her slacks pocket, "you know, actually I was fairly well tied up dealing with the School finances, so there wasn't much time.... I did go to a nearby conference for university CFOs. The venue was nice, but you probably can imagine what it's like being in a room full of accountants.... Oh, I see my husband has just arrived. I had better go and introduce him around," she deflected, as she went over to join her husband, feeling grateful for the opportunity to escape from the likely condescending follow-up.

As was often the case, the spouses of the ELT members had little in common with each other. Some were working professionals, others chose to stay at home, some were young with children, others childless, and others well past child-rearing. While she waited for her own husband to conclude the phone call, he had told her he needed to make, Jacqueline struggled to engage everyone in conversation.

As the wine began to lighten the mood, she did notice that the conversations seemed to grow more animated. At long last, she heard the President's prominent laugh punctuating the chatter and felt she could relax a bit. Dinner could now be served.

Once the group of twelve, including the President's AA and her partner, were seated, three on a side, around a large square table that had been placed on the patio for the occasion, over salads Hansen steered the conversation to the common denominators of small-talk that could engage people who had little in common... catching up on families, and tiresome tales of summer vacations. As the entree was served, meeting with expressions of pleasant surprise at the surf and turf combination, Knight prompted, "Can you tell us how your conversation about the bee problem went?"

"I can," exclaimed Hansen, as he saw the opportunity to regale the spouses with a story. "Let me start with a bit of background," he began, "for the benefit of those who were not in our earlier meeting..." Whereupon he recounted the summertime arrival of the bee population to the campus, the over-the-top message from Campus Safety, and the, also over-the-top, reaction of the entomology professor and the impending student protests.

"I was hoping to calm the professor down about his plan to launch a student protest," he continued.

"Why on earth would anyone protest getting rid of a beehive?" blurted Richardson's wife, who, based on an early childhood memory, had a deep-seated fear of being stung, and who, before dinner, may have taken a bit too full advantage of the open bar.

Ignoring the interruption, the President continued, "Sorry to say that my effort to bring calm seems not to have been successful. Our professor of pollinators apparently has already organized a group of students from his classes, and they're busy printing up placards with statements like 'Bees have rights, too' and 'Bee Reprieve, Humans Leave.' Apparently, they're planning to stage a sit-in and not to attend classes. They may even disrupt a few others. As you might expect of someone who studies bees," Hansen laughed artificially, "the professor has apparently riled them up by telling them that hive relocation is a contributor to hive death. He claims hive relocation can confuse the bees, that many of the relocated bees will die as a result, and that even the queen is at risk. Apparently, there's some academic research that supports his view, but other research doesn't. So... I don't know...." He shrugged, having found no constructive way to conclude the sentence.

"But what I do know is that we can't leave an active beehive in an area with heavy student traffic," he restarted. "I just wish Campus Safety would have taken care of the problem without publicizing it to the entire school community. I suppose we'll just have to wait and see what happens with the protest. Maybe it won't catch on and will end quickly."

"I wonder how much we had to spend to relocate the hive, when we could have done something simpler and less expensive," mused Martin, who was waving an imaginary aerosol can of bug spray as she spoke.

As the dinner progressed, the conversation moved to other topics, but systematically avoided the difficult issues and tensions that had surfaced during the earlier meeting.

Over digestives, the ELT members compared calendars and settled on a date and time for their next meeting.

CHAPTER 3

THE DEPARTMENT

Professor Larry Faquhir arrived at the Economics Department seminar room on the third floor ten minutes early and took a seat facing away from the window. As usual, he had arrived early and in his trademark Australian safari hat, which he used tactically for advantageous seating and to claim a bit of extra territory. Faquhir, who, in point of fact, had never been to Australia, had come to Baird most recently from three years at Carnegie Mellon, preceded by four at the University of Iowa. He had a longer history of staying at a school for only a few years before becoming disenchanted when colleagues or administrators failed to see the full merits of his various points of view. He typically dealt with his disenchantment by changing schools.

The seminar room to which he'd arrived had the feel of a richly appointed tiger-oak-paneled study, with floor to ceiling windows overlooking the quad and with an inspiring view of the nearby mountains. While most of his colleagues sought out window-facing seats that would enable them to admire the view and watch the activity on the quad, Faquhir had heard somewhere that facing away from the window reduced fatigue in long meetings. Since he was inclined to sometimes argue positions that others might not support and to drag out debate by invoking procedural and other obstructions, Faquhir felt that facing away from the window would give him a strategic advantage in any discussion that might arise.

When he entered the room, Faquhir was surprised to find Professors Rearden Koopman and Mark Nikolaidis already seated around the table, fortunately in chairs that were facing the window. Koopman, whom other faculty members surreptitiously referred to as "the oldest member," in an unintended homage to P. D. Wodehouse, sat with his fringe of silver hair cascading over his shirt collar. Koopman was not only oldest, but also longest serving at Baird. He had joined the Economics Department faculty over 40 years before, as his first appointment after completing his Ph.D. As he waited for the department meeting to begin, Koopman was browsing through the latest issue of the *American Economic Review*, a journal in which, despite his four-plus decades of scholarship, he had never been able to publish. Koopman was the kind of academic who, like a fan at a sports event, seemed to idolize the group of scholars who published their work in the AER with some regularity, and, often incongruously, he interjected their names into conversation.

Nikolaidis, the quietest and most consistently ignored senior member of the Economics faculty was a theoretician who generally worked alone. Wearing a rumpled and coffee-stained white dress shirt, Faquhir thought he seemed to be absorbed in some mathematical machinations.

Koopman, his head oscillating like a table fan as he read through wire-framed 3x reading glasses, was again disappointed with the contents of the latest issue of the *AER*. It had been many years since he'd seen any new research that, as he proclaimed whenever given the opportunity, was as transformational as some of the contributions by the noted economists of the Chicago School in the 1980s and earlier. More recently, it seemed to Koopman that even the University of Chicago had lost its way in economics research.

Despite having found little of interest in the *AER* in recent years, Prof. Koopman was firmly committed to continuing his subscription – and to receiving it in print instead of electronically, a pseudo-medium that he disdained. Koopman had been subscribing to the *AER* since he first became a graduate student, in 1972. He was proud that he had an unbroken collection of the issues since that time. Initially, the issues filled less than a shelf in his office, but now, there were several shelves. Each was filled two-deep with past issues, and with even-more-recent issues stacked horizontally atop the older ones. After even that space had been filled, the new issues began to accumulate on his desktop and in other places scattered around the office. From time to time, Koopman vowed to empty some filing cabinets of teaching materials he had not used for decades and that were oriented around textbooks that were no longer in print. He also planned to shred the old final exams from years ago, since he was only required to save past exams for one year in case of a grading dispute – something that had never happened in his many years of teaching. Disposing of old teaching notes and exams, he felt, might free up enough space to enable him to continue to build his *AER* collection for a few more years.

When Prof. Faquhir arrived at the seminar room, Koopman acknowledged him with a perfunctory flapping of his *AER*. Nikolaidis, his unkempt brown hair in unembellished contrast to a complexion free of any evidence of exposure to sunlight, gave no indication of having noticed Faquhir's arrival and studiously continued his pencil machinations.

After surveilling the room, Faquhir selected his seat, facing away from the window. Setting aside his *AER*, Koopman turned to Faquhir. "I don't suppose you pay much attention to articles in the *Chronicle of Higher Education*, do you, Larry?"

"Not really," Faquhir responded tersely, as he scanned his iPhone for text messages and new email. "Why would I?"

"Well, lately there have been several articles and letters on the use of meritocracy in making school admissions decisions."

"Really," Faquhir shrugged. "I guess that's good news. I never expected the *Chronicle* to be promoting admission based on merit.... So that sounds like a good development, especially in the current environment."

"I suspect that I was unclear," Koopman countered, setting aside his *AER* "It's just the opposite. The articles and letters are all critical of merit-based admission."

"Well... in that case, I guess I'm not surprised after all. Kind of goes along with their general tone of opposition to competition and trying to distinguish yourself by going to a better school or taking more AP courses in high school."

"I suppose, Larry.... But do you think they have a point? They argue that our indicators of merit like test scores and grades don't actually measure merit. They measure something more like achievement, but they claim that achievement can be partly due to things they would call 'privilege,' like going to the best prep-schools, so that kids coming from wealthy families have an unfair advantage. They argue that admission based on merit is tacitly racist."

"I'm sure there are people who feel that way, and maybe they do have a point," Faquhir responded, occasionally surprised by Koopman's apparent openness to new ways of thinking. "But what should be done about it? I don't think it makes sense to ignore merit... or achievement... or whatever you want to call it." Pedantically, with postured seriousness, he continued, "I get that it might give some people an edge, but we live in a competitive world, and, as economists, we know that competition drives innovation up and cost down, things that benefit us overall. This just seems like a repackaging of the same old debate.... Is it better to have a big pie with unequal slices or a smaller one with equal slices, and maybe those slices are smaller than the smallest one from the bigger pie? Surely the *Chronicle*, or the people taking the time to write for it, wouldn't argue that faculty hiring should ignore merit, or that professional sports teams should. So why should we ignore it when we decide what students to admit? If you ask me, issues of so called privilege need to be addressed at a much earlier stage than at the time of college admission. By then, it's already too late." With that, he dismissively turned back to scanning his iPhone.

But don't you think we may just be relying on indicators of merit that are easy to come by, like a school pedigree, when a more rigorous approach would be better and less subject to criticisms based on privilege or family connections? Koopman was preparing to continue the discussion but seeing Faquhir's disinterest, he hesitated. When, he wondered, had it become so difficult to seriously discuss things that matter?

In the course of this exchange, Prof. Nikolaidis had remained oblivious. Nikolaidis was a mathematical economist who had trained in one of the top Scandinavian schools of economics. In Faquhir's view, Nikolaidis's research was uninteresting and consisted mainly of applying the same mathematical model in a variety of different economic settings. Faquhir considered most of the applications of the models to be trivial or contrived, having little or no relationship to the real world settings in which Nikolaidis and others like him sought to apply their modeling skills.

It seemed to Faquhir that Nikolaidis, like so many formal theoreticians, had little interest in trying to actually understand the economic institutions to which he applied his technique. Yet, he seemed to have no trouble placing his research in top economics journals – not the *AER*, but several papers in the *Journal of Economic Theory* and the *Quarterly Journal of Economics*, two other journals in which neither he nor Koopman had ever published. Faquhir speculated that the publication success came about because Mark Nikolaidis was a member of what was essentially a club of theoreticians who cared only that the math be correct and not at all about the importance of the application or the legitimacy of the application to any actual institution. In Faquhir's view, economists other than theoreticians were often disinterested in or intimidated by the formal modeling and would generally decline to serve as peer reviewers for such research. Faquhir felt vindicated in this view by the fact that, except for a handful of theoretical gems, formal theory papers generated very few citations. Like many academic researchers, he considered an article's citation count to usually be a reliable indicator of the importance and impact of the contribution.

Before Koopman could respond to Faquhir, their discussion of merit-based admission was pre-empted when a group of three students arrived and, speaking loudly, as if they were alone in the room, began to rearrange the furniture. Puzzled by the intrusion, and fearing the potential loss of his strategic location choice, Prof. Faquhir demanded arrogantly of the students, "Excuse us, I guess you must not have noticed that this is the Economics Department seminar room and that several of us are here for a meeting. I think your little study group needs to find a different place to chat." One of the students responded that they were the Undergraduate Social Committee and had reserved the room for the next two hours. Another passed Faquhir her iPhone, with the screen opened to an email exchange with the Dean's Administrative Assistant. The message indicating that, as they had claimed, the students had reserved the room.

"Well, it seems there must be some kind of cockup," Faquhir responded, as he returned to his chosen seat and opened his laptop, where he found the email announcing the department faculty meeting. To his dismay, he noticed for the first time that the meeting location had been changed to one of the small classrooms in the basement of the building, a room that had been deliberately constructed without windows so that students would not be distracted by outside activity and could more easily see the PowerPoint slides that had become ubiquitous in teaching. Feeling slighted by the room change, he wondered what was driving the trend toward putting student wishes above the important needs of the faculty. Moreover, why should the department chair's administrative assistant be able to make room assignment decisions without consulting the faculty?

"No worries, though," he said to the students, concealing his annoyance and trying to recover from his earlier display of attitude. "You three can stay here. We'll head off any other faculty and move to another room for this time," whereupon, he and Prof. Koopman collected their materials and departed, heading for the classroom where their meeting had been scheduled. As they moved from the department seminar room toward the elevator, they passed, paying it no attention, the sign in the hall that had been in place for years identifying the door as an entrance for "Women." Below that guiding sign, on the left, a smaller font designated the door as the entrance to the "Women's Restroom," and on the right, a sign in the same font designated the door as the entrance to the "Kitchenette."

A few steps later, finding the elevator out of service, as it had been since early summer, they took to the stairs. As they walked to the room in the basement, Koopman complained, yet again, that there was never anything worth reading in the *AER* anymore and that the policy-oriented macroeconomics articles seemed not to recognize that people no longer used money for transactions, and instead just used plastic or Venmo, so that monetary macro models were no longer reliable. Moreover, the world's economies had become so connected and crypto currencies were so often used in transactions that individual countries could no longer really manage their economies. Faquhir nodded in commiseration but with little interest since he felt that macroeconomic models had never actually worked very well anyway.

When they arrived at the classroom, they found that most of the rest of the Department faculty were already there and were seated in rows that had been arranged for a lecture-style class. Seeking a new strategic advantage, Faquhir, muttering about the impropriety of allowing students to preempt their meet in the Department seminar room, chose a seat near the front, a location from which, by turning, but not without some difficulty, he could gain eye contact with most of the others in the room. Koopman, on the other hand, planning to continue browsing through his *AER*, selected a seat near the back of the room.

While they waited for the meeting to begin, Prof. Kristina Novikova had been relating to several nearby faculty members her experience in using Zoom to deal with some issues on a shared research project with a colleague who was a faculty member at Oxford. Her story was interrupted by the entry of Professors Faquhir and Koopman.

"As I was saying," she resumed, "Sylvia and I had been working through the ways we should deal with some referee comments we'd received on our paper when my dog heard a noise outside and started barking. Well, apparently, Sylvia's dog was in the room where she was on Zoom with me and heard my dog. Then her dog started barking, too! That got my dog even more excited, and she started barking back. Neither one would stop, so after a few minutes we surrendered. Sylvia and I both put our laptops on the floor so the dogs could see each other. They carried on barking at each other over Zoom for about half an hour before they tired of it, and we were able to get back to our project."

"That's pretty funny, Krista," Prof. James Noach laughed. "Good thing your colleague is in the U.K. so that the dogs would be speaking the same language."

"Yeah, and maybe you should look into getting your dog a separate Zoom account," quipped Prof. Nadir Kaur as he reached down to stroke the head of the 15-year old Australian Shepherd that he routinely brought to faculty meetings and classes, despite the dog's propensity for farting every few minutes as well as for profound shedding.

"Excellent idea, Nadir," Novikova flashed a smile and

thumbs-up gesture as the Department Chair, Robert Hill, came to the lectern and the room quieted. Glancing at Faquhir, Hill started, "Now that we're all here, I'd like to begin by welcoming everyone back to campus. I hope each of you had a pleasant and productive summer...." Whereupon Prof. Faquhir interrupted, "Nikolaidis is still not here. He was in the seminar room a few minutes ago, when we discovered that someone apparently felt that a casual meeting of the undergraduate social committee was more important than a meeting of the Department faculty.... I think Mark may have been so absorbed in his math that he didn't hear me mention the room change. I bet he's still sitting there."

"That sounds like Mark," quipped Kaur, the most senior accounting professor in the department.

The Chair, glancing at the assistant professors, all of whom were seated near the back of the room, asked for a volunteer to go check on Nikolaidis. Trevor Butler, one of the untenured assistant professors who was still struggling to publish work from his dissertation, stood and set off to find Nikolaidis. Butler, who'd been nicknamed TB by other junior faculty members, was doing all he could to ingratiate himself to the senior faculty, hoping that in the future the faculty might overlook a weak research record and support his tenure based partly on his likability and team-player demeanor.

As he walked past her seat, Abby Rhodes smiled and mouthed, "Suck-up." Rhodes, another assistant professor hired in the same year as TB, made no similar move to respond to the Chair's ask. Rhodes, who claimed her parents had named her when they were stoned and had taken to heart the Dylan line that "Life is but a joke," had already published two papers in *Labor Economics*, including a single-authored one from her dissertation. While she would not have minded going to fetch Prof. Nikolaidis, she didn't like the implicit message of an untenured female assistant professor running errands for a predominantly male group of tenured faculty.

The Chair, turning his gaze to the assembled group, intoned, "While we wait for Mark and TB, let's rearrange the chairs into a circle so we can all more easily see and communicate with each other." Fearing the loss of what little advantage his front row seat had commanded, Faquhir objected, "Rearranging doesn't seem necessary. Can't we just stay as we are?" His remark was largely drowned out by the sounds of furniture being moved. Most of the faculty were accustomed to Faquhir's unending efforts to circumspectly manipulate and control outcomes. Aware that even his simple suggestions might be motivated by an unstated and hard-to-discern agenda with which they might not agree, most of the faculty were reflexively resistant to any of his proposals.

Shortly after the room reconfiguration was completed, Mark Nikolaidis arrived, along with TB, and they took their seats in the circle. Butler, who was still panting from his rush up the stairs to the third floor, had discovered Nikolaidis still in the seminar room, working on his math puzzle, apparently oblivious to the vocal group of students, who were occasionally glancing obliquely at him. Upon his arrival to the room in the basement, without greeting or comment, Prof. Nikolaidis turned back to his work and tuned out the group.

Hill resumed, "Now that we *really* are all present, I'd like to begin our meeting with some important news. I've been working for years to secure a major gift from George Jennings. As some of you know, Mr. Jennings is an alum of the School and got his degree in economics from this department. Jennings is from the class of 1972. After graduating, he joined his father's oil wildcatting business. I'm pleased to say that Mr. Jennings has recently agreed to make an important gift to the school – a gift that should enable us to hire two economics professors into endowed chairs. I expect that President Hansen will be working with the donor to formalize and finalize the details of the gift agreement. I'm giving you all a heads-up now so you can begin thinking about who might be appropriate candidates to recruit for the chairs. However, until we get formal notice from the President, please keep this information among yourselves. I anticipate that the details will be finalized soon and that we should be able to begin recruiting for the positions later this fall."

"Now let me see if there are any questions."

Glancing quickly around the room and clearing his voice to preempt others, Prof. Faquhir opened with the kind of disingenuous praise that was common in academics, "This is a great accomplishment for the Department, Bob. We all know you've been working on this gift for a long time. I personally would like to congratulate you on the success of your efforts.... I wonder, however, about the decision to use such a gift to hire additional faculty members."

"Uh-oh. Here we go," Rhodes texted a few of the other assistants in the meeting. "I hope no one has dinner plans." Even in her short term as a member of the Baird faculty, Rhodes had learned that Faquhir was willing to filibuster until he got his way.

"Yeah, glad I brought along some reading," TB texted back to the group.

"Last year, we hired two new junior faculty members," Faquhir continued, "both of whom seem to be doing well and I'm happy to see them here today. But, at the same time," he continued, as he sought to make eye contact with as many as possible, and especially with potential allies, "as we all know, the number of undergraduate economics majors has been declining and our class sizes are down again this year. Those of us who understand the campus budgeting formula, as, having served on the school Budgeting Committee, I do," he lectured, "are aware that the tuition and fees paid by undergraduate econ majors are used to help support our Ph.D. program, as well as our seminar talks, travel, and faculty research activities. Now, at the same time our undergraduate program is shrinking, our Ph.D. program has been growing! As a result, we've already had to cut seminars, faculty travel, and research funding. I, for example, only had travel funding sufficient to cover two conferences last year. If we keep losing undergraduate students, we'll eventually be forced to shrink the Ph.D. program. If that happens, our access to graduate teaching and research assistants will have to be cut and the research productivity of the entire Department will suffer. So, my point is that unless the gift is very large... like in the tens of millions... adding more new faculty to the Department is just going to exacerbate this problem."

"What I mean to say," he continued, needlessly reiterating, as he often did "is that it seems to me there are more important things to do with the gift than to use it for faculty hiring. So... how much is the gift, anyway?"

The Department Chair, who was non-confrontational by nature, was uncomfortable being challenged, and noticeably reddened. Based on years of experience, he suspected that Faquhir was just out for himself, either hoping for increased travel support or simply trying to score points with some of the Department faculty. In this case, Hill was sure that Faquhir was well aware that the gift could not be redirected. So, it had to be one-upmanship that was behind his comments. In an effort to diffuse, Hill responded softly but somewhat defensively, "Well... it's a very nice gift... $2 million... to be contributed to the School endowment... before the end of the current year. So, the funds will be available to support the two faculty lines before any hiring actually occurs."

Glancing around the room again, to assess support and build impact, Faquhir retorted, "But, of course $2 million of endowment won't come close to covering the cost of two faculty lines... or even one line, for that matter.

When this latest remark penetrated his consciousness,

Prof. Nikolaidis put down his pencil, sat a bit more upright, and asked the ceiling, with incredulity, "How is it possible that $2 million is not more than enough to support the hiring?" Being among the more senior members of the faculty, and, given his focus on abstruse theory, a focus that garnered him no prospects of alternative employment, either in the academy or in practice, Nikolaidis was easily the lowest paid member of the economics faculty.

Before the Chair could formulate a diplomatic response, Faquhir responded. "That's a no-brainer, Mark." Making selective eye contact around the room, he continued, "The Board of Trustees only spends five percent of the endowment each year. So, a gift to endowment of $2 million would yield only $100 thousand of spendable funds per year. Even without endowed chairs, senior faculty members... even those who don't have outstanding records... will earn at least $200 thousand in salary, or probably even more. On top of that, there are the fringe benefits and research and travel support. Moreover, since these would be named/chaired professorships, we'd seek to fill the positions with outstanding scholars, so the base salary and all of these other elements could be higher. Conservatively, depending on the focus of our hiring efforts, we might be able to do it with $300 thousand per line. If so, we'd need $600,000 per year for two endowed chairs. That means that even with the gift we'd be $500,000 short.... Where would that money come from?" Faquhir asked rhetorically. "Most likely from our travel and research budgets and our Ph.D. program."

Hill knew that Faquhir's summary was largely correct, as far as it went, and that the extra money for adding faculty lines would have to come from somewhere. However, he also knew that the University President could not turn down a $2 million gift, even with expensive strings attached. He also knew that this particular donor would back away from any proposal to re-purpose the gift. An attempt to re-purpose would put the entire gift at risk. It wasn't going to happen. He needed to find a way to divert the faculty discussion from the course of action that Faquhir was alluding to.

"Yes, of course," he responded, "You're correct, Larry, that $2 million will not cover the full cost of the positions. I've already discussed this with the President and we're confident that the additional funds can be found. We expect that adding two well-known economists to the faculty will attract more students to our undergraduate and masters programs. So the extra tuition from econ students will help. We can also bring more students to economics by expanding the accounting and finance offerings the Department offers... and the President has told me informally that, in response to shifting student demand and declining grant-based research funding, a plan is being developed to reduce faculty headcounts in philosophy, mathematics, and some of the sciences. That should free up some funds to help support our planned new hires."

A couple of faculty members in the meeting were nodding as the Chair spoke. Nikolaidis had returned to his scribbling. No one spoke in support of Faquhir's argument. Feeling that he'd lost the momentum and seeing that the rest of the faculty seemed placated by the Chair's response, Faquhir abandoned the red herring of trying to refocus the gift away from hiring and switched to a new tack, the one he actually hoped would be successful. He had learned from experience that faculty could be manipulated by his first taking a position he planned to lose and then shifting to the one he actually cared about. Since it would seem to others that he was compromising, they would be more willing to do so, as well. "In any case, if we can't redirect the gift, we should be thinking now about the kinds of new faculty members we'd like to recruit. We obviously need to stay away from hiring in expensive areas like finance and accounting and focus on areas where we need to build strength. We don't have anyone on the faculty who has expertise in public economics, and with the way the economy is changing, that's an obvious need. We also don't have anyone who works in healthcare economics. Those seem to be the two areas of our most pressing needs and would not be too expensive."

"Hold on, Bob," Krista Novikova was fuming at Faquhir's transparent attempt to hijack the hiring focus but chose to nudge deferentially in a different direction. She elected to address the Chair, seeking to dismiss the suggestion from Faquhir. "You just said that we could help pay for the new hires by expanding our finance and accounting offerings. But I don't see how we can do that without hiring in those areas. I think everyone here is aware of this."

"Don't everyone go getting your knickers in a twist," in a soft-spoken British-accented English, Prof. Daniel Edwards interjected, seeking to sound objective while pushing hiring in a direction more in his own interest. "As long as we can use lecturers, it seems there's no compelling reason to connect hiring so closely to teaching. Surely we all agree that keeping a balanced faculty is more important.... Our last two hires were in areas of microeconomics. If you ask me, it seems only proper that the next turn to hire should go to macroeconomics."

Novikova was disappointed. She had hoped for some support from Edwards, but apparently he had an agenda of his own.

"Mashugana! That's crazy, Dan." Prof. James Noach translated for himself. Noach was an outspoken member of the microeconomics group who was prone to aggressive speeches, and an occasional ally of Faquhir. "If there is anything we don't need more of it's macroeconomists. It's only fiscal policy and monetary policy. With your background from the London School, Dan, I get why you'd favor macro. But there hasn't been a noteworthy contribution to fiscal policy since Keynes, or a good contribution to monetary policy since Milton Friedman. With the world the way it is today, economists who work in macro only imagine they can affect the economy to any significant degree. It might have worked a few decades ago, but not anymore. The world's economies are too interconnected. How can the U.S. Fed think they can affect anything when all of the world's economies are so tied together? If the Fed tries to tighten the money supply in the U.S. because they think the economy is overheating, companies just fund their projects elsewhere. It doesn't stop the global overheating but does make the U.S. less attractive than other countries for business activity."

"I realize that undergraduate students gravitate toward macro," he continued. "But what do they know? I think they do so for the wrong reasons. First, they do it because macro has a reputation for being much easier to do well in than micro... which is, of course, true. Second, students equate macroeconomics with the ridiculous notion of power to control the economy. I'd rather teach smart and well-grounded students than those looking for easy A's and hoping to be able to control other people's economic choices."

"Let me try again," interposed Krista Novikova, who, after her initial comment had been quietly trying to discern the mood of the silent members of the group. "It seems to me that all of this talk about hiring focus is losing track of the strategic strengths of our Department." Novikova was the more senior of the two finance professors in the meeting and sought to bring a different perspective to a discussion dominated by economics more narrowly construed. "We are somewhat unique among economics departments in offering courses in finance and accounting. I see this as a strategic strength and an important reason that we are able to attract students into majoring in econ. Yet, we only have two finance faculty members, one in corporate finance and one in investments, and we only have two accountants, one in financial accounting and one in auditing. I think we all recognize, even you, Larry, that this is barely enough to offer the curriculum we're committed to, even with our, already heavy, reliance on lecturers to cover some classes. If we're going to be adding finance and accounting courses to help with funding our operations, it seems undeniable that we need to add finance and accounting faculty."

"That would be ridiculously expensive, Krista" countered Faquhir. "So I have to disagree.... Compared to economics, salaries in accounting and finance are 50 percent higher, or maybe even more. If we're going to grow those areas, we need to do so with lecturers and focus our tenure-track hiring on core economics. That way, we could support increased enrollments in those areas and do so in a way that would be much less expensive.... So we can all keep our travel and research budgets."

"You know that's not realistic, Larry," Novikova responded, shaking her head in postured disbelief. "So I won't even bother to go into the reasons right now."

Hill considered the entire discussion of hiring focus to be premature, and now it had gone on for much too long. It was clear to him, even before the discussion began, that there would be no consensus in the Department for any particular focus. Moreover, he knew that ultimately the Department would not be able to choose the focus. The details of the gift were still not locked down, but it was certain, as it always was with major gifts, that the donor intended to have significant influence over the hiring focus as well as the suitability of the actual candidates.

Seeking to regain control of the meeting and shut down the many side conversations that had flared up, Hill reclaimed the floor. "I think we need to table this discussion for now. I've heard your thoughts and will pass those along to President Hansen. I'm scheduled to meet with him soon to work out the final details of the gift. Part of that discussion will be on setting the parameters of the search."

"Now, we have a few other items on our agenda for today, and I'd like to turn to those."

"First, we have a request from the Academic Senate to propose a member of our department faculty to serve on an ad hoc committee on what they are calling 'virtual courses'. It would be good for us to respond, and I'm hoping for a volunteer."

"I might be willing to volunteer," responded TB. "But, I guess I'm not clear on what the committee is being asked to do. What's a virtual course?"

"Well, I don't know much more about what's driving the request," responded the Chair. "I know it came from the Academic Senate committee that's responsible for approving new courses and course changes. We all know that use of technology in the classroom has been steadily increasing. Along with this trend, there have been proposals to offer courses online instead of in classroom. We all know that we had the surge of online with COVID, but now that things are more settled, the Academic Senate wants to return to normal order. A few years ago, the Senate became concerned that use of technology, especially offering classes online, might not be in the best interest of students. It seems that for many of us, the recent emergency experience of trying to teach our classes via Zoom has borne that concern out. Now that we're more or less back to normal, the Senate had directed the committee that's responsible for course approvals to look separately at traditional and online or 'virtual' courses, even if the content is supposed to be the same."

"Are you sure the Academic Senate isn't more concerned with what would be good for existing members of the faculty than what would be good for students?" interjected Professor Edwards, rhetorically. His classes were always oversubscribed, and he was not threatened by changing instructional modalities. Unlike most others, his hastily prepared Zoom-based classes during the pandemic had gone well.

"Wait a minute," interjected Prof. Rhodes, breaching the silence that was de rigueur for untenured members of the faculty. "Are you saying that any course we want to offer has to be approved by some campus-wide committee? Does that even make sense? How would a campus-wide committee even decide whether the course was appropriate...? Oh, and how long does it take to get a course approved?"

"Well, based on my experience, it only takes a couple years," Hill responded. First, we prepare and submit a syllabus for the course and the proposed copy for the campus course catalog. That gets sent to the Registrar for a technical review – such as whether there are enough contact hours to justify the amount of credit the course would count for and whether the language in the proposed catalog copy is in a grammatical style similar to that of other courses. After the Registrar approves, the proposal goes to this course review committee of faculty from all across the campus and they review the syllabus to assess such things as whether a week-by-week schedule is included and whether the amount of reading is appropriate. Typically, a new course might go back and forth with the Registrar before approval, and then back and forth with the committee before their approval. Since the committee only meets monthly and only during the academic year, that can take most of a year. Then, after a course is approved, it still can't be offered until it's published in the catalog. Catalog publication can't happen until all of the approvals are in. So all together, most courses take a couple years from submission of the syllabus until the course can be offered."

"O... M... G..." exclaimed Prof. Novikova, "I've been here for more than eight years, and I never even knew about this crazy approval process. When I arrived, somebody gave me copies of the prior syllabi for the two finance courses I teach. Since they were not too much different from what I had done in the past, I followed those syllabi the first year, but since then, I've made a lot of changes. I don't use the same books as then and the class schedule is completely different. I've never looked at the catalog description for either course, and I change the course descriptions in my syllabi almost every year.... Was I supposed to get all of those changes approved?" Glancing as Rhodes, she nodded slightly to indicate that, as a tenured member of the faculty, she would take on this issue rather than leaving it to an assistant professor.

"Technically, yes, you were supposed to, Krista," responded the Chair, but maybe we just keep that to ourselves. Some of our courses, like the ones you teach, are very connected to what's going on in the world at the time. Contents and reading materials need to change accordingly. If we tried to have all of those changes approved through the committee, our classes would be out of date even before they were offered for the first time."

"Well, then," asked Novikova, "so what is the point of even having the committee? It sounds like whatever they review can get changed even before it's offered."

Not wanting to explicitly take a position that would be clearly contrary to Academic Senate policy, Hill equivocated, "I suppose that for some departments and some courses, the concerns with immediacy and obsolescence may not be very important. Maybe for courses like classical literature, basic mathematics, history, or introductory languages, the campus-wide review could be a useful quality control."

"I'm not so sure faculty in the humanities would agree with you about the unimportance of keeping their courses up-to-date", Novikova retorted with a disarming smile. "However, even for those, it doesn't make sense to me. Our views of such things as history and classical literature... the way Native Americans are portrayed, for example... have changed over time in ways that could affect classroom teaching. Does the committee have responsibility for assuring that the content of a course is balanced and not skewed toward any one point of view? Maybe that could be a rationale."

"No!" blurted Prof. Noach, "I know that in some disciplines our school offers courses with a clear anti-Semitic slant. Presumably those have gone through this approval process without serious resistance. I think the argument there is that requiring balance would be an affront to academic freedom. And you might be surprised to hear that I agree! As an Israeli, notwithstanding their anti-Semitic slant and my distaste for the content, I think academic freedom is essential and that even so called 'hate speech' should be tolerated. I just hope for a broader environment where opposing voices can also be heard... not like what's going on these days."

"So, then, what's the purpose of this ad hoc committee on virtual courses? I still don't get it," said Butler, who was still looking for a way to gain favor with the Department Chair.

"The course review committee apparently is uncertain as to when separate approval should be needed for a course that is not offered in a strictly traditional format," responded the Chair. "They're asking the ad hoc committee to propose a definition they can apply to decide whether separate approval of a so called 'virtual' course would be needed. So, for example, if you use PowerPoint instead of a black board or white board, would that need separate approval? Or what if you show videos in class, or record some of you lectures to be watched by students while you're away at a conference? Or what if all of your lectures are available online, or you hold office hours or discussion sessions remotely using Zoom or some other platform? The committee wants guidance on how to proceed."

"This all sounds like complete nonsense," interjected Novikova. "Are we in a Kafka novel...? We seem to have a campus-wide academic senate committee that appears to do nothing much that is useful and that is now asking for yet another committee to be formed to help it in that task.... My advice to you, TB, is to forget about this ask. Leave it to someone more senior and focus on your research. If we really need a volunteer maybe Professor Koopman would be kind enough to help us out. Since he's just coming off a sabbatical, his other service may be pretty light this year."

With no visible reaction to the jibe, Koopman continued patiently peeling an orange he had been working on during the entire discussion.

Feeling uncomfortable with the confrontation, the Chair concluded, "I'll let the Senate know that we don't think we can make a useful contribution to the proposed committee."

"OK.... My remaining items are mainly just reminders – things to keep in mind as we begin the academic year."

"Most importantly, we have three faculty members who'll be up for tenure consideration this year: Kyle Phillips in economics, Sean Lopez in finance, and Lin Chang in accounting." He nodded to each, in turn. "As you know, all tenured members of the department are eligible to vote on these tenure cases. I'll be approaching some of you to present the cases to the rest of the faculty. Pease keep in mind that, if you're serving in one of these roles, you're not supposed to advocate for the candidate. Rather, you should endeavor to present the arguments both for and against tenure."

"Second, the IT office has asked all department chairs to remind their faculty member to complete the mandatory technology security training course. I hope each of you will do this without the need for further reminders from me. I'd like to add that I think you should complete the course for your own sake, not just because the University is asking."

"What are we?" burst out Prof. Noach. "Are we effing cattle...? Every time we turn around the university is insisting that we do some kind of training... IT, sexual harassment, recruitment, some kind of bullshit or other! How stupid do they think we are that we can't remember the last dozen times that we had to go through the same thing? And what's more, they don't actually care whether we learn anything... just that we spend the required two hours or so on the course. It's a complete waste of time."

"Jamie's right," Prof. Kaur joined in. "Of course they don't care if we learn anything. It's all about insurance. So they can claim they provided the proper training."

"Well, I suppose you're partly right," said the Department Chair, "but I think the IT training may be different. Indulge me in a quick story from last summer. Much as I'm embarrassed to admit, I was scammed for about $900. My wife was trying to sell a piece of antique furniture on Craig's List. She got a response from someone on the other coast who indicated they were very excited about the piece but needed to have the item shipped. They told her they'd pay the cost of shipping but needed to provide a COD payment for shipping at the time of pickup. When things seemed to be going off the rails a bit because of problems working out the details, I stupidly stepped in and took over the negotiation. The buyer assured me that they'd pay an extra $100 for the inconvenience of my having to go to the post office and get a money order for the COD payment. They sent me a cashier's check for the cost of the item, plus the cost of shipping and the extra $100. I deposited the check with Wells Fargo Bank and later even called the bank to make sure the funds were collected. After a bank employee assured me repeatedly that the funds were good, I went ahead with the money order for the shipping cost and sent it to the purchaser. So, from the cashier's check I netted the price of the item plus the $100 for inconvenience. Well, no one ever showed up to pick up the item and I didn't hear from the buyer again. A few days later I got a notice from Wells Fargo that the check was no good! Wells Fargo refused to accept responsibility for their misleading response to my questions about the deposit being good. They claimed the check was good at the time, but after it was returned to them it was not good. The net result – I was out $900. Maybe if I'd been through our internet security training recently I might not have fallen for this scam."

"Well that was kind of dumb of you," commented Novikova, "though I don't see how anything in our internet security training would have helped. Doesn't seem like a very smart move for the bank either, in light of all of their other customer relations problems, and because of how easy it would have been for them to warn their customer. I'll remember that story for my personal finance classes."

"Well, I'm going to try to be more cautious in the future," concluded the Chair. "So please, whether you think it's helpful or not, each of you, complete the training without further pressure from me. I only have one good cautionary story to tell and now you've heard it."

"Moving along... I know how you're going to feel about this third one. Human Relations has asked me to remind those of you who're scheduled to serve on any of our search committees for new faculty that you each have to complete the campus Affirmative Action training course before we can make any new hires. Also, if you wait too long for the trainings, the Affirmative Action Office could find that our search was defective and prevent us from hiring."

"Fourth, some of you are due for Sexual Harassment training. In general, most of you've been through this course several times already and I think it's usually pretty obvious what would constitute such things as harassment, bullying, or a hostile work environment. This recurring training, as you clearly recognize, seems to be something the University has been pressured into by its insurer and for financial reasons."

"Both affirmative action problems and sexual harassment problems are important for the University to avoid since they can put our federal grant funding at risk and this funding now accounts for a substantial part of our budget each year."

"Well," interposed Professor Cory Sarks, who'd been uncharacteristically silent during the rest of the meeting, "with all of that process training, it's painfully obvious that there's not much time left for our research. It seems clear that the University doesn't care about our productivity." Sarks was known to all to be difficult and a contrarian. Recognizing that he most likely was just trying to rationalize his own lack of research output, Hill chose to ignore Sarks's remark.

"Finally, there are several concerns related to the classroom. As some of you know, problems with academic honesty have been on the rise. Students from other cultures sometimes don't understand when collaboration is dishonest or when attribution to the work of others is called for. Please make extra effort to help the students in your classes to understand, and please make sure to include the Department's Academic Honesty Policy statement in your course syllabus."

"Also, in the classroom, it's increasingly important to provide for your students who, for one reason or another, need special consideration. Each of us should try to be sensitive to these needs and make appropriate accommodations."

"HR has also asked us to be careful of trigger words and to avoid microaggressions. Certain trigger words can make students very uncomfortable and microaggressions can be culturally or ethnically insulting. It goes without saying... although, I guess, I'm saying it... that you should avoid them in the classroom or, if you must use a trigger word, warn the students so they can elect to not attend that part of the class."

These last remarks were met with silence and reactions ranging from boredom to annoyance. But no one spoke. All seemed eager to leave and several had closed their laptops.

"So that covers it for me," Hill concluded. "Sorry for all

the tedious housekeeping reminders, and I'll get back to you on the outcome of my meeting with the President about the gift. I hope you each have a good and productive year."

As the meeting began to break up, "Happy Hour at the Tilted Kilt," proclaimed Prof. Edwards, who was always promoting anything British.

CHAPTER 4

HAPPY HOURS

Despite their varied interests and differing points of view, the economics faculty were a collegial group, both in their research and in their socializing. They enjoyed vigorous debate on topics of current interest. It was standard practice, after a faculty meeting, no matter how contentious, for the group to adjourn to a nearby bar or pub for happy hour. Most tenured faculty members, except for the Chair and Prof. Sarks, could be counted on to drop in. Participation by junior faculty members was more sporadic and less likely, especially after a difficult meeting.

A few pitchers later...

"Does anyone know what the fuck a trigger word is?" Krista Novikova, after a couple beers, was known for her occasional use of expletives that most of the others avoided.

"Well, I suppose 'fuck' might be a trigger word," chortled Dan Edwards.

"Then how the hell are we supposed to teach our fucking classes?" retorted Novikova, to the amusement of the group.

"'Hell' might be one, too, I think," added Edwards, "though we seem to hear it a lot these days from our elected presidents."

"I'm looking on Google and I can't find anything that says 'fuck' is a trigger word," reported Faquhir, as he continued to surf. But it does seem that almost anything to do with economics involves trigger words. It says here that 'capitalism' is a negative trigger for some people – kind of depressing, I think…. So where does that leave us? Do we have to give a trigger warning at the start of each class?"

"It's all pretty confusing to me," Nicole Stewart, a Professor of Economics, joined in, taking the discussion more seriously than the others. "We can't avoid talking about capitalism… nor would we want to. But it's hard to figure out what other words or phrases are triggers that we actually should avoid. I look online and I see all these contradictory definitions of what triggering is, and nobody seems to agree on when you should give warnings, or even if the warnings work or are helpful. But we're under all this pressure to give warnings. Maybe it's more important to avoid trigger words that have little to do with economics or finance. Like, maybe calling politicians liars… even if some are."

"I agree, Nicole. I'm not sure giving trigger warnings is even a good idea," Faquhir offered, redundantly to Stewart. "The internet's also full of references to studies about the negative impact of trigger warnings. It seems kind of silly to caution students in our econ classes that we might talk about capitalism."

"I suspect," Novikova noted, "that labeling anything that provokes action or an emotional response a 'trigger word' might have a chilling effect on fruitful dialogue. It seems to me that lately people are reticent to bring up even mildly provocative topics or to take positions others might disagree about. Haven't you all noticed…? In social settings, doesn't it seem like people just try to stay with safe, noncontroversial topics like families, vacations, popular TV shows, and other bullshit? I'm bored almost to death with such drivel. I'm starting to think that we should want to do the opposite, we should want to engage in conversations that might challenge us or make us feel uncomfortable. I think we're all better off if we're exposed to different points of view, even if we sometimes feel uncomfortable. It makes us think more critically about other perspectives… and about our own…. Now, more importantly, could someone please pass me that pitcher?"

"I agree with you, Krista. I wonder if all the focus on things like trigger words contributes to the woke sorting by race, gender, political views, whatever, that seems to be going on now. If everyone you know thinks and acts like you do, it's harder to be triggered. But, still, maybe there's something.... Maybe we should pay more attention to avoiding microaggressions." suggested Nadir Kaur. "It seems that a goal of aggression, micro-, macro-, or whatever, is to stop people airing other points of view."

"Maybe not even that," challenged Edwards, "A while ago the University of California published a list of words and phrases they considered to be microaggressions. Apparently, if we were at a UC school, we'd be cautioned against what they call 'The myth of meritocracy'. We're supposed to try to avoid using phrases like, 'The most qualified person should get the job,' or 'America is the land of opportunity.' Now, maybe those ideas really should be challenged, but not, I think, in a way that seeks to shut them down or dismiss them. I wonder if, maybe the act of labeling something a 'microaggression' is actually the microaggression."

"Yeah," added Faquhir. "That's an interesting thought, Larry.... There was also something bizarre from Amherst a while ago. I thought it was weird enough that I saved it on my iPhone.... Here it is.... According to something they called a Common Language Guide, capitalism is... get this", he laughed... "'An economic and political system in which a country's trade and industry are controlled by private owners for profit, rather than by the state. This system leads to exploitative labor practices, which affect marginalized groups disproportionately.' I guess the first sentence is factually accurate, but the second seems pretty judgmental and designed to shut down pro-capitalism speech. So which is the microaggression? Speaking of the benefits of competition or labeling capitalism a system that leads to exploitation of labor...? I know which way I lean on this."

"And there's more... that same Guide also defines pay equity as, 'The concept that all people should be compensated equitably based on their work, not their race, gender or another marginalized social identity,' which seems fine... but then it goes on to cite the statistic that 'White women make $0.82 on the dollar compared to men.' But it makes that comparison without controlling for such things as job related risks or a variety of other factors. Maybe the gap would still be there, but the absence of controls in the comparison seems intellectually dishonest to me. Now, that doesn't sound like a microaggression, but it seems to have the same effect. A male who tries to point out the unscientific nature of the simplistic comparison runs the risk of being labeled a male chauvinist or misogynistic. It's all starting to sound like some sort of religion.... You have to accept all of the beliefs without question or be excommunicated."

"In any case," Faquhir continued, "it seems that someone at Amherst jumped the gun. The School quickly pulled the document from its website.... Probably mainly just concerned about losing donor support, I suspect, and not really recanting the sentiment."

"Really?" exclaimed Jamie Noach, who'd been half-listening, "capitalism bashing like that would never happen in Israel. What schmuck came up with that idea? This seems like an attack at the very core of economics.... How can we even teach if we can't stress the benefits of capitalism, opportunity, and merit...? Why do students even come to college if they're not seeking to improve themselves, to gain some sort of competitive advantage in whatever discipline... or however they define themselves? I'm certainly glad I'm at Baird instead of at the UC... or, apparently, at Amherst."

"I don't know," said Reardon Koopman, who was always delighted to show up for happy hour sessions, but rarely spoke.

"I suppose there may be something to this concern about microaggressions.... I know it really angers me whenever anyone describes the economics faculty as being 'Older than dirt....' I know the comment is pointed at me and a few others... but, and let me say unequivocally, I AM NOT DEAD WOOD! I'm still research active... still effective as a teacher... and still carry my share of the water.... Though... funny story... June and I were out walking our dog a few days ago and June stopped to chat with another woman who was out with her dog.... I couldn't quite understand why she made no effort to introduce me.... Anyway, when their conversation broke up and we resumed our walk I asked her who the women was. Turns out we'd just had her and her husband over for dinner a couple days earlier." Over laughter, some choking, and a bit of spraying beer, he finished up. "So, sometimes, I admit," he blushed, "there is a senior moment for me... but, like I said, I'm still able to do my part."

"That was really the point I was trying to make," said Edwards. "Referring to senior faculty as 'Older than dirt' seems to have no constructive purpose, unless, I suppose, you think it's better for students to be taught by younger faculty and you're trying to get the more senior ones to leave.... So, maybe the notion of a microaggression is reasonable if application of the term isn't too broad."

"I agree," Novikova said. "And maybe the way to deal with it is to push back with, for example, evidence that senior faculty continue to be productive... challenge the misperception. But unfortunately, it seems that the people who come up with terms like trigger words and microaggressions want to apply them as broadly as possible or only selectively.... For sure, there are racist people, but it seems that the term now is so broadly applied that it's mainly being used to shut down dialogue that could actually bring about real progress.... So where's the opposition to using the racist label as a microaggression?"

"I have to say," continued Koopman, recovering somewhat from his outburst and recovering his normal skin hue, "that I really do enjoy these informal get-togethers. It seems to me that, for the most part, unlike most on-campus meetings, no one here has a hidden agenda or holds back on saying what they really think. And no one's being labeled for the things they might say.... Thanks for allowing me to vent a bit. Now... shall we order another round?" he proposed, though, based on his prior remarks, he was already feeling the effects of the preceding ones.

"But wouldn't you agree," argued Novikova, returning to the focus of the discussion, "that all of this political correctness over trigger words and microaggressions is actually working against what is supposed to be the ultimate objective? Intense competition may well be the best way to level the playing field for everyone. After all, you can't discriminate on any basis if doing so would mean hiring people who are less qualified, and if hiring the best qualified is the difference between a successful enterprise and a failure.... I know I'd not like to believe that I got to where I am because of my gender. I think I got here because I focused my education on finance, and finance is a highly sought-after specialization. Until fairly recently it's been a male dominated field, but we all recognized that this has been changing, partly because more women have chosen to take up the technical challenges of the specialization."

"That's a good point," began Edwards, striking a serious tone. "But of course you'd agree, wouldn't you, that our world of human endeavor isn't quite the same as the Darwinian ideal of competition in the natural world. We don't actually have the intensity of competition that drives the fittest to survive and the others to fail. Our economic and social organizations... and even our regulations, create what you might call 'slack....' And when there's slack, non-economic discrimination can survive unless some steps are taken to restrain it.... It's bloody good, if you ask me, that we teach our students the pure arguments of the competitive model, but I think we all need to recognize that we haven't reached a point where we're free of discrimination on whatever grounds."

All the while, Larry Faquhir was listening to the banter, studying his colleagues, and taking it all in. He was seeking to identify those he could rely on to support his point of view in the upcoming hiring and tenure discussions and those who would most certainly be of a different view.

In an effort to flush them out, as there were no untenured faculty members present, he sought to change the topic of discussion, "What do you all think of our candidates for tenure this year? It's not clear to me that all of them are deserving."

"If you ask me, they're all a bunch of millennial wusses," Koopman barged in. "In my day the only way to get tenure was to work your tail off in producing good research. It seems like now we're all into so-called work-life balance. Here's a news flash... work *is* part of life."

Novikova had grown accustomed to Faquhir's efforts to control the outcomes of tenure decisions, and of his disdain for finance, and especially accounting. She chose to ignore Koopman's alcohol-induced outburst and, identifying Faquhir's question as an attempt to find allies who would oppose the tenure cases in those disciplines, she sought to close down the shift in discussion. "I think I may have had one too many to discuss such a sensitive matter right now... and isn't it a bit inappropriate to do so before our formal meeting?"

Edwards, recognizing the tension a discussion over tenure cases would create, and not liking the idea of discussing promotions in a public bar, joined in. "Yes, by all means, we do need to have this discussion, but I'm afraid it wouldn't be proper to do so here, in public, over several rounds of ale, when we're all talking much too loudly. I also need to be heading out."

Faquhir was defeated in the first round, and the group called for their tab and dispersed, postponing the tenure fight for another day.

All but Prof. Edwards were headed to their homes. Edwards had an evening meeting scheduled on campus with an Econ Ph.D. student whose dissertation research he was supervising.

***

At the same time as most of the tenured members of the group at the Tilted Kilt had departed for the pub, Mark Nikolaidis was headed for the Cambridge Inn, a restaurant in town that, over the years, had become a popular meeting place of faculty. As he arrived, he found Professor Jennifer Morris waiting in the lobby and they took a small booth near the bar. Morris was a Professor of Mathematics, and Mark had found that his interests often had more in common with some members of the Mathematics Department than with most members of his own. Nikolaidis had first encountered Jennifer at the Cambridge Inn, when, by chance, they both happened to be there at the same time and had decided to share a table for dinner. Nikolaidis learned that Jen often came alone to the Inn for dinner when her husband, Joseph Gardner, a member of the Physics Department faculty, was away at a conference.

Mark and Jen struck it off well in their first meeting and each felt they'd benefitted by discussing their work with the other. As it turned out, Prof. Gardner loved conferences. Attending them, he claimed, facilitated the collaborations of the large research teams that were a common feature of research papers published in his area of physics. Though it seemed more likely to Jennifer that he just liked the travel and socializing over physics topics. So, Mark and Jen had become regular diners at the Inn. Neither was particularly concerned about the inference others might draw from their not-infrequent meetings. In recent years, it had become more common, at the Inn and elsewhere, for male and female faculty members to meet over a drink or a meal to discuss matters of common interest.

Since that first meeting, conversation had remained centered around their work and on-campus matters. After the usual business small talk, conversation over this early dinner took a different turn. "How about if we share a bottle of chardonnay?" Jennifer proposed.

Mark's initial inclination was to decline or to propose a cabernet, instead, since he didn't much care for chardonnay, but he ultimately responded, "Of course, should I ask for a wine list, or do you know of something you'd like?"

"How about the "Rombauer?" she replied, "I had it once and it was very buttery and quite delicious. I noticed it earlier on the wine list."

After a glass of wine and continued small talk about their respective departmental tenure cases, dinner arrived, and the conversation took a turn. Have you heard about Professor Andres Collings in Sociology?" asked Jennifer. Over a puzzled look from Mark, she continued, "Apparently, he was placed on administrative leave because of a complaint by one of his female students that he'd tried to pressure her into something sexual."

"Really?" responded Nikolaidis. "So I guess he must not have done so well on the harassment training.... I know Collings a bit and wouldn't have expected something like that of him.... He always seems to be championing women's causes on campus. Maybe it's actually just a student disgruntled over a grade or something."

"I don't think so, Mark," Jennifer continued. "Apparently the complaint came from a colleague. I think the School wouldn't have put him on leave without some pretty clear evidence and maybe some confirmation. I'm not a bit surprised. It seems to me that it's often the most outspoken champions who are the most flagrant offenders.

"Of course, you never really know who starts these things," she went on. "It's been a few years now, but I do recall one of my undergraduate students coming to my office much more often than usual. He even, at one point asked me out for coffee, which I foolishly agreed to.... When I arrived, he presented me with a box of candy and asked if we might, sometime, meet for dinner instead of just coffee. I sent him away, of course, and the term ended shortly after, thank God.... It seems to me that we always need to be a bit on guard for such things."

"I completely agree," rejoined Mark. "I haven't had anything quite like that happen, but I suppose my demeanor could be off-putting to many students.... Students almost never come to my office hours, and I have a policy of always keeping my door open during office visits, but otherwise closed.

"I did hear, recently, that during a term when Dan... Prof. Edwards, that is... was teaching some upper-level undergraduate courses, he came to work one morning and found a pair of women's panties tacked to his message board.... I'm guessing from a student... and that he probably has a good idea which one. I've noticed that his office hours seem to attract quite a few students, mostly female. I think it's the Oxford accent that he puts on that does the trick for him, even though he grew up in Liverpool, and was mostly educated at the University of Manchester."

As the gossip-studded conversation continued, the bottle they had shared was emptied.

"How about if we each order one more glass of wine," proposed Jennifer?

Mark, realizing that Jen, clearly, was not ready to leave, beckoned for a waiter.

"You know, all this talk of faculty trysts has me wondering a bit about Joey," she began, moving to what was really on her mind. "I know his conferences are important to him professionally, but I've started to think that's not the only reason he goes to so many. Lately, it seems that he may be doing so to get away from me.... I think there may be something going on, as you hear so often happens when people are away from their spouses.

"The people who attend the Physics conferences he goes to include a lot of regulars, and an increasing number of them are women. I'm starting to think there's someone else."

"I'm sure that can't be true. You're a very attractive and interesting woman," Mark consoled. "There's no way he'd want to jeopardize your relationship. I only wish I could say the same of mine."

Jennifer already knew that Mark's relationship with his wife was one of convenience. He worked at the university and brought home the pay checks. She worked at home without explicit pay. He was always busy with his academic pursuits. She had a full calendar of duplicate bridge, book clubs, volunteer social work, and, of course, shopping and maintaining the household. In fact, she was far better than he at such things as replacing non-operating light switches and leaky toilet flappers. Anyone would have been. So they rarely saw each other except for a few minutes in the morning and at some dinners. Tonight was her bridge night, a night when Mark would routinely come to the Inn for dinner. Lately, they'd discovered that even their vacation interests were divergent and so they generally vacationed separately, if at all.

"Well, I'm sure your relationship's just fine, Mark... probably a lot like most people who've been married for a few years and have grown comfortable with their lives," she responded, knowing that what she was saying was unlikely to be true.

"I think not," Mark responded, leaning forward and making penetrating eye contact with Jen, "but I have to tell you, that aside from my research, these dinners with you are the thing I most look forward to.... Well... it's getting a bit late, and I am feeling the wine and the press of work, so perhaps we should call it a night," Mark demurred.

"Yes, Mark, I, too, look forward to these dinners... and probably should be getting along," Jennifer affirmed, reaching across the table to touch his hand. "But let's do this again soon."

"Yes, let's. I'll pick up the check this time, Jen, so you can head on home. I don't need a ride tonight, the walk's short and maybe will help me get my mind back on my work."

***

The dinner between Mark Nikolaidis and Jennifer Morris ended around the same time as the department happy hour was concluding and Daniel Edwards was heading back to campus to meet with his student.

"Hi, Professor!" exclaimed Rebecca Prescott, as she saw Edwards enter the hall.

"Hi, Becca, I thought this might be a good time for me to get an update from you on your dissertation progress.... Give me a second to open my office."

She was looking quite fit, he thought. "Why don't we sit over here," he proposed, gesturing toward the seating arrangement and coffee table in his office.

Becca took a seat on the small sofa, crossed her legs and reached up with both hands to toss her dark brown hair back over her shoulders, after which, she leaned forward expectantly, and began, "OK... so I have a draft of what I think will become the first chapter.... I know I need to keep polishing, but I hope that within the next couple of months I'll be ready to begin sending it out to schools as my job market paper. That way I'd have it ready in time for interviewing with schools at the January meetings.

"So… that's good, Professor… but I'm struggling a bit on what I hope will become the rest of the dissertation," she continued. "I'm hoping you might look over my draft and let me know if you think it's ready," she smiled. "And maybe we can talk through the problems I've been struggling with on the rest of the dissertation."

"Cracking!" exclaimed Edwards. Which drew a puzzled look from Rebecca. "Sorry… I mean very good."

"It's great to hear that you're on track for the job market season. I'll read it over quickly once you send it to me and I'd be chuffed to send out a few letters of introduction with my recommendations for interview. Now, how can I help on the rest?" Again, Rebecca was puzzled by the unfamiliar colloquialisms, but thought his tone sounded like he was offering to support her applications.

"Maybe I can just show you some of my results…" Rebecca stood and handed him a few pages of computer printout. Leaning over his shoulder, she began pointing to a few problems, all the while her breast was brushing against his upper arm and her hair grazing his neck.

Daniel found that he was having trouble concentrating on the work, but it really didn't matter anymore. It was enough, he knew. Game on! "Let me have a few days to study this and think of how we might tweak things a bit. Let's meet for dinner on Friday and we can proceed from there with these pages."

"Perfect!" she smiled bashfully, relishing her power over the professor, and knowing that as long as the relationship lasted, he would make sure her dissertation was a success.

CHAPTER 5

IN THE OFFICE

Since assuming the presidency of Baird four years ago, Thomas Hansen had found that his work consisted almost entirely of meetings and appearances. Most of the days when he was on campus were filled with meetings: individual or group meetings with his administrative staff, meetings with individual department chairs, cathartic meetings with small groups of students or faculty members (who usually were unhappy about something), meetings with prospective students and their families, and meetings or almost daily phone calls with trustees. When not in the office, the President was likely to be in an off campus meeting with a key donor or prospective donor or to be making an appearance at an on- or off-campus event.

And, of course, there was the occasional corporate board of directors meeting. Some of the School trustees had arranged his board appointments as a way to sweeten the inducement for him to accept the Baird presidency. They had done so even though, with his chemistry background, he had little expertise that was relevant for either of the corporate boards on which he served.

Hansen sometimes wondered how best to describe his job at Baird. Externally, he knew his job was to promote the University. Internally, it seemed he was supposed to be mainly a listener and consensus builder. In contrast to his own perception, it seemed that others mainly thought of him as a vision setter and decision maker.

Hansen knew there was little truth to the view of him as either vision setter or decision maker. Sure, he could have his own opinions and could promote some actions and downplay others, but ultimately, no person could legitimately claim to lead a University. Most of the consequential decisions of the University could only be reached through collaboration and compromise. Anything that mattered required buy-in from someone – the trustees, the faculty, the students, the administrative staff, a key donor, or maybe all of them. The same was true of vision-setting. He could, of course, articulate a vision for the University, but not really his vision. Rather, the vision, if it could be called that, had to emerge organically from the interplay among the various constituencies. His real role, it seemed, was to try to find the common threads and to articulate whatever vision emerged. President Hansen was confident that he could not truly advance a vision of his own and could not sustain an important decision that was not broadly supported.

Even something like selecting a provost, which, on the surface, was his prerogative, was beyond his ability to control. Faculty and staff members, students, and trustees were always well-represented on search committees at that level and, realistically, an appointment could not be made without the broad support from such a committee. Moreover, unless the provost was sensitive to the will of the faculty, it would only take a significant slip-up or two to precipitate a mutiny. Hansen recalled a recent story in the *Chronicle* of a provost who, in an effort to reduce administrative overhead, had attempted to merge that university's colleges of humanities and sciences into a single college, a plan that was overwhelmingly rejected by the faculty members of both colleges. Having failed at that attempt, the provost had sought to centralize the faculty hiring process, taking cherished decision-making authority away from the individual departments. At that point, the faculty had rebelled, and the president had been compelled to accept the resignation of the provost or risk losing his own position.

The reality, Hansen believed, was that there was no such thing as the leader of a university. There was just a confluence of forces that were all tugging in somewhat different directions. He often felt that, like a ship under power but battling a crosswind and a tidal flow, a university would drift in the average direction of the discordant vector forces. If the crosswinds or tidal flows were strong enough, the ship could drift off course, make no forward progress, or even founder under the will of the competing forces.

As he reflected, his mind turned naturally to the financial wellbeing of the school and the concerns raised in his last meeting with his ELT. Clearly, the very top universities could function well under the confluence of forces of faculty governance, board pressure, and the like. They might drift off course a bit, but their financial cushion would protect them from serious harm. He wondered, however, about the less-financially-strong colleges and universities, and, in particular, about Baird. Heather Martin's comments in the ELT meeting were foreboding, but nothing really seemed as serious as she was trying to suggest. Moreover, she had been appointed by the previous president and clearly felt no loyalty to Hansen or his different ideas. He needed a CFO who would buy into his ideas, help sell them to the Board, and help find the resources to pursue them. That, at least, would be one less force to contend with and try to manage.... But that would have to wait.

Turning to his calendar, Hansen noted that today was nothing unusual. It was filled with on-campus meetings, beginning with an early one with the Chair of the Economics Department.

***

"Come on in, Robert," said President Hansen as he welcomed the Economics Department Chair into his office. "Can I offer you coffee... or maybe a bottled water...? Oh, hey,

I heard the good news that your daughter's been admitted to Dartmouth. Congratulations on that, and please also convey my best wishes to Sarah." Hansen, as always, sought to strike a casual/personal tone with faculty members who were serving in administrative roles. Prior to today's meeting, as per usual, his Administrative Assistant had briefed him on Hill's family and his daughter's recent admission to Dartmouth.

"Yes... I'll have a coffee, thanks," said Hill. "And, yes, we're quite pleased with that outcome, and especially Sarah is. But we're still wondering how we'll pay for it." Dartmouth was Sarah's first choice, partly because it has its own ski mountain, so she applied early decision. Based on her scores and academic record, she could get into almost any school, and with some good aid offers. But, because she applied early decision, she could only apply to one school. So Dartmouth didn't have to compete to get her to accept. "We'll be paying full tuition... quite a stretch for us. Maybe I'm being too cynical, but I sometimes wonder if schools at the level of Dartmouth are using their early decision programs to help them meet their budgets or to boost financial aid awards to non-early decision students. I think I remember having seen some economics research that supports this possibility."

Hansen already did not like the way the conversation was going. School financing and early decision policies were too close to home for his comfort. So he sought to redirect, making a mental note that he needed to be careful commenting about college admissions. "Yes... well, I'm sure you're pleased with her admission, and you must be relieved that she's finished with her search."

The personal exchange out of the way, he questioned, "I trust the year's off to a good start in the Economics Department. Any concerns I should be aware of?"

"No new concerns," Hill replied. "We do still face significant challenges in staffing our classes with appropriately qualified faculty members. In fact, that's the reason I asked for this meeting. I think we have a potential solution."

"Good to hear," responded the President. "What's up?"

"Well, you may remember that I met with you last year about one of our alums and his possible interest in supporting the Department with a major gift," Hill began. "I'm happy to report that our alum seems ready to move forward on this and that he'd like to fund two endowed professorships in economics. I'm hoping you might be able to meet with him to sort of close the deal. I'm certain he's almost ready to act, but that a meeting with you would get us over the final hurdle and help shape the gift in the best way."

"That's very good news, Bob, and of course I am happy to help out in any way I can. Tell me a bit more about what you'd like me to do."

"Well... maybe we should talk a bit about the academic focus of these prospective new faculty lines," Hill began. "I teed this up in our department meeting earlier this week and mentioned that we currently have no faculty members who work in a couple of specific areas, but I didn't see much support in the meeting for those as a focus of hiring. Naturally, there was no consensus among the faculty," he shrugged. "The macroeconomics faculty wants to hire more people in macro, and the microeconomics faculty wants more in micro. But recent hires have been in micro, and we seem to be fairly well covered in macro. The most compelling arguments I heard were from our economics outreach areas into finance and accounting. One faculty member pointed out that we only have two financial economist and two faculty members who work in accounting. Student interest in those areas has been growing and I personally have found that it's very difficult for us to do a good job of staffing our finance and accounting classes with so few core faculty members in those areas.

So maybe those would be the most useful. I think George Jennings... our alum, that is... would be open to funding endowed professorships in those areas," Hill concluded.

Hansen, feeling the pull of the competing forces he had been reflecting upon earlier, was immediately concerned about the proposed focus. Finance and accounting were both expensive areas in which to try to hire. Considering everything – salaries, benefits, and research support, filling those two lines could cost the University almost a million per year, even after support provided from the donor's gift. At the same time, he did not want to lose the gift. Raising support from donors was one of the main benchmarks trustees used when they evaluated the performance of a university president, even if the fundraising actually ended up costing the university money.

"Sounds good," he said to Hill. "Please let your alum know that I'd like to host him for a lunch on campus and that my AA will be in touch to make the arrangements. I'll see what I can do to get us over the finish line."

Closing off the discussion, the President asked, "I know you have a few assistant professors in your department. How are they doing – do they all seem to be on track for tenure?"

"We do have several," responded Hill. "Three are up for tenure this year. I think they're doing okay, but, as I'm sure you know, it's never certain how department faculty will go on tenure cases. We also have a couple of juniors who were hired more recently. It's a bit too soon to know about them, but they come from strong Ph.D. programs, so I am optimistic."

"Well, I do hope it works out well for all of them." Not really caring about the response to his question, President Hansen stood, signaling that the meeting was concluding. As he escorted Prof. Hill to his office door, he concluded, "Please send my AA your alum's contact information soon, so I can follow up quickly. Oh... and, again, extend my congratulations to Sarah."

In the minutes before his next meeting, the President reflected on the additional challenges the gift would create. It would mean a significant increase in the personnel costs in the Economics Department, a department that he believed was already in good enough shape so that additional hiring was not really needed. Yet he obviously could not decline such a gift. For sure, some of the trustees would learn of the prospective gift and would see not closing the deal as a failure on his part. The suggested finance and accounting focuses were particularly concerning. Perhaps he could, at least, limit the near-term damage to the School's financial performance by steering the donor into less expensive disciplines within economics.

**

President Hansen's second meeting of the day was with his Vice President for Operations, David Gomez. Gomez arrived in a sweatshirt, denims, and work boots.

Taking note of the attire, Hansen was glad to see an opportunity to keep the meeting short. He had never developed the ability to interact well with blue-collar workers, and wasn't that basically all that Gomez was? "I can see you've been busy in the field, Dave... so I don't want to take too much of your time," the President began.

"Yeah," responded Gomez, who went by 'David' and was never happy to be called 'Dave', "but the work will move ahead fine for a while without me on site. That damn water feature for the new dorms is turning out to be a problem."

Dismayed, Hansen queried, "Nothing too serious, I hope, Dave?"

"I guess," Gomez shrugged. "The original construction wasn't quite level. So when we tried to add water, we found that the slope was pretty obvious and that the water feature wouldn't work properly. We also discovered a significant leak somewhere so that the autofill line seems to run pretty much continuously."

"That doesn't sound good," said Hansen. "What are we doing about it? I hope there's an easy fix."

"Well, we're gonna need to relevel the fountain – maybe reconstruct some parts of it. Depending on where the leak is, we may need to jackhammer part of the fountain to get access," Gomez responded.

"That sounds expensive," prompted the President, still hoping for more positive news.

"Count on it," responded Gomez. "Maybe a couple hundred grand, I guess. But we're not sure yet."

Two hundred thousand dollars," exclaimed the President. "Who's responsible?"

"Don't know," responded Gomez, shaking his head. "The landscape architect was selected by the donor. He's blaming the concrete contractor for not leveling the fountain, but the contractor is blaming the architect. We don't know yet about the leak.... Could be a bad installation of the plumbing or maybe someone like the concrete contractor or the landscaper who did the rough grading broke a pipe somewhere. I wish we'd never got into this. Large water features are always a problem... but what're ya gonna do when a donor asks for something?"

So, the year had just begun and was already $200 thousand over budget. But it could have been worse, Hansen reflected.

"Let's set that aside for now, Dave," he responded, "and look for an easy and less expensive fix."

Gomez looked at the floor, telegraphing his doubt that the fix could be easy and inexpensive.

"You probably know," continued the President, "that the ELT met earlier this week. Among other things, we were discussing last year's budget overrun. A big part of the overrun was that we overspent on facilities and maintenance. Heather Martin thought you'd be able to fill in some of the details on the cost overrun and also mentioned," Hansen fibbed, "that you thought you could operate within budget this year. So, I'm hoping we can get in on budget and maybe even make up some lost ground."

"Not gonna happen," Gomez pushed back, shaking his head. "I'm not sure what gave Heather the idea that we could operate within budget. It's not so much that we were over budget last year. The truth is more like that we were under-budgeted.... The same thing happened the year before and it looks like this year could be even worse, not even considering the fountain mess."

"Let me fill in some background on the shortfall last year. You know, our new dorms were completed in early summer and are now almost fully occupied by the entering class... By the way, if you haven't seen the dorms, you might wanna take a quick walk-through. They really are quite impressive... The architect, who was selected by the donor, who, by the way, only funded about 10 percent of the cost of the project, did a great job, even though his fee turned out to be quite a bit higher than anybody expected. We did have some changes to the building design that were unplanned. Those changes caused us to run over the construction budget on the project. So, it's partly the architect, partly building construction costs, and now the effing water feature."

"That new dorm was our main capital project for the year," Gomez continued. "Aside from that, we followed our established facilities renovation and maintenance schedule, including the planned replacements and upgrades to computers and classroom technology. You probably recall that we established an annual budget that we felt should enable us to renovate, replace furniture and fixtures, upgrade or replace classroom instructional technology, laboratories, vehicles, and other equipment like photocopiers, and replace personal computers on schedules that were designed to maintain our competitiveness with peer schools."

"That all makes sense," Hansen commented.

"Well, yeah, but the main reason we ran over on maintenance is that over the last few years, it's become increasingly difficult to adhere to the planned schedule and still stay within budget. If you ask me, we have a two-sided problem. First, adhering to our maintenance and replacement schedule has become more expensive than we'd projected. Second, for some things like instructional technology, the projected frequency of required upgrades has turned out to be too low. So we've been falling behind on maintenance, remodeling, and replacements."

"I see, Dave. Well, maybe we can reconsider some of those schedules and stretch some of them out a bit to free up some funds for other uses," Hansen responded, declining to focus on the problems resulting from deferred maintenance.

"I'm not sure doing that would help much," Gomez pressed. "We're just not getting to everything we should. For example, because of budgetary limitations, some of our older buildings are still in need of asbestos abatement and earthquake retrofitting; some are not ADA compliant; and some are not adequately insulated with such things as dual-pane windows. If we defer a few of these projects this year we might be able to catch up a bit and replenish the reserve. Longer term, however, I think we need to reassess whether some aspects of our schedule can be adjusted. If we can't do that, which seems likely to me that we can't, we're going to have to commit some additional resources to facilities each year."

President Hansen felt he was getting nowhere with

Gomez and decided to press harder. If he could push things off for a few years, the long-run would be someone else's problem. "Well, fortunately, we're not a public university, so some of the things you just mentioned are postpone-able. Before we go down that longer-term course, let's talk a bit more about how we might reduce expenditures this year. How about slowing down routine maintenance a bit? I'm sure we could save some money that way."

Since it seemed that the President was not hearing him, Gomez tried again, "Well, that's what we thought a few years ago. So, we slowed down back then, and now all of that deferred maintenance is coming back on us. It's worse than if we'd just stayed on schedule. Instead of deferring even more, we really need to catch up, but we're not even attempting to do that, so probably things will just continue to get worse in the future."

Even as he was describing the problems, Gomez felt he was trying too hard to put a brighter spin on the situation than it deserved. He believed that there was little, if any potential to find slack in the maintenance schedule and that it would not be long before problems associated with the deferred maintenance would become apparent to others, including students and Board members. He also did not see much opportunity to postpone planned improvements that were outside the normal maintenance schedule. Without some strategic refocusing he expected that problems related to the facilities budget would only worsen.

"I agree with you," Hansen equivocated, and, of course, I recognize that we need to rethink the schedule and do more to maintain and improve our physical plant. But, as I said, those are longer term issues. Now, just focusing on this year, what do you think we can do to bring the expenditures back into line with the budget?" Hansen demanded.

"You mean other than increasing the budget?" Gomez

questioned rhetorically. "Well, we could cut back on all of the seasonal planting and other sprucing up before campus events like convocation and commencement. That would save quite a bit, but still not balance the budget."

"But, of course, we can't do that," responded the President, who was convinced that the seasonal planting was important to the school image and was concerned that the trustees might notice that the campus was looking tired. He needed to keep up appearances, no matter the cost.

"Well, here's a suggestion I haven't heard from anyone.... Maybe we could rethink the library. It's not clear to me why we even need to have a library anymore, at least not such a large one.... Maybe we should close it." Gomez was only half joking but knew the suggestion would be quickly dismissed. Nonetheless, he continued, "Whenever I'm in there for some maintenance issue, it seems that almost no students are there, just untouched stacks of old books and journals. The students I do see at the library are almost all in the coffee shop we added a few years ago. But we only did that to try to get students to use the library... and the coffee shop is a money loser since most students don't seem to want to go to the library just to meet over coffee. Seems like a simple stand-alone coffee shop would work as well or better, especially since almost everything you can find in a library is available online now. I don't see much point in devoting all of that space to storing books. If we closed the library, we could cut back on library staff, and we probably could convert the space to classrooms and offices, both of which we actually do need... and even keep the coffee shop, if that seems valuable."

Hansen was taken aback at the bluntness of the suggestion, not that he hadn't had some of the same thoughts. But there was no way the University was going to close its library, even if it was so underutilized. A proposal to close the library, he knew, would be met with outrage by both faculty and trustees, albeit not by the students. And it quite possibly would put Baird on the front page of the *Chronicle*. Those of his generation simply could not conceive of a university without a library. "You're joking, of course, David," he responded. "We're not closing the library."

"So... no change to the planting or physical plant, I guess," Gomez concluded. "Maybe someone should consider raising tuition or reducing financial aid.... If we can't cut our expenses, maybe we can increase our revenues."

Hansen, feeling he was accomplishing little and becoming increasingly frustrated by the bad news, sought to bring the meeting to closure with a final push. "I realize this will be a challenge for you, David. Please just do what you can to control and limit expenses. We need to manage through this difficult time, but I'm sure things will improve fairly soon."

With a resigned shrug, David Gomez stood and headed for the door.

***

As he steered Gomez toward the outer-office door, President Hansen saw that John Cook was waiting, intently focused on today's *Wall Street Journal*. Hansen generally found little of interest in the *Journal* and wondered if Cook did, or if he was just posturing.

Cook was Baird's Director of Career Counseling. In the President's view, the mission of the University was only tangentially related to placing its graduates. Certainly, at the undergraduate and masters levels, the School's mission was to produce well educated, well rounded, and thoughtful graduates, without a particular view towards career. But Hansen recognized that in some disciplines school rankings were heavily influenced by so called "placement success." Moreover, placement success was among the most frequent queries he received from trustees and alums. Indeed, it was for these reasons that the Office of Career Counselling had been established. Still, cutting back here could help to address the budgetary concerns he was facing.

Although, except at the Ph.D. level, Hansen did not personally have much interest in the placement of Baird graduates, because the interest was so high among the school's important constituents, he knew it was imperative for him to keep informed and to avoid actions that would attract attention.

"Come on in, John," he invited. After a handshake and exchange of greetings, he turned to his reason for the meeting. "I thought that since we're starting into a new academic year, it'd be a good time to touch base with you as to how things are looking on the placement front."

"Hmm..." mused Cook as he straightened his jacket and sat up a bit straighter, "I'm not exactly sure how to respond to that. We do have some statistics on employment after graduation, but, as you know, placement, per se, isn't our focus. Post-graduation employment numbers go up and down with the economy. During hot job markets, our employment stats are pretty good, during slow period we tend not to hear from former students. The non-responses suggests that they're still looking for work. This past year wasn't a great one for finding work, so we didn't hear from many of our grads.

"To answer your question, I guess... we do try to factor out these economics fluctuations by comparing our record to the records of our peers. We all had declines in post-graduation employment last year, but Baird's experience may have been a bit worse than the average. That could be due to many things, such as how much effort we put into getting the responses, differences in the majors of our graduates compared to peers... things like that."

"What I can say... I think you already know all of this, Tom... is that, in our Office of Career Counseling, we offer a full range of services to help students prepare for, seek, and find employment. Unfortunately, most students don't take advantage of what we have to offer. Maybe that's part of the reason for the lower placement numbers. Students these days seem to think that by searching the internet or figuring it out for themselves they can learn how to do such things as write a good resume or communicate with a prospective employer. What they want is for us to act like headhunters. Of course, we can't do that. We can't, for example, recommend one student over another or provide services to some students that are not available to all. When there's high demand to interview with a particular recruiter who's visiting campus, we can't rank or help the recruiter to rank the prospective student applicants."

Why was it, Hansen reflected, that people in career counselling never wanted to accept responsibility for placement success? Maybe, like so many others, they sought to avoid accountability, or agreeing to any sort of metric that could be used to assess their effectiveness. Hansen didn't really care about the counseling role that seemed to consume so much time and effort. The questions he got from trustees were always about placement success. And Cook's rationalization about student reliance on things like the internet was not helpful since that behavior would have affected all schools, not just Baird.

"So, John, as we've discussed before, it sounds like there's a bit of a disconnect between what students would like from your office and what you provide. I have to say that I can sort of empathize with the students... and I can understand why they might not see much value in career counseling, per se, as you say. There are many links on the internet to websites that offer advice on such things as what to put in a resume, what to put in a cover letter, and how to dress for an interview. Maybe, in the connected world of today, these kinds of services would be more economically and effectively outsourced. I'm guessing that people working in your office may be reticent to question whether their work is actually valuable. Most of our trustees and important alums seem to think that we do need to be concerned about placement. So I wonder, again, if there might be something Career Counseling could do to bring its services more into line with student and alum expectations." As he reflected on the discussion, Hansen continued to question whether, in the face of increasing financial pressure, the School's expenditures on career counseling afforded an opportunity to cut down on the deficit. "Maybe there are some services your office provides that we can do without, so we can focus on the ones students demand and maybe we can save a few dollars at the same time.

Cook countered that his office actually needed more funding, not less. "It's possibly true, to some extent, that we're not meeting student needs," conceded Cook. "But the problem is that students expect there to be career counselling resources on campus and even focused career counselling in some disciplines, especially at the masters level in the professional schools. On top of everything else we do, we don't have the resources for focused career counseling. So, without more resources we just do the best we can."

Hansen found himself debating whether to press harder on the need for the Office of Career Counselling to cut back its expenditures. But he could see he was getting nowhere with his efforts to get voluntary cuts from Cook, and he knew that cutting back administratively would not sit well with some of the Trustees. He'd have to find other ways to reduce expenditures or else prepare the Board for another shortfall.

***

The President's final meeting before lunch was with his General Counsel, Gloria Moreno. As he prepared for the meeting, Hansen reflected on the changing times. Only a few years ago, the Office of General Counsel at most universities was staffed by a handful of individuals and much of the necessary legal work was outsourced. But that no longer seemed possible. With increasing reliance on government funding, increasingly complex compliance requirements, and increasing reliance by faculty, staff, and students on litigation, the administrative staff involved in legal matters - staff under direct or indirect supervision of the Office of General Counsel - had exploded.

In Hansen's view, a primary reason for what was now being called "university administrative bloat" had occurred in direct response to the increasing legal complexity of operating as a university. Moreover, the disproportionate growth of administrative staff relative to instructional staff actually understated the trend. What used to be fairly simple, faculty driven, processes of hiring and promoting faculty now were heavily overseen by general counsel staff. But, since faculty were unwilling to relinquish their historical roles in hiring and promoting, the amount of faculty time that had to be devoted to preparing legally defensible records of the hiring and promotion processes had exploded. Baird University was no exception to the general trend, yet Hansen hoped that his General Counsel could help address the budget concerns.

"Good morning, Gloria. I hope the year is off to a good start for you. But I suppose you've heard about this beehive thing.... With luck, we won't get sued over it," he joked.

"Yes," she responded. "I don't think the bees pose much of a threat. But, sorry to say, there are some interesting other matters that I can't discuss," she laughed. "Let me update you about the ones that I can."

Hansen knew that Gloria would seek to protect him and the University from possible legal exposure by avoiding topics that could become the subject of litigation, so this was nothing unusual. He would eventually learn of any matter about which he might be personally exposed or be called to testify.

"I just got back from a conference on dealing with sexual harassment claims," Moreno began. "The conference was attended by many from other schools who serve in my same role. It was organized largely in response to the well-known Dear Colleague letter that came out a few years ago from the Department of Education and more recent developments. It seems that pretty much every school is in a state of confusion. One federal administration tells us we need to substantially change how we deal with accusations of sexual harassment or risk losing the federal funding we receive through grants and the like. But, after we spend months on implementation, another administration comes out and says to forget about that. You can go back to your old ways... and now it looks like that may also change. It's clear that higher education has been drawn into the skirmish over how schools should act to assure due process for both the accusers and the accused."

"Given the unsettled state of affairs," continued Moreno, "I found that most schools plan to stay fully staffed up to deal with sexual harassment complaints. The initial Dear Colleague letter triggered an increase in complaints, and we had to staff up to deal with them. The demands on our resources were further elevated when the 'Me Too' movement encouraged even more individuals to make complaints. As a result, Human Resources was a contributor to last year's operating shortfall. We now believe this development and others related to the handling of personnel matters demands a permanent increase in the Human Resources budget. Otherwise, we'll continue to run deficits."

"And now it looks like we may have another looming issue over free speech," she continued.

"Well, I don't see how that can be a very big deal. Universities have always promoted free speech and diversity of ideas as long as it doesn't cross over the line into hate speech," Hansen responded.

"Yes, but one person's free speech can easily be

another person's hate speech," she responded. "In addition to the obvious complaints about protecting guest speakers on campus and balancing the presentation of points of view, if this catches on, we could see students suing the university because they felt that certain professors were intolerant of their different points of view and either publicly humiliated them or punished them in their course grades. We could see faculty members who were denied tenure or promotion suing because their intellectual focus was in conflict with the views of faculty colleagues who were involved in the decision. Look at the mess the University of North Carolina got into over the 1619 Project and tenuring Nikole Hannah-Jones."

"Yes, I see the problem, of course," responded Hansen. "But at least it's not here yet, so I hope we can wait to see how the matter develops. It's not something we can add to the budget this year."

"It's your call, of course, Tom, but I am concerned that this could come upon us quicker and more forcefully than we might expect," Moreno concluded.

"Well, I suppose we can look into the HR budget for next year as part of our budgeting process," Hansen responded." He was eager to move on.

"One reason I wanted to meet with you, Gloria, is to ask for your help in bringing this year's budget into balance. In the past, it seems to me that we've had to invest considerably in the software and systems that we use to assure our compliance with such things as harassment training, affirmative search processes, and the like. Now that we have those systems in place, it seems that we should be able to cut back on staffing in those areas and rely more on the systems. I'd like to know what you think is possible."

"I wish that were true, Tom... that the systems could operate with fewer personnel... but unfortunately, it goes in the opposite direction. In faculty search, for example, our improved processes enable us to generate more applicants for open positions, and the software calls for a lot more information from applicants than would have been provided in more traditional searches. All of that data takes time to manage and if we're not diligent in our follow up, we could lose diverse applicants who, for whatever reasons fail to complete their application files. We need to reach out to those applicants to get them to complete their files. Beyond that, we can't really trust the faculty members who are involved in the searches to treat applicants equally. We know that some faculty members put weight on the school from which an applicant earned their Ph.D. But focusing on pedigrees could cause some diverse applicants to be passed over inappropriately. So we need to carefully monitor all of the search committee decisions about whether to advance an applicant to the next step in the search process."

"I have to say, Gloria, that I'm a bit surprised that you don't think we can trust the faculty to identify the best qualified applicants," Hansen responded. "I recognize that there could be a small number of people on search committees who are biased in one way or another, but the entire search committee is involved in the decision so I think that problem should largely take care of itself."

"Maybe, but even if that's true," Moreno rebutted, "we have to produce a search record that we can defend legally in the event of a lawsuit by an applicant. We can't do that without a lot of oversight."

"I see," said the President. Well, in any case, please go back and take a hard look at your staffing and what you can do to cut back. Maybe a hiring freeze in the areas under your supervision. That would probably reduce our staff somewhat over the course of the year and would be very helpful for meeting this year's budget target."

"I'll take a look," Moreno equivocated. "But I'm not too

optimistic that we can accomplish much, and I am concerned about the free speech matter."

"Okay, please just do what you can," concluded the President in frustration.

A depressing morning, reflected Hansen, as he headed out for a stroll on campus before lunch, hoping the walk would brighten his day.

CHAPTER 6

THE DEPARTMENT

With the fall term underway for a couple weeks, following a mostly undisturbed lunch where she had been reviewing the research paper that was scheduled to be presented at the next Economics Department seminar, Krista Novikova had just left the Faculty Club. Strolling across campus, reflecting on her concerns about the empirical analysis in the paper she had just read, she was headed for the 1:00 PM meeting of the Economics Department faculty. As she was leaving the Club, she had encountered President Hansen, who apparently was on his way to a late lunch. Without stopping to talk, Hansen had given her a familiar nod of recognition. Krista reflected that, while he recognized her, the President was unlikely to know her name or even that she was a member of the economics faculty. She was untroubled by the President's disconnectedness. She hoped he was meeting with a potential donor or Trustee who could help address some of the financial concerns the School seemed to be facing.

On stepping outside the Faculty Club, she noted that the flowers that had been planted for the start of the academic year were already losing their vibrancy and looking leggy. The first signs of the end of summer were also apparent in the hint of fall colors beginning to show in the tree leaves.

Novikova was an exceedingly popular professor and as she walked across campus, she occasionally was greeted by undergraduate students who had done well in one or another of her classes. Mixed among the smiled greetings, of "Hi, Professor," was the occasional presumptuous "Hi Krista". Such familiarity from students seemed to have become more pervasive in recent years, and Novikova was not sure it was a good development. She knew young professors often encouraged students to use first names, as they were striving for friendship rather than professional bonds with their students. She was experienced enough to know that such familiarity could undermine respect and diminish the control a professor needed to have over the classroom, something that could be especially important for a young professor who aspired to be an effective teacher, unfortunately, even more so for a young female professor.

One student she recognized from last year silently ogled her as she walked across campus. She recalled that the student, a member of the school lacrosse team, had seemed to consider himself a "stud" and had unabashedly stared at her during class meetings and shown up at her office at unpredictable times when few other faculty members were around, sometimes broaching topics that were borderline inappropriate.... He was probably the student who gave her a hot chili pepper rating on RateMyProfessor.com.... Did he actually just wink when she sensed the leer and glanced his way?

Unthreatened and unimpressed by the juvenile, she continued her walk, reflecting, now, on the agenda for the day's meeting. She'd heard that the Chair had received the go-ahead from the President to begin recruiting for two new faculty members in anticipation of the promised gift from the alumni donor. Novikova believed it was critically important that those lines be focused on hiring in finance and accounting, but she also recognized that getting the Department to hire in those areas would be a challenge. How could she nudge the faculty to a decision to recruit in those areas and forego others, especially with Faquhir and maybe Sarks tugging in the opposite direction?

The other matter on the agenda was the three tenure cases, including one each in finance and accounting. None of the cases was clear-cut. Novikova had her own views but was unsure how to convince the others. The faculty vote on tenure cases, though only advisory to the campus Academic Personnel Committee, was critical, and without a clear majority of support from the Department, the probability of a negative outcome on tenure was high. Losing a faculty member in either finance or accounting might be even more damaging than not hiring in those areas.

As she continued her walk, her attention was drawn away from the pending meeting by an encounter with the small group of diehard students who were still protesting the beehive removal. She was pleased to see that the group appeared to be losing steam. She recognized that college students seemed to have a need to seek out things to protest and about which to try to effect change, but this one seemed particularly inane. Perhaps, she rebuked herself, she lacked a proper appreciation of the importance of bees.

Entering the building, as the elevator still was not working, she took the stairs to the third floor, grimacing as she passed the entrance to the Women's Restroom/Kitchenette, and wondering how such an insensitive conjunction could survive for so long in a university environment. Upon entering the Economics Department's conference room, Krista found that most of the other faculty members had already arrived. A few minutes later, the Department Chair called the meeting to order. "As this is a special meeting with a narrow agenda, and because we need to act quickly, I'd like to dispense with approval of the prior meeting minutes until our next regular meeting, and, given the narrow focus of today's agenda, I don't think there's much need for anyone to take minutes this morning."

"With due respect, Mr. Chair," interjected Professor Cory Sarks, condescendingly, "I object to postponing minutes approval and especially to not taking minutes in this meeting.... I'll accept postponing, even though it's highly improper to proceed without first approving the prior minutes, but I strenuously object to there being no minutes taken in this meeting. Either this is a faculty meeting or else it's just some kind of social gathering with no specific purpose. If it's the latter, I have more important things to do.... But, if it's the former and if there will be voting, we need to have properly prepared minutes."

No one in the room was particularly surprised by Sarks's rigid insistence on process. They had grown used to his ongoing efforts to disrupt and derail almost any attempt at forward progress. So this was just more of the same.

"Very well," responded the Chair, seeking to avoid confrontation with Sarks and feeling the need to get the group moving ahead quickly on faculty recruiting. "Can I ask if there's anyone here who would volunteer to take the minutes?"

Sarks quickly responded. "Well, I suppose we are expected to be talking about recruiting. As we all know, faculty recruitment is one of the most important actions this Department... or any department, for that matter, can undertake. For that reason, I am willing to prepare the minutes of this meeting but please, Mr. Chair, do not expect me to do so ever again."

"Supercilious asshole," Abby texted the other assistants, including a GIF of a sleeping sloth. TB stifled a laugh and texted back, "If you knew about him would you still have joined the Baird faculty?" Abby texted back a GIF of Mama June signaling thumbs down with both hands. Kyle Phillips texted back an applause GIF of Leonardo DiCaprio at the Oscars while Lin Chang did her best to look attentive.

"Then perhaps, if it's okay with you Cory, we can move forward."

Though Hill had been taken off guard by the insistence on minutes being taken, he felt that by accepting Sarks's offer he had avoided a potentially disruptive, time consuming, and largely pointless diversion into procedure and interminable appeals by Sarks to inaccurate interpretations of Robert's Rules. The Chair suspected that Sarks was possibly up to something. Otherwise he would not have volunteered. But, at this point, Hill could not see what possible harm could come of having Sarks take meeting minutes. It seemed ironic, Hill felt, that Cory was addressing the importance of faculty hiring. He was, in all likelihood, the worst faculty hiring mistake the Department had ever made, and possibly the worst that had ever been made at Baird. If there was ever a reason to question the practice of tenuring faculty, Sarks was the strongest case in point.

Professor Sarks had a good pedigree from a highly regarded economics Ph.D. program and had started his academic career at a leading university. With a solid early-career publication record, he was awarded tenure at that school. Subsequently, for reasons that were unknown to the Baird faculty at the time of his hiring, Sarks had decided to leave. Given his prior tenure at a more-highly ranked school, he was hired with tenure at Baird. Unfortunately, no one involved in the faculty search that culminated in his having been hired had bothered to check informally with his references or look into the details of his academic record. Eventually, the Baird faculty learned that Professor Sarks's prior colleagues actually threw a party to celebrate the fact that another school had been careless enough to actually hire him away. When asked, occasionally, about their mainly positive letters of recommendation, some of the letter writers questioned Baird's apparent inability to read between the lines as to what had gone unsaid. Some expressed a concern that Sarks might be able to breach the confidentiality of their letters, and, out of concern with retaliation, had avoided putting certain things in writing.

Reflecting on the hiring disaster that was Cory Sarks and that predated her joining the Baird faculty, Professor

Novikova felt there were two lessons the Department should have learned: first, be wary of hiring candidates that seem too good to be true, such as a candidate moving from a more highly ranked school to a weaker one, and second, don't rely on the written reference letters.

Since his arrival at Baird more than a decade ago, the School had come painfully to understand the reasons for celebration at Sarks's former school. He had proven to be a constant disruptor of the smooth operation of the Department. In Department meetings, he was capable of completely derailing almost any discussion if it was headed in a direction he did not support. He was willing to filibuster meeting discussions endlessly until other faculty members grew exhausted and simply gave up. He was known to threaten junior faculty members with negative tenure outcomes if they did not vote in support of his views. He would generally not respond on a timely basis to requests from the Chair for an indication of teaching preferences for the coming term, but once the teaching schedule was largely set, he would demand revisions to accommodate his own preferences, which often seemed to be designed to be contrary to the overall interest of the faculty to provide the best education the Department could for its students. He was known to demand that junior faculty members collaborate with him on research, and he actually expected these junior colleagues to undertake the full project with only occasional prodding from him. Since coming to Baird, his research output had been almost non-existent, and a few students had complained about his biases and even some more personal and unwanted overtures. Sarks's reputation for obstruction was well-known on campus, to the point that he was never asked to engage in campus or school service. Although he would sometimes volunteer for committee service at the campus level, because of his reputation for disruption, his offers to serve were never accepted.

With almost no research, recognizable problems in the

classroom, and no significant service, Sarks refused to compile the annual record that would be the basis for his own routine performance reviews, and he generally participated negatively in the performance reviews of his colleagues. Sarks blamed his lack of research output on what he claimed was a lack of significant research support and on conflicts created by a teaching schedule that did not suit his needs for research time. He dismissed the negative comments about his teaching as racially or ethnically motivated targeting and blamed his lack of service on the unwillingness of those involved in committee selection to include him, even though he had volunteered.

In light of all that, Hill felt himself fortunate to have largely deflected the matter of minutes-taking in the current meeting. "I expect that this can be a short meeting, today, and that there'll be plenty of time for the department personnel committee to meet after. We just have one item to discuss, that some, perhaps all, of you already know about. I met with President Hansen recently and he's approved our proposal to search for two new chaired professor hires. The actual hiring is still contingent on the donor coming through with the gift that I mentioned in our meeting at the start of the year, but at this point it seems pretty likely that the gift will happen. So we've been authorized to go forward with the search."

"Given that, I think now would be a good time for us to get organized and to focus our efforts. We have much to do. Most pressingly, we need to prepare the position announcements so we can get them placed in time for informal interviews at the upcoming meetings. Related to that, those of you who still haven't completed your affirmative recruitment practices training, please do so quickly. We can't actually start screening applicants until you all have finished the training. As we determine the focus of our recruiting efforts, some of you may know of prospects we might want to consider. Once the ads are placed, I hope you'll reach out to them and encourage them to apply. Since these are going to be chaired positions and prospects may not want their current schools to know they're looking around, we need to be very careful to keep the applicant list confidential."

"I'm afraid I must object, Mr. Chair," Sarks interrupted arrogantly. "As we learned from our recruitment training, it's against policy for any of us to reach out to specific individuals and encourage them to apply for the positions."

"Unfortunately, Cory's actually right about that," Larry Faquhir commented. "The HR people argue that reaching out to people we know is unfair to the people we don't know, and tends to perpetuate so-called good old boy networks and so could be implicitly racist and sexist. Personally, I think that while the concern has some legitimacy, the prohibition on reaching out is an absurd over-reaction.... When we search, we're trying to find and hire the best people.... We might reach out to people we know to encourage them to apply, but there are many checks on the process that help to assure that the ones we hire are the best from the pool of applicants. We all know that there are people who won't apply unless they get some encouragement and feel they'd be welcome. So if we don't reach out personally, I think we're unlikely to build the strongest applicant pool we can."

"Well, it's a fine line," the Chair concluded. "While the search committee has to treat all prospects the same, we, as individuals are also entitled to tell anyone we care to about our open positions. Now, why don't we move the discussion along?"

"Before we do, can we back up for just a minute?" asked Faquhir, "What, exactly, did the President say, Bob? Did he put any limits on the search other than that it would be for tenurable professors who would be deserving of holding endowed professorship positions?"

Hill and others on the faculty, recognized immediately that Faquhir was hoping to guide the search effort in a direction that served his own interest.

"Yes," Sarks joined in, seeing the potential to gain a temporary ally. "Yes, Bob, what *did* the President say?"

"Well..." began the Chair, seeking to buy some time before speaking, "I first tried to summarize for him the discussion in our last meeting. I mentioned that there are some areas, like public economics where we have no faculty, and I reviewed our recent hires in microeconomics and our coverage in macro. The President seemed to want to know where our needs were most pressing, so I told him about the growing staffing shortages in accounting and finance. President Hansen didn't get very specific about fields for hiring, but it did seem to me that he was supportive of hiring in those areas, so my impression is that we would do well to look for good candidates in finance and accounting."

Professor Novikova was pleased with the direction and was somewhat relieved that it appeared she had the support of the Chair and would not have to take a strong advocacy role in trying to get the faculty to "do the right thing" as she saw it to be.

"I guess I'm a bit confused," demanded Faquhir, who was not in favor of the direction the Chair seemed to be proposing. "I think we asked what the President told you... but it sounded like you just gave us the opposite: what you told the President. I, for one, would still like to know what the President told you. Did he actually say we needed to focus our search on finance and accounting or was he just listening?"

"If you'll allow me, I'm trying to tell you what happened... to give a more complete picture of the discussion," the Chair defended. "I recall suggesting that we search in those areas, and he seemed supportive, but I don't remember specifically what he said."

"So, as far as we know, he told you nothing about hiring focus, but you tried to steer him.... By what authority,

Mr. Chair, do you seek to speak for the faculty of the Department?" Sarks challenged. "We all recognize that you are the Department Chair, but as we all know, that doesn't mean diddle. It clearly does not mean that you can speak for the Department faculty. It sounds to me like you were just expressing your own opinions, but, as it relates to hiring focus, your opinion is no more important than that of any of the rest of us. When it comes to faculty hiring, you have one vote, as do we all. As near as I can tell from what you've said, the President didn't really commit to anything except that we could go ahead with a search to fill two professorships."

"In this instance, I find myself in agreement with Cory," jumped in Faquhir, who occasionally found Sarks to be a convenient ally, but still wanted to show some distance. "We never had a vote, and really not much of a discussion. So it doesn't seem that there was much basis for you to propose any particular hiring focus to the President."

Others in the room had been silent during this exchange, most wanting to avoid inserting themselves into the confrontation between the Chair and two vocal full professors. Only Professor Novikova showed any sign of concern. Her suggestion at the previous meeting to hire in finance and accounting was now under forceful attack, even despite the Chair's apparent support. At first, she had expected that settling on the hiring focus she sought to achieve would not be easy, but then, when Hill summarized, she had relaxed. She was not surprised, now, to see that Faquhir and Sarks were the most outspoken against it. Hoping that Hill would show some backbone, she chose to keep her powder dry for the time being and to look for a better opportunity to advance her position without seeming to be too much of an advocate.

However, to Novikova's dismay, the Chair, seeking to defuse the situation, back-peddled. "Well… of course we might be able to search in other areas… and I can speak with President Hansen about that possibility…. So maybe the best thing to do at this point would be to reopen the discussion of hiring focus and see if we can reach agreement.... Would anyone care to begin?"

"Hold on a second," responded Professor Faquhir. "Before we get into such an open discussion, I think we need to decide how we're going to decide. My suggestion is that we start by going around the room and see what suggestions people have for hiring focus. Then we can have some open discussion to see if we can narrow the list, and after that we can vote on specific areas of search."

Most faculty members in the room, especially those who were more experienced in dealing with Faquhir, recognized that in proposing to solicit a diverse array of opinions and preferences he probably had some undisclosed agenda in mind. But beyond inferring that he opposed hiring in finance and accounting and hoped to foster open conflict among the faculty, they could not discern what his agenda might be.

"I fully support Professor Faquhir's process suggestion," commented Sarks. "I've noted in the minutes that we have decided to discuss the options and then to decide on the hiring focus by faculty vote." Despite the mischaracterization of what had transpired, no member of the faculty felt compelled to get into a protracted argument with Sarks as to what actually had transpired and what belonged in the meeting minutes.

"Very well," said Hill, who apparently had failed to notice that Sarks had just mischaracterized a possible approach proposed by Faquhir as one that had been decided upon by the faculty. With resignation that the meeting was going to take quite a bit longer than he had hoped, he opened the discussion. "Who would like to begin?"

"Can we assume that in any case finance and accounting remain on the prospective focus list?" Professor Novikova queried, seeing the coalition that seemed to be forming between Faquhir and Sarks, and feeling that she could no longer remain silent.

"I think you can," responded the Chair.

"I also feel compelled to caution everyone," Novikova continued, "that voting would not necessarily lead to an outcome that would be best for Baird. I don't think there's any serious disagreement that finance and accounting are the two areas of our most pressing need. Yet, if faculty members vote their own self-interest and not what's most important for the School and our students, voting might lead us into hiring in areas where we already have strength and plenty of capacity."

"Not so fast, Krista," interjected Faquhir. "As we discussed in our prior meeting, these are very expensive areas in which to hire, and if we were to do so, it could easily draw resources away from support of our Ph.D. program and our research and travel budgets."

Several others in the room nodded their agreement with that sentiment.

Predictably, Professor Noach proposed that the hiring focus be on microeconomics. "I think we need to build on our strengths," he began. "We can't try to be good at everything. It's much better to strive for excellence in a few areas. We have a pretty strong contingent in micro, but some of us are near retirement and with our recent junior-level hires in micro, we need more senior leadership."

"Rather a nice argument, Jamie," responded Edwards. "I agree that we shan't be able to cover all areas of economics, especially when we've already branched out into accounting and finance.... Be that as it may, there are some core areas where we simply must do well. Macro is key among them. We didn't hire in macro last year and it would be most unfitting to forgo hiring in that area yet again."

The Chair turned toward the whiteboard and, in blue

erasable marker, made two bullets. Next to the first, he wrote "microeconomics," and next to the second, "macroeconomics."

"Well, that pretty much covers all of economics," whispered Kyle Phillips to Lin Chang, not recognizing that with her degree in accounting, she might not see his attempted humor in exactly the same light as he.

"Can you add a couple more bullets to the list you're building, Bob?" asked Novikova. "One for finance and one for accounting. As our Chair has said, and I strongly agree, these are the areas of greatest teaching need."

"Well, I disagree about adding those areas," said Faquhir. "We can't allow the so-called teaching needs of our students to drive our tenure-track hiring decisions."

"I completely agree," Sarks pounced. "With good microeconomics foundations, our students will be well-prepared for pretty much whatever comes along. If the need arises for them, they can master what they need to in finance or accounting on the job or by self-study. Moreover, we can always staff classes with part-time folks from nearby public schools or community colleges, or even practitioners since accounting and finance are such practice-oriented disciplines."

"Well, you may agree, Cory, but I certainly don't!" bristled Novikova, who had reached her limit on the academic elitism towards disciplines having anything to do with practice. "Sometimes, Cory, the things you say suggest that you actually know almost nothing about finance.... Quite a few of the more recent Nobel Prizes in Economics have been awarded to academic scholars working in finance," she challenged.

"Yes, yes, Krista, we all know that, but then what does the Royal Swedish Academy of Science really know about which scholarly contributions are important and which are not?" interjected Professor Noach. "In 2008 they actually awarded the prize to Paul Krugman, who turned out to be totally wrong, and look where he is now... writing newspaper columns and a regular focus of ridicule by people who actually know something. He's a total whack job who hasn't done a speck of research in years."

"I'm not sure what that has to do with anything," Novikova resumed somewhat more measuredly and not wanted to be diverted into a corner of trying to defend awarding the Nobel Prize to Krugman. "But in any case, it's absurd to believe that finance is not a serious academic discipline. And it's wrong to assume that students with enough economics don't need to be educated in finance. I insist that finance and accounting remain on the list we're building."

"No need to get all snippy, Krista," responded Professor Nikolaidis, failing to recognize that his interjected use of the term, "snippy" would not be well received by Novikova. "But what about the expense of hiring in those fields? I think perhaps we should be focusing on less expensive areas like economic theory."

"Actually," fumed Novikova, "I think you get what you pay for. We need to look at faculty hiring like any investment decision. What do we get if we hire another theoretician? Most likely we get someone who can only teach certain classes that are not very popular to begin with, and who writes papers that are rarely read or cited by anyone else. How many alums can you think of, Mark, who have decided to make important gifts to the School because of how pleased they were with their classes on economic theory...? I'll tell you – none."

"But what about finance?" she continued, a bit more calmly. "If you look over a list of our important donors, I'm sure you'll find that many of them work in such finance-oriented areas as investment banking and venture capital. Sure, the School has to pay more for faculty members who work in those areas, but the extra investment pays off in high returns from supporters of the School later on. Something similar is true of accounting, but in a different way. A very large fraction of our undergraduates go to work in the big accounting firms and go on to support the School later on in their careers, through donations and especially by hiring our students. So let's not exclude finance and accounting from the search just because they're expensive in the short run. I suspect they're the best investments we can make. And besides, we aren't making the investment. We don't have a separate department faculty salaries budget that we have to live within. That's the President's problem... to find a way to finance the positions. Moreover, I don't see that hiring in those areas would have any different effect on our departmental research and travel resources than would hiring in any other area. It's still two more professors to support."

"Let me say one more thing," she continued forcefully, seeking to cater to the self-interest of others in the room, "we all benefit when we hire people at high salaries. In my experience when econ departments are housed in B-schools instead of humanities, the higher salaries in business disciplines help pull up econ salaries. I think the same thing happens when econ departments branch out into areas like finance."

"No need to throw a wobbly, Krista," weighed in Professor Edwards. "I'm sure most of us agree that finance and accounting belong in the list we're building. I think we have a balance of strengths that is quite good, and I suggest that we not balls it up by hiring in specialty areas where we don't currently have some strength. So, like our Chair said, we don't currently have anyone who works in public economics.... But perhaps I differ with our Chair in that I believe we should keep it that way.... If we need to offer a course or two in public economics, it seems to me that's where we should be looking for a decent freeway professor."

"Freeway professor?" Professor Nikolaidis questioned, having never heard the term.

"Stop acting like such a prat, Mark," responded Edwards. "You know... someone who has no full-time faculty position or at least has one with compensation too meager to subsist on, and who teaches on one side of town in the morning, the other in the afternoon... and yet somewhere else in the evening."

"Colleagues... I think we can do without the pejorative attitude toward those of us who are dedicated to teaching," interjected Sarks, who was, himself, known to seek out opportunities to supplement his salary through adjunct teaching at nearby schools. "If you ask me, people who teach at more than one school do so because they're being sought out for their expertise, which is beyond that of many faculty members who focus excessively on research." Sarks had previously been officially reprimanded for having taken a teaching appointment at a foreign university during a paid sabbatical leave from Baird.

"I think Dan's right," commented Nicole Stewart, who had a reputation for not commenting in faculty meetings. "Let's not add confusion to the search by opening up to fields that are unrepresented among our current faculty. Quite a number of trendy subdisciplines have sprung up recently because they're topical... economics of climate change, gender and economics, for example. I suggest that we not focus our search so finely that we're limited to considering economists who only work in narrow and trendy subdisciplines. Most of us with general econ training can easily move into such areas if the research questions are of sufficient interest and importance. But if we hire specifically in a subdiscipline based on what's in fashion, we're likely to end up with someone who'll only work in the narrow area... even if, after a few years, the research questions become uninteresting."

"Niki's right," said Professor Koopman. "I've been around long enough to have seen quite a few good econ departments destroyed by losing focus and spreading too thinly. We need to avoid the allure of trendy fields and stick to the core."

"Well, this has been an interesting and, I hope, a useful discussion," the Chair attempted to conclude after a lull in the exchange of views. "So it seems clear that there's no support for hiring in a subdiscipline where we don't currently have some strength, and it appears we've identified four possible areas of focus. How shall we proceed to narrow things down further?"

"Maybe we can do a straw vote where we each rank the alternatives from four to one, with a rank of four being best," suggested Nikolaidis, innocently.

"I don't like the idea of ranking," responded Noach. Ranking suggests that the difference between ranks three and four is the same as that between ranks one and two. Maybe some of us think the best choice is ten times as good as the second best, but the others are all pretty close together. That kind of concern would suggest that we each just vote for the one we most prefer. I think that would be a better approach."

"Yes," said Edwards. "It would be… if we each had a clear favorite. But what if we each think three of the areas are pretty good, but one is really not? If we feel that way, your approach wouldn't work well."

"If I may suggest," began Professor Faquhir. "We can use a hybrid system. Let's first just vote on whether any of the areas is clearly not an 'acceptable' one in which to hire," using air quotes to set off the term. "If we get a majority saying one is not acceptable, we could drop that one from further consideration and then go on to see how we might further refine the list. Let's try that."

"So, you're suggesting that we each just vote like we think we should try to hire the best qualified candidate, except that there might be one area that we think should be excluded. Is that what you mean?" Koopman asked, as he felt himself becoming confused by all of the discussion of voting methods.

"Not really," responded Faquhir. "I'm just trying to see if we can narrow down the list a bit. Maybe later we might want to consider the option of hiring the best qualified candidates without regard to field."

Krista recognized that Faquhir's proposal was simply a veiled attempt to shift the voting focus away from finance and accounting, but it would be hard to argue against some kind of voting as a way to decide on focus. She chose to remain silent, expecting that the tactic proposed by Faquhir would not succeed, hoping others would see through the ploy

Having learned from experience that there was little point in debating with Faquhir over procedural matters such as this one, the faculty acquiesced. "Let's just vote," proclaimed Sarks.

"Wait," responded Koopman. "I'm confused about how we're supposed to vote. What's the question?"

"Simple, really," answered Faquhir. "We have four areas of potential interest, as we all know.... We're trying to decide whether one or more can be dropped from further consideration. I suggest that each of us have one vote, and that we each vote for the one area we most want to drop from further consideration."

"Okay, I guess," responded Koopman. "So a 'yes' vote is actually a 'no' vote, a vote to drop the area. Seems kind of upside down. But then how will we know if a field gets enough votes to be dropped?"

"Good question," rejoined Faquhir. "I propose that if an area gets a majority, we drop it, but otherwise leave it in. That way we would drop any area that was opposed by a majority of the faculty."

After hearing no dissent from that suggestion, Hill asked for a show of hands. But Novikova, recognizing that some of the untenured faculty might feel pressures to vote in particular ways, quickly interjected, that the vote should be by secret ballot.

Sarks hastily responded. "I don't see the need for secrecy. This is a simple matter... and a secret ballot would just be a waste of time."

Novikova countered, "According to our by-laws, Cory, as I'm sure you know, if any faculty member requests it, a secret ballot is required. I'm requesting a secret ballot." Sarks was exactly whom Novikova was concerned about. Given his past record, she felt that some faculty in the room would fear retaliation and would either try to vote as they perceived Sarks would want them to or would abstain. Even with the secret ballot, the Department was a small group, and she knew there was a reasonable chance that Sarks would be able to make a good guess as to how the assistant professors each had voted.

Following the discussion, a secret ballot was prepared, distributed, and collected. With twenty faculty members in the room and voting, none of the four choices received a majority. Microeconomics and macroeconomics each got four votes of "unacceptable," accounting and finance each got six.

"Well," commented Novikova, "that didn't work too well, Larry.... We don't actually know how many of us think any of the fields would be an acceptable area in which to search." In an attempt to shine some light on the hidden objectives of Faquhir and Sarks, she proposed, "How about if we vote again, but this time, we each vote on the acceptability of each area. You can vote that only one is acceptable or that more than one is... or even that all four are."

After the usual arguments against the approach and questions about how the results would be used, a new ballot was prepared and distributed. As it turned out in this round, one faculty member had voted that only microeconomics was acceptable and one had voted that only macroeconomics was acceptable. The other 18 had voted that all four areas were acceptable. The Chair, Novikova, and most others suspected that Professors Faquhir and Sarks were the two who were seeking to game the outcome, Faquhir favoring macro and Sarks favoring micro.

"So, I guess that didn't help us much, either," observed the Chair.

"I disagree," countered Sarks. "There are two fields with lower vote totals than the other two. Based on that vote we should drop those two.... We should drop finance and accounting, from further consideration."

"No way," retorted Professor Novikova. "We'd agreed that this was just a straw vote on acceptability. If we thought we were going to use it as an exclusionary vote, we quite likely would have voted differently. If we now use the results of this vote to exclude fields, even if they got majority support, we'll be giving complete control over the search focus to the two people who voted only for their pet disciplines and against all the others... even though all four field got overwhelming majorities." Novikova was upset that she seemed to have already lost the attempt to focus on accounting and finance, and even more so to see the move toward dropping those disciplines from consideration by reinterpreting the prior vote. How could her colleagues be so self-oriented and care so little for what would be best for students?

"I'm afraid we just made an important mistake," she continued. "I now agree with Larry. We should have decided how we were going to decide before we even started voting. That was a mistake. Let's not make it worse by using the latest straw vote to exclude disciplines. Let's go back and try the ranking approach that Mark first suggested."

Feeling empathy for Novikova, and not wanting to be led by either Faquhir or Sarks, the group acquiesced. Following another secret ballot where each person was to rank the four fields, four for best to one for worst, so that with 20 people voting the maximum total points for any field was eighty and the minimum was twenty, accounting and finance each got fifty-five points, whereas micro and macroeconomics each got forty-five. The Chair summarized, "Well, I think we were hoping that by this approach we might find a strong consensus to drop one or more of the four fields from further consideration. Clearly, that didn't happen. In fact, as it turns out, accounting and finance are the winners, whereas in the prior approach micro and macro were the winners.... I don't think we can drop any of them."

"Ok," said Nadir Kaur, who was growing tired of the meeting. "If we vote on acceptability, micro and macro come out on top. If we rank, finance and accounting come out on top. Let's just each vote for the one field we would most want to hire in, so we can save some time for the personnel committee meeting."

"Thank you for not referring to accounting and finance as the 'losers in the first approach,'" joked Novikova.

After the fourth balloting attempt, the votes came out three each for each of the four fields. All of the assistant professors and some others, fearing that their votes would be too easy to discern had decided to abstain. In frustration, the Chair concluded, "Like I said before, I was hoping we could narrow this search down. We did decide not to move into new subdisciplines, so I guess that's something. But beyond that, we've been at this for an hour and a half, and we've made no progress. I'll report back to President Hansen that the Department faculty would prefer to have an open search that includes consideration of candidates from all four areas. I don't like doing that, since we're likely to get back to the same problem once we've identified acceptable candidates from all four areas, but it seems that at this point, this is the best we can do... especially without knowing more about the donor's preferences."

"I was hoping we'd be able to finish both the department meeting and the personnel committee meeting before lunch," he continued, "but this one has taken much longer than I expected.... Let's take a break for lunch and to deal with email and other things, and then the tenured members of the faculty can reconvene at two PM for discussion of our tenure cases." Hill felt strongly that finance and accounting were the right focus and hoped that the faculty would eventually get to that realization, but he did not see how it would come about.

Novikova was disappointed in the results of the meeting, if only the assistant professors had had the courage to vote, she believed the outcome would have been different. Still, she had at least overcome attempts by Faquhir and Sarks to control the search outcome for now. She would just have to do her best to make sure the finance applicant pool was as strong as it could be.

Sarks and Faquhir separately were each satisfied that they had managed to keep the search open rather than focused on finance or accounting, and that subfields of no interest to them had been excluded. Now, the politicking and arm-twisting could begin. There would be other opportunities to narrow the search in directions they each preferred.

CHAPTER 7

THE DONOR

As the Economics Department faculty meeting was breaking up, President Hansen was straightening his desk in anticipation of the arrival of George Jennings (class of '57), he was reflecting on his objectives for the meeting. He had already contacted the Office of Advancement for Jennings's bio, knew that he had graduated with a degree in economics and, after that, had gone on to join the family business. He also knew that Jennings Oil had struggled during the '50s and '60s and into the '70s, until Saudi Arabia had recognized its overwhelming share of crude oil production and formed the OPEC Oil Cartel. The Jennings oil fields in Texas were marginal producers, extracting mainly high viscosity Medium to Heavy Crude Oil. Many of their wells were shut in and not producing during the era of low gasoline prices that preceded the formation of OPEC. In early 1974, thanks to Saudi Arabia, the price of crude oil from the Jennings fields more than tripled and production from the fields had more than doubled.

By the end of the 1960s, in the decade or so since his graduation from college, George Jennings had risen in the organization and had replaced his father as President of the company, with the father remaining as CEO into the mid-1970s. So, fitting the pieces together, George had been lucky, gaining his leadership position just in time to benefit from the oil price run-up. Since that time, except for a few brief episodes, crude oil prices had generally remained high, and George had become a billionaire. He was easily capable of making a substantial gift to the University. The Office of Advancement had pegged him for a major gift in the

$25 to $50 million range. So, while locking down a couple million to support chaired professorships in economics would be nice and would be perceived by most as a significant accomplishment for Hansen, he aspired to do better. Maybe if he could land a truly major gift that would help with the University's increasingly troublesome budget problems and would enable him to move ahead with his aspiration to provide need-blind admission with loan-free financial aid, a move he thought was necessary in order to maintain Baird's status and to put him on the radar for a presidential appointment to one of the elite universities.

Upon being notified by his AA that Mr. Jennings had arrived and that his assigned host from the Advancement office was just leaving, Hansen came into his outer office to greet him. Jennings, he found, looked a bit like a heavy-set version of Lyle Lovett. He was dressed in a summer-weight pick-stitched tan suit with an open-collared French blue shirt, and Justin hand-tooled cowboy boots that showed signs of hard use. He held an El Presidente Silverbelly Stetson in his left hand. "Welcome back to campus, George," Hansen enthused as he took in the view and extended his right hand. "How can it be that I've been here for four years and we've not previously met? Somehow it seems like every time I was able to make it to Texas you were away on business." In reality, while Hansen had made a few trips to Dallas and Austin, he had never been to West Texas, and certainly had never aspired go there.

"Well, it's nice to finally meet you, too Tom…. I can call you that, right?" he said, shaking the President's hand with a grip more aggressive than necessary. "Tell you the truth, the last few years have been a busy time for me, and it's been hard to focus on some of the things I care greatly about. I finally got an opportunity to be in this area and I'm really happy to be back on campus. I've been hearing from a few alumni friends that great things are going on at Baird and I'd like to see what I can do to help out in some small way."

President Hansen knew that there was nothing alums liked more than getting back on campus and interacting with a few students and faculty. Jennings, he expected, would be no exception. "I see that we've put together a busy schedule for you today, George, and that I have to turn you back over to your host in a couple hours. Now, if it suits you, I have a golf cart waiting for us downstairs so we can take a quick campus tour and then we have a lunch reservation at the faculty club. I should be able to get you back here by 2 o'clock or so.... Shall we head out?"

"Great. I'm eager to see what all is new. It's been almost a decade since I was last on campus, so I'm especially looking forward to my meeting this afternoon with a group of students in the Economics Department.... I hear the gender mix of econ students has changed quite a bit since my time."

As they were driven around the campus on one of the School's electric carts, the President was busily pointing out the sites that he hoped would bring back fond memories for Jennings. The driver knew from experience and training to avoid the more austere and utilitarian buildings that had been constructed in recent years and to concentrate on historical and iconic buildings, campus water features, athletic and recreational facilities, and the new dorm – focusing especially on areas with high student traffic. The tour timing was strategic, as well: a window of time when most students were between classes and meeting for lunch or socializing on the quad.

President Hansen could not help but notice that Jennings seemed far less interested in the campus physical plant than in checking out the co-eds, which, he believed, was one of the main reasons many donors liked to visit the campus. Jennings, he found, was amused by the beehive protesters and recalled that during his time, the issues students were rallying about seemed to have been more consequential – the civil rights movement, the beginnings of the Vietnam War. When he mentioned the contrast, Hansen responded that there were some other matters about which students these days cared greatly. Race and gender continued to be hot-button issues and environmental damage had become a major concern. Noticing that Jennings seemed to flinch a bit at the mention of the environment, Hansen wondered if he'd just committed a serious faux pas.

When they arrived at the dorms, Hansen felt compelled to comment on the construction delays and to try to paint a word picture of how the site would eventually appear. "Well, I come from oil country, you know," Jennings interrupted, "where everything looks like it is under construction all the time, with rigs, wells, pipelines, and refineries scattered about. I'm sure you'll get this sorted out. Looks to me to be very close to being finished."

"Yes, I believe it is.... I'd really like to get to West Texas sometime for a tour of your facilities.... So, how's the gasoline business going these days? I know from filling up my car that the price seems to be holding up. So I suppose Jennings Oil's doing pretty well."

"Yeah, I guess gasoline prices maybe do seem high," responded Jennings. "But that's gasoline and we aren't really in the gasoline business.... We extract crude oil. We're a non-integrated producer so we sell to refiners who make the final products. There's a lot more than crude oil that goes into the gasoline you're buying for your car." It was clear to Jennings that Hansen, despite his chemistry Ph.D., was fairly clueless about the industry, so he launched into a tutorial. "Our crude oil's mostly what they call Heavy Crude. Compared to what comes out of Saudi Arabia and some other places in the U.S., our product is messy, hard to handle, and high in content of things we don't like, like sulfur.... Refiners won't pay nearly as much for our crude as they will for Light. They have to do a lot of extra processing to make a saleable product and, especially here in the U.S., they have a bunch of environmental restrictions that make the processing expensive. On top of that, there are both state and federal taxes on the gasoline you buy at the pump. Have you ever looked at the stickers on the gas pump that set out how much of the price is taxes?" Jennings asked rhetorically. "I can tell you that it's a lot. Even in Alaska, which has more oil than they know what to do with, it's more than 30 cents per gallon and that doesn't include all the hidden taxes that are levied on crude and refined product producers.... Long-story-short, anymore, I don't actually know too much about what's going on in the oil production side. I spend most of my time now on the environmental issues that are threats to my company."

They rode on in silence for a brief period before the tour ended at the Faculty Club. The Club was in the older section of the campus, away from the dorms and much of the student activity. The building exterior was of the same argillite stone as the main buildings on the quad. The interior was of tiger oak, richly stained a dark honey brown. Some of the faculty were clustered around a bar that resembled an old English pub. Others were working their way through a buffet line or seated at cloth-covered tables with traditional wood chairs. Jennings and Hansen were greeted by a somewhat casually dressed host and were shown to a private dining room of the same wood and with a tapestry covered floor and oil paintings of the original campus on the interior walls. The ten-foot windows were paned with antique-looking clear glass and overlooked the quad.

Instead of the buffet that was open to faculty members and their guests, Jennings and the President were offered table service. They ordered from menus accordingly. Over an aperitif, Hansen steered the conversation to less-controversial small-talk that gave him time to recover from his blunder and to promote some of the University's work on environmental issues. As salads were served, he decided it was time to try to get back on track and launched into a serious discussion of what Jennings could do to support the School. "You must be very proud of what you've been able to accomplish with your degree from Baird, just as Baird is proud to have you as an alum. I hope you could see from our tour that the campus is doing pretty well. That said, there's still a great deal more that could be done with more resources. You mentioned that you're interested in learning what you can do to help the School, George. So maybe we can explore that for a few minutes."

"Well, sure we can, Tom. It's something I've been pondering about quite a bit. And I think you know that I've been speaking with the Chair of the Econ Department, what's his name, Dr. Hill, I think, or something like that. He gave me some ideas about faculty hiring that we might want to explore further."

"Yes... well... of course, funding some new faculty hiring would do a lot to boost the stature of the Economics Department.... But maybe before we go to that, we can talk about an idea that would be of great value to our students, campus-wide, especially those who're struggling to afford their education." Seeking to sift the focus to his pet projects, he launched in. "You probably know that there's been increasing concern about the affordability of college education. The most highly ranked schools and some of our peer schools have taken steps to address that serious social problem. Many of those schools, including almost all of our peers, have moved to what's called need-blind admission. Schools with need-blind admission don't consider an applicant's ability to pay tuition when they make admission decisions. Those schools effectively guarantee that adequate financing will be available to the student. The financial aid to those students might include a combination of scholarships, work-study commitments, and loans. More recently, public attention has focused on the high debt burdens some students accumulate in the course of completing their degrees. Some of our peers have addressed the concern by promising financial aid that's debt-free. I'm sure you can see that the combination of need-blind admission and debt-free financial aid is an expensive proposition but very important for many students.

"I'm sorry to have to admit that Baird has lagged a bit behind some or our peers on this, as we haven't yet committed to either need-blind admission or debt-free financial aid. We're just not quite there in terms of our ability to move those initiatives forward. A major gift that was focused on student financial aid could get us a long way there. I'm wondering if that initiative might be of interest to you. A significant gift could enable us to launch a named scholarship program, help to maintain our stature with our peer schools, and might also be a nice visible way for Jennings Oil to build some goodwill."

Leaning back in his chair and setting aside his fork, Jennings responded, "I can see that would be good for Baird, Tom. But it sounds like you're talking about a big number, one that's more than I can do at this time. You probably know through your development people that my wife of 27 years passed away a few years ago and that my children with her are both doing quite well, but maybe you haven't heard that I remarried four years ago to a wonderful woman. We have a two-year-old daughter and Tiffany's pregnant with a new baby that's due in a couple months. At this point in my life, I need to make sure that Tiffany and our children are well-cared for. So, for now, I'd just like to focus on what I can do for the Economics Department."

"Fuck," Hansen thought to himself. How had Advancement failed to fill him in on Jennings's apparently young bride and new family? Richardson was going to hear about this screw-up before the end of the day.

"Well, before we go back to that, maybe just one more thought. I know you see the value of a Baird education and the importance of helping to support the Baird students who are in need. We do have a planned giving program that would enable you to defer a major donation until after your family was well provided for...." Even if the gift was deferred through such an arrangement and would not help to rectify the immediate financial situation, Hansen knew that it would still be included in his own measured performance.

"Hold on Tom. You seem to be operating with some misconceptions. So let me lay it out more clearly for you," Jennings flared. "First, while I enjoyed my time here as a student, it was mainly the party atmosphere that appealed to me. I recall that Baird was ranked as the number one party school by one of the girly magazines in the year I accepted. And the girls on campus at the time were pretty hot.... Too bad there weren't more of them then, like there are now," he mused. "Beyond the fun, I can't say that I really got that much out of the education. I did pick up a bit of finance and some accounting that were somewhat useful in my personal life, but not much beyond that. Now, maybe you think that Baird is somehow responsible for my business success... but not really. The plain truth is that I got really lucky on the timing of my move into the company presidency. If not for OPEC, we might easily still be the struggling company that we were in the '60s."

"Second, I know what planned giving is. My kids' schools are already after me for that, but my company's basically an oil wildcat operation. It wouldn't take much of a change in oil prices or environmental regulations to totally destroy us. Given that, I'm not ready to consider any kind of planned giving arrangement."

"Third, and this is the most important point, this is a family decision. I want to support Baird, but I also want to be sure Tiffany's on board with whatever we do. She's agreed to a couple million. That's as far as I'm willing to press."

"So, bottom line, I came here to meet with you about funding a couple of chairs in economics. And given the educational benefits I got from Baird, and my discussions with that department chair, I think I'd be interested in supporting chairs in accounting and finance. I'd like them to be named in honor of my parents, one for each of them. How does that sound, Tom?"

As Jennings concluded, their entree's arrived and the two ate in silence for a few minutes. It was clear to Hansen that he needed to back-peddle, but now he was actually in trouble. Funding chairs in those areas would make the School's financial problems worse, not better. Maybe he could at least control the damage by getting Jennings to focus on areas in economics that would be less expensive to staff. "That sounds like a wonderful way for you to honor the memory of your parents, George. So let's think along that track a bit. My only concern is that the specific focus on finance and accounting may not be what would most benefit our students. We already have some good faculty members in those areas, including some early-career people who'll be coming up for tenure soon. If they get tenure, as I expect they will, we'll be pretty well covered in those areas for the foreseeable future."

Most of what he was saying, he knew, was not exactly true. The School could use more faculty in those areas but hiring would be very expensive. And, while it was true that there were untenured faculty in those areas, he had next to no information on the likelihood that they would receive tenure. The real driver of his efforts at this point was to avoid an increase of a few hundred thousand dollars in annual operating losses that would arise if the hiring focus couldn't be changed.

"Well, I'm not totally locked in on finance and accounting," Jennings responded, having calmed down a bit. "I heard what you were saying earlier about student interest in the environment. Maybe it'd be better to think about those areas. I'm sure my parents would've agreed, and, given my position at Jennings Oil, the environment has to be a major concern of mine, too. It also would look good for Jennings Oil to be supporting education in those areas."

Hansen was relieved. It appeared that Jennings had stumbled upon one of the areas where hiring was cheap. So maybe the financial hit would not be too great. "Let's work on that, then," he said. "Is there anything more specific you have in mind?"

"There sure is," Jennings's features hardened noticeably. "I hate all of this environmental crap that's going on now about how carbon-based fuels are destroying the earth. Sure, there's some truth to it, but what's the alternative that's both affordable and doesn't impact the environment? It takes a lot of energy to manufacture a solar panel, the materials that go into the panels are toxic, and large solar farms disrupt the natural environment. Wind farms kill birds, and most people think they're eyesores. The amount of energy supplied by wind and solar is also unpredictable... subject to the whims of nature. No one's really in favor of nuclear power, even though nuclear may be the most efficient and reliable energy source."

"Don't get me wrong," Jennings continued, "I'm not saying we should forego alternatives to carbon-based fuels entirely, but no one's doing the cost-benefit analysis. Students need to be educated on both the pros and the cons and need to learn to think about the choices more rationally and less emotionally. So it seems to me that a faculty member who focuses on environmental economics could be a good addition to the economics department and could do some good."

"And then, maybe, a chair in the economics of the oil and gas industry would be another good addition, something like the University of Oklahoma has.... As I mentioned this morning, I have to spend almost all my time holding off new regulations that could kill us. It's easy for our elected officials to pick up votes by championing legislation or regulations that drive up our cost and reduce the supply of carbon-based fuels. I think we need a voice of reason on that front, as well... someone who can help voters to understand the full consequences of regulating the energy sector."

While he was grateful that discussion had moved away from the more expensive disciplines, Hansen was dismayed that Jennings seemed to be proposing hires who would go against the popular views of most of the faculty. He was also concerned that if new hires really did what Jennings seemed to want, it would be nearly impossible for them to attract any significant grant funding. But, of course, scholars who worked in those areas generally knew that major funding agencies like the Department of Energy would only fund research that they expected would produce results popular with voters. But maybe, if the School could find pro-environment candidates in those areas, it would work out okay. It might be best to follow this emerging path of least resistance and to hold off on trying for something more ambitious or less controversial. "I think we can work with that," he said. Let me have our Advancement Office follow up with you to iron out the details."

"I see we are getting close to the time when I need to get you back to the office for your afternoon schedule, but we do have time for coffee and dessert if you care to."

"Not a coffee drinker," replied Jennings, who was unimpressed by Hansen and eager to bring the meeting to a close, "and Tiffany's pressing me to lay off of the desserts. If we get back a bit early, I have a couple of calls I should return."

As they headed back across campus and Jennings admired the scenery, Hansen was reflecting as to how he would break the news to Economics Department Chair Hill that the plan Hill had to fund endowed chairs in accounting and finance had not quite worked out as expected.

CHAPTER 8

HARVARD SQUARE

When faculty members wanted to break away from group lunches with colleagues at the Faculty House, they most often chose the Harvard Square Café. The Café offered a light lunch menu with outdoor table service in a heavily planted garden, and enough water features to assure the privacy of conversations. Coming from the contentious Economics Department meeting over hiring, when Prof. Novikova arrived at the Café, she found that Heather Martin had already arrived, claimed a private table, and was sipping a glass of some sort of white wine. With a brief hug and European-style double-cheek kiss, she joined Heather at the table. "Wine looks like a good idea after the meeting I just came from... but let's not talk about that," she said as she ordered.

Krista and Heather had gotten to know each other five years before, when they had served together on the search committee that was responsible for the appointment of Thomas Hansen as Baird's President. During their time on that committee, they quickly discovered that they shared a common view of the candidates the headhunter had surfaced. Both had opposed Hansen's appointment, but they had lost the argument to the then-serving chair of the Board of Trustees, who had forcefully insisted that Hansen was "the real deal." They both were dismayed by Hansen's apparent naiveté about the economics of higher education and school finance. Both felt that he owed his appointment to a carefully cultivated veneer of shallow "smart talk" about social issues, his postured commitment to liberal education, and the appearance of wanting to regain the fading glory of Baird University. Since that time, they both had felt vindicated in their concerns. The Board Chair who had driven the decision had long-since moved on.

"I've been looking forward to an opportunity to catch up," said Heather. How was your summer?"

"Very nice... and a welcome break from campus," Krista responded, "especially with pointless meetings like the one I just experienced.... Now, about last summer, one of the European finance associations held its annual meeting in Glasgow. I was on the program and presented some of my latest research, as well as discussing a couple of other papers.... So, I was pretty busy during the conference, but also was able to spend some personal time touring parts of Scotland and even into England."

"Let's order, and while we wait, I'll give you the Cliffs Notes version."

With salads nicoise on the way, Novikova sketched out her summer. "After the conference, I drove along the western shore of Loch Lomond to Fort William, which is a small town most of the way to Inverness. The drive along the Loch was spectacular but scared the you-know-what out of me, especially for an American unused to the narrow and winding roads bordered by irregular stone walls that seemed like an emery board ready to file the rough edges off the side of the car, or sheer drops from literally the very edge of the road into the lake. While the white-knuckle drive along the lake shore was terrifying, it could have been even worse... like I could have ended up in the lake.... Oh, and when I arrived at the Glasgow airport, the car rental company offered to upgrade me into a larger car at no charge. Fortunately, a friend had mentioned that when he rented in Ireland, the roads were so narrow that when he returned the car he had to pay for damage due to a lot of scratches from branches of some kind of hedges that were growing next to the road.... I suspected that Scotland would be

138

no different... turns out I was right! With hindsight, I can see why the rental company might have been pushing the upgrade to a bigger car."

"So, Heather, back to my story... just north of Fort William, I stayed for a few days at the Inverlochy Castle Hotel, a stone mansion that was built in the 1800s. From there, I spent an afternoon hiking on Ben Nevis, and another day driving via Loch Ness up to the Culloden Battlefield, from the late 1700s and into Inverness, which is quite a beautiful setting. And maybe the best part of the trip was that I didn't think about Baird even once for a couple weeks."

"Any sighting of Nessie?" Heather asked with mock seriousness.

"That was actually one of the funnier things along the drive. The Loch is really nothing special compared to others in Scotland. There's a small museum/tourist stop along the western shore, where you can see pictures of purported sightings and an old two-person submarine that apparently was used by somebody to search for the monster. The best thing at the museum was probably the ice cream. But how could you drive past Loch Ness without checking out the museum?"

"After returning to Glasgow a few days later, in a car that, amazingly, was still undamaged by the narrow roads, I headed south to the Lake District of England and spent a few days there hiking in the hills around the lakes. Of course, I had to stop in at Hill Top House, which is Beatrix Potter's cottage overlooking Lake Windermere. My favorite stop on that part of my trip was the town of Lanark, which I came to on my way to the Lake District. Lanark is a fully-restored cotton mill town from the days of the industrial revolution. Given my economics background, I found the development around the mill fascinating, and something I couldn't hope to see in the U.S."

"But, enough about me, as they say. I know how self-absorbed it sounds when someone goes on about their latest trip." Krista felt sure that with her commitment to the University and her family obligation Heather would stay close to home. "How about your summer? I know you're always busy dealing with the School's finances, but I hope you were able to find some time for yourself."

"My summer was ok, Krista, but before we get into that, I couldn't help noticing that when you first got here, it seemed that you were troubled about something... maybe related to the department meeting you mentioned."

"Well, that's quite perceptive of you, Heather, as usual.... We did have a difficult and, I have to say, pointless meeting about recruiting. I wonder why it is that faculty members, including some in my department, seem unable or unwilling to step away from their personal interests and just do what would be best for the school. But let's set that aside for now.... I really want to hear about your summer."

"Sure, but let me just say that I suspect the people in your department are not so different from others on campus... or anywhere, for that matter. This group I belong to... that Hansen likes to refer to as his Executive Leadership Team... is anything but a team. It's just a small group of key administrators, each of whom seems to be focused on what's best for them... excluding me, of course," Heather joked about herself even though Krista knew that Heather's commitment to doing what was best for Baird was absolute. "Why the confluence of conflicting interests should work to the benefit of the School escapes me.... But enough about that."

"Now, let me get back to your question.... I did spend a few days at a conference for college and university administrators that was nearby. But, as I'm sure you know, I'm not much of a traveler.... I can't help but feel personally responsible for Baird's financial soundness... and being away from it for more than a few days just makes me too uncomfortable.... It's just the way I'm programed, I suppose."

"To be honest, Krista, I found this past summer a bit disconcerting... more so than in previous years."

"So, what happened?"

"Well, nothing much really and certainly not much that was unexpected. It's just that our finances for the year didn't come out too well, not as well as we'd hoped. Or, maybe I should say, they were worse than expected.... I can't go into detail, but you do already know that we were anticipating running a deficit for the academic year. When it was all in, things turned out to be a bit worse that we thought they would be."

"Really! Was it anything in particular, Heather?"

"Not really. We did have some unexpected problems with the new dorm project, but it's hard to think of a capital project that comes in on budget, so that's nothing new. But there are other problems... with enrollments and financial aid... and a few other things that are making my job harder. A lot of people are running over budget and there's no accountability. I sometimes feel forced into the position of having to push back on everyone's plans and aspirations... and, to put it mildly, that's making my job less fun, and more uncomfortable."

"I'm a bit surprised," Heather continued, "that even after four years, that weenie, Hansen, still doesn't seem to understand the importance of the financial health of the School. Or maybe he just chooses not to understand. He seems to think we can just do whatever we want, and that the finances will take care of themselves. So, I increasingly, find myself in difficult conversations with him."

"Oh, I'm starting to get the picture, Heather.... But can't you find a few others in the Administration who also see the problems and can help absorb some of the pushback...? And what about the Trustees? Don't they see the problem? Can't some of them help?

"Unfortunately, I don't think I can enlist their help. Like I was saying earlier, it seems to me that the others in the Administration, mainly the members of Hansen's ELT, all care more about their own fiefdoms than about the financial health of the School. The Provost wants to hire more faculty, the head of admissions wants to admit more students, even if doing so would require more financial aid, and the head of advancement wants more resources for development but has not been able to boost giving to the School. And I can't really go directly to the Trustees, though some of them do ask.... But it's not my place to tell them of my concerns."

"That all sounds awful for you, Heather... but maybe now that the academic year is underway, maybe Hansen and some of the others will be busy on other things, and that'll give some time for things to settle down."

"I guess so," Heather responded unenthusiastically. "I suppose we'll just have to wait and see."

"Well, of course I'm not as close to all this as you are, but it does seem like there are some positive developments on the financial front," Krista continued. Apparently, we're close to landing a major gift for hiring in my department. Ironically, it's that gift that led to the tensions and in-fighting in the faculty meeting I just came from."

"I hadn't heard about the gift," Heather responded. "We'll need to see how that works out. Sometimes gifts come with enough restrictions that accepting them actually makes our financial condition worse. But, of course, while Hansen might try to negotiate for some flexibility, like most other university presidents, he's not going to turn down a gift just because accepting it would make the financial situation worse," she scoffed. "His performance is gauged by the Board mostly on the basis of fundraising, not fiscal management."

Seeking to move off of further discussion of university finances, Krista tacked. "I had a bit of my own annoyance to deal with this past summer, let me tell you."

"I made the mistake of agreeing to serve on a Faculty Senate committee that's responsible for making preliminary assessments about alleged violations of the Faculty Code of Conduct," she continued.

"Usually it is not a busy committee. We only need to engage if there are allegations of misconduct and those are pretty rare. But, last spring, university Administration received a complaint alleging that a faculty member in one of the sciences... I'm being deliberately vague here, since I don't want to breach any confidentiality obligations.... Anyway, the allegation was that this faculty member was upset about something and threatened to kill several faculty colleagues before, themselves, committing suicide."

"Really!" exclaimed Martin. "I've never imagined that such a thing might happen at Baird."

"Well, it did.... I suppose it could happen anywhere.... But the thing that gets me is how the whole thing was handled by my committee. Our job is pretty simple... sort of like a grand jury... we're just supposed to make a preliminary assessment of whether the allegations, assuming they're true, would appear to violate the Code of Conduct."

"But how could threatening to kill colleagues not be a violation? That makes no sense to me."

"I know.... Right?" responded Krista. "In this case, when we received the complaint from the Administration, we also received copies of statements from several faculty members who reported that they'd heard the threat and felt that it might have been made seriously. We also received a copy of a response from the person alleged to have made the threat, conceding that they were angry but could not remember whether they had made such a threat or not... So, not really a denial."

"That seems pretty open and shut as far as your committee's concerned. So, I suppose the person was removed?"

"One would think... but our chair and some members of the committee are fixated on 'process'," countered Krista, setting off with air quotes. "Although the allegations would be an obvious violation and were not even disputed by the respondent, our committee procedures suggest that we should go back to the Administration and ask for more information. So all we could do in our first meeting during the summer was to draft a letter to the Administration asking if there was more evidence.... We had to do that even though there clearly was none."

"I don't get it," Heather reacted. "What more evidence could there possibly be that would make the incident not a violation?"

"I completely agree, Heather.... It's obvious... but nonetheless, that's what we did. So two weeks later, the committee had to meet again to be formally notified of what we all already knew... that the Administration had no additional information."

"So then, I guess, after that you could move forward to make a recommendation."

"Well, again, one would think.... But, again, not so. Instead, our 'procedures' as interpreted by some members of the committee seem to suggest that we're supposed to ask the respondent for comment or any information they might have. So all we did in that meeting was we voted to do that... to ask for a response to the allegations.... So then another three weeks went by, and we got a message from the respondent, but the message just reiterated what the person had stated in the earlier response. It provided no new information.

"The back-and-forth took weeks and seemed rather pointless. Given the strength of the evidence that came to us along with the original allegation, it's hard to conceive of there being anything that would lead the committee not to believe there was a prima facie violation.... So we finally did get to vote to refer the matter for a full investigation... but the whole process took almost two months.... It was kind of surreal hearing the committee chair and some members congratulating themselves on the committee's adherence to process, even in the face of an obvious case, and one where delay could have had tragic consequences."

"Wow... we all know that university faculties pay great heed to process, but your committee seems to have taken it to a whole new level."

"Oh... Heather, I just realized what time it is," Krista exclaimed as she stood to leave. "I have another meeting in a few minutes and I need to get back to campus.... It was nice to catch up a bit after the summer. I'm sorry to rush off and I hope we can do this again soon.... It seems cathartic for both of us," she laughed. "Let me send you an email and we can put something on our calendars."

CHAPTER 9
THE DEPARTMENT

Following their break for lunch, the tenured members of the Econ Department faculty were re-assembling in the conference room. Some had arrived early and were opening their laptops to review the tenure cases they would be discussing and to check email. Professor Koopman was among the first to arrive and, after recovering from his climb up the stairs, was studiously typing something on his iPhone. After pressing "send" on the iPhone, the following message, addressed to the facilities manager and copied to econfac@baird.edu, appeared in the email boxes of all his colleagues.

Hi Ron,

At this stage, I would prefer if you would STOP with the emails of hope and just advise us when the elevator is actually working again. There have been too many disappointments. I will be surprised if it works by the end of this term – like last term. On the positive side, I am getting my steps in....

Cheers,

In the stream below Koopman's message was the following message from the facilities manager:

There appears to be some light at the end of the elevator tunnel.... After shipping difficulties, the parts are now in the hands of our local elevator technician, who should be on-site to install tomorrow.

With any luck, we'll have our elevator back soon.

Sorry for the inconvenience and thanks for your patience

Ron

Winded by her dash from the parking lot and the stair climb, Krista Novikova entered and took a seat at the table around which the others sat.

"Did anyone happen to hear the latest on our student matriculations?" asked Professor Noach. "I heard that applications to Baird were down this year and that matriculations were down even more. But it seems to me that our class sizes in econ have been increasing. Seems to me that these larger and larger classes are hurting our students. So I think we need to be hiring and growing the faculty." In the context of the Personnel Committee meeting soon to be underway, Noach's comment was a not-so-subtle reminder of the cost of denying tenure to the assistant professors who were up for review. No one bothered to respond.

The meeting, like the earlier one, was chaired by Prof. Hill. "This morning's meeting took quite a bit longer that I expected, so I feel that we're now under some time pressure. We don't have the luxury of deferring this meeting since our recommendations on tenure are due. Let's try to be expedient if we can. As you all know, we have three cases to consider: Kyle Phillips in econ, Sean Lopez in finance, and Lin Chang in accounting. I hope we can finish this meeting by five or six. Toward that end, I'd like to call upon a senior person in each area to present the case for the tenure candidate in their area. Let's start with Phillips. Jamie, I know you've reviewed the case. Would you mind taking the lead on this?"

"Well, of course I do mind... we should all review each case carefully... but I'll do the spiel.

"So, here goes.... Phillips got his Ph.D. from the U of Maryland about six years ago. His research is mainly on topics related to industrial organization. He has three papers in top-tier econ journals and a handful of others in journals a bit below top-tier. Overall, it's probably enough for tenure. The rub, if there is one, is that the top-tier papers are all from his first few years here and are all coauthored with senior people from Maryland, including with his dissertation advisor. The more recent work is with more junior faculty and hasn't placed as well. Overall, I think three top-tier papers and some other work is enough for tenure. His teaching seems to be okay – not great, but who among us can claim to be a great teacher? And his service is okay for an untenured faculty member. So I think Phillips is deserving of tenure."

"I'm not sure I agree with you, Jamie," Cory Sarks picked up the discussion pre-emptively. "Like you said, those three pubs in A journals are all coauthored with senior people. How are we supposed to know whether he contributed much more than just running the computer? I think the failure of his later papers to place well is strong evidence that he's not driving the research. I'll be voting 'no'."

"Well, I think it's unfair describe those papers as 'failures', Cory," countered Noach. "The journals are good, and sometimes even very important work appears in them."

"Sorry to say that I also am likely to be a 'no' vote, but not for the same reason as Cory," Larry Faquhir commented. "I think the output's okay up to this point, but I'm not very optimistic about his future productivity. He has a couple of papers under review at good journals, but they were submitted just before the deadline for preparing his tenure case. That's a red flag to me. I suspect those submissions were premature and will be rejected by the journals, and I don't see much evidence of an ongoing commitment to high quality research."

Discussion of the research continued for some time, each faculty member seeking to influence the outcome, but none having any material effect on the views of the others. The one thing that was clear was that only Noach had gone to the trouble to actually read the papers and attempt to evaluate their contributions. The others relied mainly on journal placements, even though all would concede that placement is not a particularly reliable indicator of the importance or impact of any given research paper.

As the discussion of research seemed to be drawing to a close, Nicole Stewart picked up, "While I do have some concerns similar to Larry's, I'd find it hard to oppose tenure for Kyle.... I have to put some weight on the contribution he makes to the diversity of our Department. I see him meeting with quite a few students of color and he seems to be an effective mentor and role model for some of our students. Also, I think racial and ethnic differences can be a significant impediment to forming effective research teams. So, I plan to vote in favor of tenure."

"Hold on," Sarks rejoined. "I think it is highly improper to allow the fact that Phillips is black to affect your vote. Either his record is good enough or it's not.... In my view, it's not."

"I disagree," argued Stewart. "I don't think we can be colorblind when we consider such consequential decisions, and we can't be rigid. If a person can contribute to our academic mission in ways that others can't, we can't simply dismiss that, and if a person is disadvantaged in research collaboration for reasons that are not reflective of innate ability, we can't ignore that either."

After further discussion of the tenure case, including a scattering of comments on minor concerns about his teaching, sometimes based on the written comment of only one student, the Committee voted and moved on to discussion of Sean Lopez, deferring the announcement of all vote outcomes to the end of the meeting.

Novikova, who had been mainly silent in the Philips discussion, took the lead. "Sean's degree is from the University of Texas, also from around six years ago. He's been at Baird ever since. The research record, in my judgment, is very solid.

He has two single-authored papers in top-tier finance journals, and two other coauthored papers in a journal that many schools consider to be top tier. He also has a couple other papers under review at top tier journals, both with positive revision requests. Beyond that, he has quite a pipeline of work in progress. I think there's no question that he'll continue to produce important research that will place well. I don't see anything to be concerned about in either his teaching or his service."

"But we can all see that the published research... only two papers in top-tier journals... doesn't clear the bar," Sarks interjected. "He has two, but we expect three."

Recognizing that Sarks would use any argument to try to avoid tenuring candidates in finance or accounting, Novikova responded, "I strongly disagree with the notion that tenure is given simply by counting only accepted papers in top-tier journals. We should be trying to grant tenure to people we think are good scholars. Tenure is basically a prediction that the candidate will continue to be a good and productive researcher. It's not a reward for past work without regard to future potential. Lopez clearly demonstrates that he'll continue to be productive and that he's committed to quality work. Moreover, even if you want to rely on just counting completed work, I think you need to factor in co-authorship and can't ignore papers that may not be in so called top-tier journals. Lopez's top-tier papers are both single authored, whereas Phillips has two other coauthors on each of his, and Lopez's other papers are in journals that, if not top-tier, are only slightly below. In fact, his most cited paper is in one of those journals. So it's not true that we can rely solely on top-tier placement as the indicator of the impact of a paper."

"Say what you want, Krista," retorted Sarks, "But I believe... and I think others will agree... three top-tier papers is the minimum standard. I'm going to vote against."

Others in the meeting were largely silent on the case since Lopez was in finance and most of them were in economics. Their views of the tenure case were hard to read.

After rehashing some of the arguments in the debate over Phillips, and some scattered comments on Lopez's teaching and service, the group voted, at 4:45, and turned to the final case, that of Lin Chang. Discussion was led by Nadir Kaur, who, as an associate professor, was still the most senior in the accounting area. "This should be an easy case, I believe. Lin earned her degree from the University of British Columbia and has four top tier accounting journal papers including one that's single-authored, and she has a nice mix of other work."

"I don't think research is the concern in this case," interjected Sarks. "Though I am not sure why we need to be considering tenure for another person in accounting anyway. It seems that we should mainly be able to cover these practitioner-oriented classes with local accountants. I also don't really see much of an intellectual contribution in accounting research, even in so called top-tier accounting journals. The more critical issues for me are her poor records of teaching and service. Her teaching evaluations are below the department average and there are some comments from students that her courses are too difficult, that her answers to questions are confusing, and that she's hard to hear and hard to understand. Also, while I think it's okay for an assistant professor to have light service on campus, we should expect a good degree of professional service. Chang doesn't appear to be very active as a reviewer, and she's not on any editorial boards. She also doesn't seem to have attended any national academic conferences in the last couple of years. That's not the record of a team player, and I don't think we can accept it."

"In her defense," rebutted Kaur, "you seem to be ignoring the reality that most of her teaching is in required accounting classes and that course evaluations for required and more technical classes are normally on the low side. You also may be ignoring that she took parental leave a couple years ago and is now raising a young child as a single parent."

"Well, I don't think family responsibilities can compensate for ineffective teaching or low service. I plan to vote against this case," Sarks responded.

"Of course you will, Cory. Why would we expect anything else?" Kaur reacted angrily.

No one was particularly surprised that Sarks was consistently voting against tenure. That had been his practice for a long time, as had been his tendency to jump in with arguments against tenure as soon as possible in each case. The main question was whether his arguments would carry much weight with others who had not spoken. In the case of Chang, Kaur was concerned that some of the other faculty members might agree with Sarks that tenuring faculty in accounting was a mistake, and that Chang could become a victim of that attitude. Subsequent discussion elevated his concern.

After the ballots on Chang were collected, the votes on all three candidates were counted. To the dismay of pockets of faculty members in the room, none of the candidates received a clear majority vote. Phillips got a plurality of positive votes, but the negatives plus the abstentions outnumbered. Lopez and Chang both got slight majorities of negative votes.

The Department Chair, who had avoided arguing for or against any specific case, summarized, and commented that the lack of support for junior faculty members with good records was disturbing and did not bode well for the future of the Department. "He concluded, "It's approaching five. I'll prepare the department letters describing our deliberations and summarizing the vote outcomes and distribute to you by email for comments, but given our vote, it seems unlikely that the campus will be positive for any of our candidates for tenure. We are probably going to lose all three."

"Before we break," Krista Novikova reflected as she

glanced about the room, "I have something to say about our process here today.... I believe we've just voted to deny tenure to three perfectly well-qualified candidates, and we did so, not so much based on the merits of their candidacies but on a variety of other things that might be grouped under the general heading of academic ethnocentrism. It seems likely that some votes against Chang and Lopez may have been based on resentment of salaries in finance and accounting or the view that those disciplines are not academically pure. As for Phillips, I can't help but wonder if the negative votes, to some extent, reflect a desire for sameness. I'm not sure why a model for making tenure decisions where everyone is focused on placing their research in top tier journals and downplaying the importance of mentorship and effective teaching is a formula for making the department as good as it can be. Maybe we'd do better if we were to allow people to differentiate themselves based on all three dimensions that we seek to evaluate... research, teaching, and service.... Maybe I am being too pragmatic, but competitive enterprises do best when their employees specialize... not when they all try to do exactly the same thing. Perhaps there's a lesson in that.... Just a thought."

"That would never fly," commented Sarks. "Even if we wanted to do that... which, by the way, I do not... that model would never be accepted on campus. We might try to argue that so-and-so is a great teacher and therefore we should tenure him or her... or them... based on teaching excellence and we might, in that case, be less concerned about there being a modest contribution to research. But, the Academic Personnel Committee of the University would never accept such an argument, and certainly the Provost would not."

"All I can say," responded Novikova, "is that what we're doing now is not working. Maybe we should try harder to promote a different model. We can start by changing our own thinking about tenure cases. If we don't, I suspect we're our own worst enemy."

CHAPTER 10

THE CAMBRIDGE INN

Professor Edwards returned briefly to his office, before heading out to the Cambridge Inn for his scheduled 6:30 meeting with Rebecca Prescott. He found Rebecca waiting in the foyer of the restaurant. Edwards did not consider himself to be up to speed on women's fashion, but nonetheless thought his student's attire might be a bit over the top. The Inn was a casual dining venue, where many of the patrons arrived in their work clothes. Becca, in contrast, seemed dressed for an evening out. She wore a lacy top that revealed about as much as it concealed. The top was tapered to a tight waist that accentuated her figure, before draping over a snug-fitting black skirt. As she stood to greet him, he noticed that she was wearing a pair of red high heels. In addition to a sequined clutch, and, in apposition, she held her laptop and a few sheets of paper.

"Hi, Professor," she smiled a greeting. "When I got your message that you'd be a few minutes late, I thought it might be a good idea to reserve one of the booths in a quiet part of the restaurant."

"Wicked," Edwards responded, meaning that he approved, but he realized he had been drawn to the colloquialism by Becca's attire. "I'm famished, so let's get to our seats and order."

At their table, Rebecca ordered a vodka martini, remarking, "I love these, but I always get a bit loopy from them, so I think we should try to complete discussion of my work quickly, and then we can enjoy the evening."

Edwards, who had opted for a cask ale in the British style, was unsure what exactly Becca had in mind, but it seemed apparent that he would not need to work too hard on moving the relationship forward. Probably, he could just play along and leave it to Becca to make the overtures.

As they worked on their salads and waited for their meals, Rebecca, assisted by her laptop, led Edwards through her most recent work. He acted appropriately impressed and made a few constructive suggestions. "I think you're very close and should be able to develop a good job market talk in time for this year's job meetings." He chose not to mention his concerns about the obvious problems with the writing. The empirical work was all good, of course, since he had proposed the research question and laid out the methodology. But the writing, so far, was weak. The research question was poorly motivated, and the literature review was sketchy and disjointed. Edwards suspected that it was about as good as Rebecca could do, so why make an issue of it?

"By the way," he queried as their entrees were served, "have you heard that the American Economics Association wants schools to stop holding candidate interviews in their hotel rooms?"

"I hadn't, but I have to admit that interviewing in hotel bedrooms does seem a bit awkward."

"Yes, I suppose so, but we've been doing it that way for decades, and it seems to have been working okay. I do remember a time, a few years ago, when we'd been interviewing applicants solidly for two days… 45 minutes per candidate with a 15 minute break in between. By the end, I was so exhausted that I was doing my part in the interviews while lying on the bed. My recollection is that it worked okay, and no one seemed very concerned."

"The alternative doesn't seem very good either. The Association would like us all to set up small spaces in a large hall and conduct our interviews there. You can be sure that many schools won't go along. Maybe they'll forego the hotel room, but might, instead use a suite with a separate living room, or interview over a meal. I'll be interested to hear your experiences with this change."

As the dinner was drawing toward conclusion, the focus of conversation returned to Rebecca's dissertation.

"I'll get to work on finalizing my paper, Professor. When do you think we should meet again? There isn't too much time before I'll need to start sending out my work."

"Yes, we do need to push things forward and will probably need to meet a few times," responded Edwards. Unfortunately, I'll be out of town next week to attend a professional meeting in Key West. So maybe afterward...."

"Key West!" Rebecca exclaimed. "Have you ever been there? I hear it's beautiful and very interesting. I'd love to go there sometime."

"I have been, and it is beautiful on the beaches... though I can't claim to be a fan of their conch chowder. I'll stick with my childhood favorite... fish and chips with salt and vinegar and top it off with a brown ale."

"Listen," he continued as they each tendered credit cards for their separate portions of the tab. "I just had a thought that might work out. I'm scheduled to chair a session at the meeting... something about the challenges that crypto currencies may pose to the effective implementation of monetary policy."

"There are three papers scheduled to be presented in my session. For each one, I had selected a discussant to critique and present a different view on the paper. As it turned out, one of the scheduled discussants had to cancel so I was planning to handle that discussion on my own. I already have some comments prepared, but perhaps you'd like to fill in for the discussant?"

"It sounds interesting," Rebecca responded, but it wouldn't give me much time to prepare.... Still, I'd really love to see Key West."

"Yes, it's a bit tight," Edwards pressed, "but I was going to say that if you're interested, I can provide my notes and draft slides... so it wouldn't be too much work.... On the plus side, I think it could be a good way for you to get some exposure to the academic community and would give you a nice line to add to your c.v. I'm not sure if you know, but the School sets aside funds to help graduate students cover the cost of attending professional meetings. They would probably cover coach airfare, a basic hotel room in the conference hotel, and some incidentals. With you being on the program, your meeting fee would be waived by the association. It's pretty late to be trying to get financial support for attending a meeting that's only a week away, but I think I can work it out, if it's something you'd like to do."

"Yes!" Rebecca exclaimed after a moment of reflection. "I'm sure I can rearrange a few things in my schedule and would love to participate, and to check out Key West."

"Wonderful," Evans replied, evenly. "I'll go to work on arranging the funding tomorrow and will send you a copy of the paper and my notes and slides. In the meantime, you should make your travel arrangements."

"What a fantastic opportunity," she continued. "I can't thank you enough, Professor, and I promise I won't disappoint."

Edwards wondered how broadly he should interpret Becca's last comments.

"What do you think I should wear?" she asked.

"Well, people wear all different things to those meetings... but probably what you have on tonight would be a bit over the top for an academic conference. Maybe just dress like most of the women do, who come here to present their research in our seminars... a well-tailored black suit over a professional-looking white blouse, and black low heels or flats."

"Mostly Asian women, I think.... But, yes, I can do that," Becca nodded. "I already have that outfit since it's what I was planning to use for my job interviews."

As they headed for the door, Edwards happened to notice Mark Nikolaidis sitting at a table with a woman he did not know but who looked familiar. The two of them were sharing a bottle of Rombauer Chardonnay and seemed to be engrossed in conversation.

As they exited the restaurant, Becca squeezed Edwards's arm, and parted with a kiss on the cheek.

***

Inside the restaurant, Mark Nikolaidis and Jennifer Morris were engaged in a conversation that seemed uncharacteristically intense. Jennifer's husband was attending another conference and she was convinced that he was seeing someone from another school.

"I'm sorry to cry on your shoulder," Jennifer said. "I was planning just for a pleasant evening out and away from my self-centered thoughts. But I don't seem to be able to help myself. Even when I'm not home, my thoughts keep going to Joey. What's he doing right now? Is he with someone? Is he even thinking about me...? It's like an obsession, but I'm a professor of mathematics... I should be able to get beyond it and control my emotions."

"You're a brilliant woman, Jenn. I'm sure you know, at some level, that your intellect and your emotions are two separate things. So there's nothing wrong about the feelings you're having. But I will say that I know Joseph... not well, but well enough, I think… and I'd be very surprised if there's anything going on."

"Yes, of course, Mark, at some level I know you're right. He lives a life of the mind and is so cerebral that it seems implausible that he'd be having an affair. Still, I can't seem to help myself…. I just know that something's not right. I think it would help if he'd talk more about what he's doing at those conferences he's always going to. But when I ask, he just says that the discussions he was involved in were too esoteric to be of any interest to me. He doesn't seem to understand that sometimes I just need to hear him talk, even if what he says sounds like gibberish to me."

"Oh," noticed Nikolaidis, "it seems we're out of wine. Shall I order another bottle? Do you think it'd be too much… or maybe just a couple more glasses?"

"Under the circumstances," Jennifer responded, "nothing could be too much for me tonight…. Let's do it," she laughed.

As they worked their way through the second bottle, the conversation remained on a personal level, almost without retreat into the realms of teaching, research, or campus politics.

Eventually, they decided it was time to move on. After paying the bill, they headed for the street.

I was planning to walk home again tonight, but I'm unsure of the wisdom of leaving you to drive home on your own, Jenn. Are you feeling okay, or would you like me to drive you and then walk home from there?"

"I'm unused to such chivalry these days," Jennifer replied. "I am concerned about my ability to drive home right now, but I don't want to ask you to walk from my house to yours. Perhaps you could just drop me off and then take my car to your house. We can then sort things out in the morning."

"That'd be fine, and it would save me a walk in any case."

So they headed for Jennifer's car. Upon their arrival, "Your driving was fine," Jennifer commented. "Much better than I could have managed at this point. But would you like to come in for a coffee before you leave?" she asked.

"Coffee sounds good," he responded, and they headed for the front door.

"Actually," Jennifer said, after they were inside, "I don't think I'm quite ready to be alone with my thoughts. I was hoping the wine would help, but not so much. So how about a brandy?"

"That would be nice," Mark responded.

"Wonderful," if you can excuse me for a few minutes, I'll be right back. The brandy's above the wet bar. Could you pour us each a glass… and make sure mine is extra-large?

When Jennifer returned to the living room and lit the fire, she was no longer in her work clothes, but instead had changed into a black satin lounge outfit and velvet sandals. Sitting next to Mark on the sofa, she reached for her brandy with one hand and placed her other on his thigh.

"Cheers," she said as she leaned into his shoulder and drew up her knees.

CHAPTER 11

THE EXECUTIVE LEADERSHIP TEAM

"Thank you all for rearranging your calendars so that we could meet again as a group," began President Hansen. "I was hoping to finish this up sooner, but my own calendar made it difficult to find a time. In any case, here we are again and I'm happy to report that the incident with the beehive has finally been resolved... we can all safely walk about campus without being accosted by either bees or protesting students."

"When we broke last time, we had just finished Heather's recap of the School's financial situation and you'll recall that we'd identified several concerns. I'd like to pick up, as best we can, where we left off. I don't think we need to go back over all of the financial details from the last meeting. Maybe we can just start right in."

"So, David, I'm sure you remember that one of the concerns in our prior meeting relates to our financial aid expenditures last year. I wonder if you might have some thoughts as to why our aid expenditures ran over budget?"

Knight decided to equivocate and pass at least part of the buck to someone not in the room. "Well, for some reason... I don't know why... we were very slow to get updates on our applications, offers, and acceptances from IT. We did have some people in our office who were just learning the enrollment management software system, but it seems that there were also some problems in IT. When I finally did receive some stats from them, I found that we were well below our enrollment target compared to the same time in the prior year, so most of my time since discovering that, up until the start of this term, was focused on enrollment management and trying to make sure we ended up with about 4000 students to start this year."

"Yes," interjected President Hansen, "it's really rather remarkable how you're always able to come so close to hitting the final numbers of students we're aiming for."

"Thanks," Knight smiled, "but it's really just a lot of experience and some attention to detail over the summer."

"As to why the number and quality of applicants were down relative to prior years, it may just be part of the general tightening of the market. I've heard that a few other schools are reporting declines in their applicant pools, as well. In past years, it seemed that we didn't need to work very hard to generate large and strong applicant pools. Our reputation alone was enough to yield a rich pool. Possibly, we need to reexamine that premise... that passive recruiting is enough... and put more resources into building the applicant pool by outreach to high schools and maybe some direct marketing to students we'd like to recruit."

"When I first got the stats, it was also apparent that our admission rate was low as a percentage of applications and that acceptances of our admission offers were low as a percentage of admission. The low admissions percentage seems to go along with the overall decline in the number of applicants, and I think the solution is the same – more resources devoted to building the applicant pool, with an emphasis on quality."

"So," questioned Martin, who was concerned about planning for the next year, "do you really think recruiting for this year was just an aberration and that next year we'll be back on track?"

"That may very well be," responded Knight, glad for the unintended help he was getting from Martin's question. "The decline in our acceptance percentage last year may be partly due to some new staff in our office being slow to process applications. Sometimes they waited for an application file to be fully complete before communicating with the applicant. So, they were slow to make contact with obviously good applicants just because the applicant's file might have been missing something as tangential as a reference letter. I suspect that we may have lost some good applicants to competitors before we even took a serious look at their files. Of course, the low percentage at the time may also partly reflect a general increase in competition to get the best students."

"I'm pleased that, despite these challenges, we were able to meet the enrollment target for the year. I do need to acknowledge, however, that achieving the enrollment target was not without some important costs. One of them, and Heather alluded to it at our last meeting, is that we had to be pretty aggressive with financial aid offers. When I noticed the acceptance problem, we began by reviewing all of the outstanding applications to see if there were some that had been overlooked but could have been admitted. We contacted admitted applicants who hadn't responded and sweetened our aid offers. For those who had accepted offers from other schools, we tried to use the sweetened aid awards to persuade them to rescind their prior acceptances and to come, instead, to Baird. When neither of those approaches worked very well and it became clear that we would still fall short of the enrollment target, we went back, again, through the files of applicants we'd rejected, and we took a harder look at qualitative factors that could counter low GPA and SAT considerations. By doing that, we were able to reach the enrollment target, but we did so at some cost to the GPA and SAT statistics that will, no doubt, be reported by *U.S. News* when they come out with their best colleges and graduate schools rankings. I think there's some risk that Baird will fall out of the top 50 private universities list."

"So, if I am understanding," interjected the President, obviously fuming over the stream of excuses but still trusting in the track record, "you think the problems you experienced last year are behind us and that we can count on better result next year on the quantitative factors and the aid awards. Is that what I hear you saying, David?"

"Yes," said Knight, who did not like to hear the summary articulated so concisely or so inaccurately. "The bright side is that I think this decline in our stats is temporary. We plan to redesign and revitalize or recruiting efforts, which will cost some money. In doing so, we expect that we can build a bigger and stronger applicant pool so that we can be more selective with our future admissions decisions and bring our financial aid expenditures back into line, even after the extra expense." Knight was unworried about making such a commitment since, from experience, he was confident that many intervening events over the course of the year would provide ample cover for a missed target.

"I'm personally planning to represent Baird at a number of college recruitment fairs, both in the U.S. and internationally. We're also planning to retain an advertising agency to help us work on name recognition and recall.... And of course, we'll do all of the usual things like paying for placements of our banner ads in key outlets and buying mailing lists from the College Board."

"That's all very interesting," interjected Martin, who remained skeptical and was again beginning to feel the effects of the adrenaline rush that her budget review talk had previously triggered, "but do you have any evidence of the efficacy of the things you're planning to do, like attending college fairs, placing banner ads, and buying mailing lists? These all seem like pretty expensive ways to generate applicants, and none of them seems to have much to do with getting an applicant to the point where they accept our offer. Might it be more effective to focus more of the effort on the applications we receive and on getting those applicants to accept... maybe by getting to the applicants sooner, getting them to visit the campus, attend a class session of one of our star lecturers, or connecting them with current students or an alum?"

"Well, at this point," retorted Knight, whose face had reddened noticeably. "I want to keep all of our options open. We don't have good records of what has worked in the past and what hasn't. So we plan to try pretty much everything. One thing we can sort of rely on is that if other schools thought doing something like attending college fairs wasn't valuable, they wouldn't be attending."

"Maybe that's right," said Martin, "but I can think of plenty of cases where an employee unquestioningly continues to perform a worthless task just because that's what he or she was told to do, and they either never questioned the assignment or didn't want to call attention to it.

"I'll give you an example…. I've noticed that the employee benefits office holds weekly webinars for faculty and staff who are approaching retirement age. That means someone in benefits is spending much of their time in these webinars. And if you want to get the information from one of these webinars, you have to sign up and attend in real time. Since the webinars are not recorded, there's no way for someone to view them except by joining the session. Might it not be less expensive and more valuable to faculty and staff to hold fewer of these and to make the recorded sessions available to all? But no one in HR seems to have any incentive to challenge the way this it being done. Seems to me that it's make-work that is keeping someone employed when a better and less expensive alternative is available."

"I don't know about student recruitment, and as you recognize, you don't have the data. But my guess is that many of the things we and other schools do to attract students are actually not worth doing. Now, I'm not suggesting that we shouldn't do them, but I do think we should be testing their efficacy. For example, if we attend a college recruitment fair, why not keep a list of whom we met with, whether we're interested in them, whether they applied, and whether they actually matriculated? I do recognize, David, that this kind of simple record keeping wouldn't definitively show that attending these fairs is valuable, but it might produce evidence that doing so is not valuable if, for example, if none of the prospective students from the fair applied or matriculated.... Or it might show us that attending certain fairs is not valuable."

"Whatever," bristled Knight, "I guess we'll just have to wait and see.... But I'd like to point out that I've been involved in student recruitment for decades. So, I think I can be trusted to make these choices correctly without the need for some pseudo-scientific process that would take our attention away from actual recruiting."

Martin would not give up. "Yes, 'wait and see' makes sense when we're just trying out different things, but I think it works best if there are some pretty clearly stated expectations of what sort of measurable results would justify continuing the activity beyond the trial period."

The President, feeling the tension rising in the room, decided it was time to move on. "Okay, then, David, what I'm hearing is that you're confident that you can reverse the trend in the quality of admitted students and bring us back into budget on our aid awards. Does that sound about right?"

"Well, yes, especially if we implement the plan I alluded to," responded Knight, "barring any future surprises, of course." As he was responding, Knight had no idea how he would be able to achieve this expectation. He had portrayed the declines as partly systemic – due to declining applicant pools nationally, and intensified competition, and partly due to some addressable operational problems on campus. He knew, though was unwilling to say, that at least part of the problem was that the School's reputation had been slipping in recent years and the decline was beginning to show up in the applicant pool.

"Thank you, David," said President Hansen. "I think we need to keep moving our discussion along so we can wrap up at a reasonable time. Jonathan, I realize you're still new in your role as VP for Advancement and that you've had to focus on rebuilding your staff and turning things around. Still, I hope you can bring us some good news on the development front and maybe let us know what you think Advancement can do to help close the budget gap we experienced last year."

"Well, yes, it's true that we've had quite a bit of staff rebuilding to do," responded Richardson, looking down at a few notes he had scribbled on a pad, "and we're close to being fully staffed, now. We've also reached out to our known donors to rebuild relationships. Many of those donors had committed to future gifts, but some have not followed through and we're working to get them recommitted. We have a new Assistant VP for Alumni Relations to fill my prior role and I've been working on a smooth transition of responsibilities from my prior work there."

"Good to hear your group is getting back up to speed, Jonathan. So, maybe you can tell us what we can expect from your office over the next year?" asked President Hansen.

"Well," Richardson continued, "as you know, the percentage of alums who donate to their school is an important factor in the rankings of some academic programs. Our giving percentage has been on the low side in recent years and we're working to get that number up. I'm hoping that we'll get the percentage up somewhat this year by increasing the number of alums making small donations. While I don't expect much change in the dollar value of alumni giving the increase in alumni giving could help with student recruitment. We're also working hard on major gifts, but in most cases, I think we're going to need to rebuild the relationships… and as you know, these relationships usually have to be cultivated over a long time. So it can be quite a few years before they come to fruition."

"Any of these major gifts on the horizon, Jonathan?" questioned the President, "So that they might help us rebuild the endowment this year?"

"I'm optimistic," responded Richardson, who was not making eye contact with anyone, "that there could be a few… but we never know until they actually happen, and some major donors will wait until the School has a capital campaign in place before they'll donate."

"It's good to hear that we can count on receiving at least a couple of major gifts this year," misinterpreted the President.

As he was responding to Hansen's questions, Richardson became increasingly uncomfortable, and felt that the President was setting unrealistic expectations. If any major gifts came in this year, it would mainly be due to the luck of timing… the unexpected death of a wealthy alum who had included a bequest to Baird. It seemed that university presidents and trustees could never accept the reality that short run or even sustained operating shortfalls could not be offset by redoubling efforts to bring in donations. Endowment needed to be viewed as much more of a steady state means of support. With major donations happening pretty much at random times. Temporary operating shortfalls could be weathered, but targets needed to be set based on a steady state that was in balance. It was looking like Baird's shortfalls were becoming chronic.

Richardson did know that some potential major donations were on hold until the next capital campaign. Most donors did not want to contribute unless others were also doing so, and a capital campaign helped to build the sense of a collaborative group commitment to support the school.

Unfortunately, a campaign was not on the horizon for Baird. Such campaigns generally took years to arrange, and normally would not even be announced until the school had already received commitments for about half of the campaign funding target. So if Baird wanted to launch a $400 million campaign to bring it in line with its peers, it would need to already have identified about $200 million in donations that it could count on to start. Baird was not even close to being able to do that. Maybe a total campaign of $100 million was achievable, but such a campaign would be embarrassingly small. It looked like it would be quite a few years before a campaign would be warranted. Even then, many of the gifts that came in would be earmarked toward special projects that the donor wanted the School to pursue, projects that were not necessarily in the best interest of the University and might even make the budget shortfall worse over time.

Hansen was already aware of most of what Richardson reported since he met regularly with the head of Advancement. Still, he felt reporting to the ELT was important and helped shield him from blame for poor fund-raising performance. "Thanks for the update, Jonathan. Please keep us posted and let me know of anything I can do to help," concluded Hansen. "Now maybe we should get all of these numbers out of our heads and spend at least a few minutes on the academic side, can you bring us all up to date, Jim? And maybe let us know what's behind the increase in faculty salaries that Heather told us about last time."

"Yeah, well, I think the year is off to a pretty good start." The Provost always sought to strike a diminutive pose in meetings with the President and administrative staff. "We did have hiccups in a couple classes where the faculty members who supposedly were teaching them were found to be off at a conference in Bali and 'forgot' to notify anyone. Other than that, and the usual start-of-year problems with classroom instructional technology... oh, and the beehive... as far as I know, everything's going smoothly."

"Let me first comment on what happened to faculty salaries last year. The increase in spending on salaries was caused by unexpectedly high resignations of faculty and the offsetting need to hire new faculty. The faculty members who resigned unexpectedly were generally making below-market compensation and were able to find higher-paying positions. To replace them, we had to pay full market salaries for the new hires. Possibly, our policy of limiting salary retention offers to only those with written competing offers is not keeping salaries down in the way we had hoped. I wonder if being more preemptive would actually slow the growth rate of our expenses for faculty salaries and benefits."

"So, where is their loyalty to the School?" Knight challenged. "They only teach a few classes per year, and more often than not, when I try to call them, they're not in their offices.... They have their summers free, when we're at our busiest in Admissions, trying to reach our student recruiting targets... and they get sabbaticals every few years, which just give them more time to vacation at some foreign school. Seems to me they have a really great deal and should be happy where they are, and loyal."

This was an old argument, Provost May felt, and did not call for a response. Administrators who had never taught at the college or graduate school level and had not undertaken a serious research program would never understand that the best faculty members, when they were not teaching or preparing for their classes, were working pretty much all of the time on their research.

"We do have some looming problems that I should mention. We're beginning to see a structural imbalance between the interests of our students and the disciplines of our faculty. This is indicated by low enrollments in certain disciplines, and very crowded classrooms in some others.

Students now seem to want more focused education, more technical and practical education, and are disinclined to enroll in the softer and more traditional disciplines. Since some broad knowledge in the humanities seems important to a well-rounded education, and because of the misalignment between faculty focus and student interest, we've already modified our degree requirement to encourage humanities enrollment. I'm not sure we can go further in that direction."

"We probably need to think about downsizing the faculties in some of the humanities and fine arts, and increasing faculty in the disciplines that are feeling the most severe enrollment pressure. If we decide to move in that direction, we can do so over time and pretty much balance teaching demands across the campus. The problem, as Heather alluded to at our last meeting, is that the people we'll need to hire are going to be more expensive than those who leave. Given the trends, we may need to think about closing down or merging some departments and maybe eliminating some Ph.D. programs. Since we haven't discussed it and because I know it won't sit well with the faculty, I haven't indicated to faculty that we might eventually need to make some adjustments."

"Yes, and the faculty wouldn't be the only ones resistant to such a move, Jim," remarked Hansen. "Some of our more influential Trustees are champions of various disciplines in the humanities or fine arts. They're strong supporters of the importance of a liberal education and will push aggressively against any change that appears to downplay those disciplines. Before they'd be willing to consider something like closing down a department or eliminating a Ph.D. program, they'd need to be convinced that there are no other solutions.... I'm not sure they can ever be convinced. So let's make sure we think through all the options before we make any move toward closing departments."

As he said this, Hansen knew there was no way the

Board would approve closing a department and no way the faculty would be supportive of closing a Ph.D. program. They would need to come up with a different solution.

"Okay, so, maybe now would be a good time for me to segue into a discussion of what I've been doing to improve our financial condition" Hansen continued. "Last year, I spent quite a bit of my time meeting with major donors to maintain their support for the University. As part of my development efforts, Jacqueline and I made a trip this summer to Japan and Hong Kong. We met with several very successful alumni to explore their potential to become important donors to the School and with broader groups of alums to help us in our efforts to prospect for good students."

Aware that the development focus was now on him, the President continued, "As Jack mentioned, landing a major gift is a long game. We start with an overture and an invitation for them to return to campus for a hosted visit and maybe to meet with some of our students, and we move on from there." Reflecting on the incredible evening one of the alums had shown him to in a Kyoto geisha house, and the penthouse dinner he'd had in Hong Kong with the president of an important Chinese bank, he continued, "I plan to return to Japan and Hong Kong next year to continue to develop these relationships. I'm optimistic about their potential success. Perhaps, on that same trip, I'll also find opportunities to visit with prospective donors in Shanghai and Singapore."

As the President described his summer travel, Richardson reflected on his discussions with Hansen as to the fruitlessness of these visits. He knew the alums would show the President a good time, but that in their cultures significant gifts to universities were almost unheard of. In reality, this was just a Presidential junket. The President and his wife traveled first class, stayed in the finest hotels, and ate at the best restaurants. The meetings, he knew, accounted for only a small fraction of the time on the three-week trip.

"Back here, at home," President Hansen continued, "I've been working with several deans and department chairs to secure major gifts that can be used to fund endowed professorships. One meeting that I recently concluded is with an alumnus of our Economics Department. The Department Chair had indicated that the alum was willing to fund two professorships. I confirmed that over a lunch with the donor and am now working out the details of the gift."

"I think that about completes the agenda we'd hoped to cover at our meeting last month. I'll ask my AA to get in touch with each of you to schedule another meeting for later this term so we can check the status of all the things we've been discussing. I see it's still a few minutes before cocktail hour, but maybe we can forgive ourselves for getting an early start. Let's adjourn to the bar. Please, help yourself to whatever you like."

CHAPTER 12
THE TRUSTEES

President Hansen had a practice of driving into the city on occasion to meet informally with the Chair of the Board of Trustees. Those meetings normally took place at the University Club, where, because of his role as Baird's President, Hansen maintained a University-funded membership.

Trevor Alexander had risen to the position of Board Chair two years earlier, after the prior Chair, the one who had overseen Hansen's appointment, had stepped down. The former Chair was an Executive Vice President of an East Coast pharmaceuticals firm and was attracted to Hansen's chemistry background. The current Chair was much different. Alexander was heir to a family fortune earned in the fashion industry and was actively involved in several philanthropic pursuits that he managed around a schedule of extravagant vacations. Baird University was among these.

Hansen, with his background in the sciences had little rapport with Alexander, whose interest was clearly more in supporting the arts. Nonetheless, these somewhat regular meetings were an important way for him to try to maintain a reasonable alignment between the Board's aspirations and the School's direction. Their first meeting of the academic year, a preview before the meeting of the full board, was normally devoted to a status report on the most up-to-date financial results and new enrollment statistics, as well as on setting out some initiatives for the year.

This time, they had agreed to meet over an early cocktail, since Alexander had another of his philanthropic engagements scheduled for dinner. After an exchange of greetings and the usual perfunctory and disinterested inquiries into family – for which, Hansen had, nonetheless, prepared, with the aid of his AA – Hansen turned to the task de jour. "I take it, Trevor, that you received the documents I had emailed to you on the financial report for last year and the start of the current year."

"Yes, yes, of course, Tom," replied the Board Chair, "but, as you know, I'm not much of a numbers person, so how about you just tell me how things are going."

This was the kind of response Hansen had expected... had hoped for... since spinning was easier when the spinnee was not doing any reality checking.

Hansen, while he wanted to do well by Baird, was more focused on his own personal agenda – to be appointed to the presidency of a more prestigious research university than Baird. Hansen knew that to achieve his goal he would need to be able to show some tangible achievements from his time at Baird. He also knew that achievements that could be realized in the short-run could sometimes come with significant long-run costs. However, any longer-run costs would generally be overlooked and would have little, if any, influence on his ability to move to higher office. An attentive, well-informed, and committed board of trustees could be a check on such personal ambition, but with Alexander as its Chair, the Baird Board could not really be considered to be attentive. As was common at many universities, most of the current Board members would acquiesce to the Chair or would want to direct the University into pursuit of their own personal aspirations and pet projects.

Seeing the opportunity to advance his own agenda, Hansen began, "Okay, let me summarize, if I may?"

"Of course," derided Alexander. "After all, it's what we're both here for."

Hansen chose to ignore the jibe. "Well, as I think you

know, we did have a bit of a budget shortfall over the past year. That was due mainly to four things, most importantly, we had a bigger faculty hiring year than expected. Second, our gifts fell off a bit due to the turnover in the development office. We also had some turnover in our student admissions that led to some overspending on financial aid. And finally... no surprise... there were some cost overruns in the capital cost of the new dorm project that the Board had approved a couple years ago... prior to your term as Chair."

"As I think you recognize, these are all transitory or aberrational problems that should be rectified next year. The building project will be over, our staffs in Admission and Advancement will be more experienced and up to speed, and because our hiring was high last year, we can be less ambitious this year."

"Yes, yes... I see... of course," the Chair responded. "That all makes sense to me.... So I expect that we'll see better financial performance this year."

Having skated through the financial results and having skimmed over the looming problems, Hansen was ready to move on to his agenda for the current year. He was glad to see that Alexander apparently was also ready to move on.

"So, let's turn to the current year, Tom," Alexander posed. "What do you think we should be seeking to accomplish."

"Well, let's start with a couple of housekeeping matters that I think we can deal with quickly," Hansen responded. "Our student demographics and interests have been changing in recent years, as they have at most schools. Yet our educational profile hasn't been keeping up, and may even have drifted in the opposite direction."

"I'm not sure what you mean by that, maybe you can elaborate," Alexander responded, pushing back from the table a bit and striking more of a confrontational posture.

"Sure.... Increasingly, these days, our students are seeking more quantitative education and are less willing to commit their time to broad-based education that includes very substantial commitments to the humanities and the arts. Don't take this the wrong way, Trevor," Hansen began, hoping to placate the Board Chair. "We're firmly committed to the concept of a liberal education, but maybe we've taken it a little too far. Except in our required humanities and arts courses, enrollments are quite low. We offer quite a few sections of classes with enrollments of ten or fewer students. So it's pretty expensive for the amount of education we deliver."

"And, Trevor, doesn't it strike you as a bit odd that we devote substantial resources to our many humanities Ph.D. programs and arts MFA programs? In effect, we encourage students to pursue these degrees by paying them to attend, and then, when they do, and when they complete the degrees, they discover that it's almost impossible to find relevant employment. More and more, we see two people sharing a single faculty position and splitting the salary at a school that is unexceptional, to say the least. It seems to me that we could go a long way toward improving Baird's financial condition by keeping a solid list of basic core courses in these areas, while rationalizing some of the degree programs, and especially some of the Ph.D. programs. If we did that, we could maintain our commitment to liberal education and also respond to the demands of our students for more tools-based and quantitative education."

Hansen expected that this could be a hard sell and that he might not get all the way there, but he hoped to gain enough flexibility so that he could devote more resources to the kinds of initiatives that would demonstrate his effectiveness as a university president.

He was unprepared for the level of push back he was about to receive.

The Board Chair was silent for several seconds, staring into his drink. As he sat, Hansen notice the vein in the Chair's temple pulsing. Alexander's hand was visibly shaking as he picked up his drink, took a sip, and placed it down. Glaring at Hansen, he began, "You do know who I am, Tom.... At least I thought you did.... My family's committed to the arts and humanities. That's the source of our family success. It's what we care about. It engenders the values we wish to instill in college-age youth.... My family's commitment to the arts and humanities is why I'm serving on the Board of this institution. I personally have no interest whatsoever in any repositioning of the University that would diminish the arts and humanities."

Hansen struggled to maintain composure, "Well... of course, we'd never want to take any action that would detract from the University's mission to provide a liberal education to our students. But we do, also have to deal with the reality that the needs of our students are changing."

"Look... I get it..." Alexander responded, "that increasingly, there's a shift toward professional and technical education.... But there'll always be an important role for educating students in the arts and humanities. Society will always need good writers, artists, actors, and dancers. I, and a number of others on the Board, expect Baird to be a leader is educating students in those areas. If the current profile of Baird students is drifting away from our mission, it seems to me that, instead of hiring different faculty, you need to refocus your student recruiting and admissions policies and practices on students whose aspirations are consistent with the mission. I can promise you," Alexander threatened, "that a majority on the Board would not support abandoning the School's very strong commitment to humanities and the arts."

Hansen had come to the lunch hoping for at least some accommodation to the changing needs of students. Such a shift would have freed up resources that he thought he could redirect into initiatives that would draw attention to his leadership. Clearly, he was getting nowhere with that. In fact, he suspected that his attempt might lead the Board to reaffirm its commitment to the outdated mission. While Hansen still wanted to pursue his agenda, he would have to do so in ways that would not require Board action. Although he could not close down academic programs without Board support, he could allow faculty resignations and retirements to shrink departments in certain areas and could cut back on funding the support of Ph.D. students in those areas. Recognizing that, he changed course.

"Perhaps," he began, "we can think about what we can do to attract the kinds of students you're speaking of. As you know… and like I mentioned earlier… I believe, an important factor driving students away from humanities and arts majors is that education at a private university like Baird is quite expensive and the prospect of relevant employment is low. Many of our students have to borrow heavily to finance their education and they can't justify doing so except in areas where the prospects of employment are good. I think we could materially shift the profile of our students if we were to commit to need-blind admission and debt-free financial aid."

"Now, that is an idea worth considering," responded the Board Chair, who also was seeking to reduce tension. "Can you elaborate a bit? Wouldn't it be pretty expensive to go to that approach?"

"Well, sure it would cost us some, but maybe not as much as you might suspect. I think the trends in higher education, and our commitment to the mission are pushing us in this direction. As I'm sure you know, a number of the top private universities have already committed to need-blind admission with loan-free financial aid. By doing so, those schools have been able to attract more applicants who truly seek liberal arts educations and also have been able to build a more diverse student body."

"That sort of cream skimming skews the applicant pools of schools like Baird toward more professional education. So if we want to maintain our liberal arts focus, we need to compete more directly with those top colleges and universities."

"About the cost... I don't think it'd be as significant as you might expect. Bringing more students into the arts and humanities wouldn't be expensive since most of the classes in those areas are currently under-enrolled and could handle more students with no increase in cost. And being need-blind and debt-free would probably increase our applicant pool so we could cut back on some of the direct costs related to student recruiting."

"That all sounds good," replied Alexander, "but what about the reduced tuition if financial aid is loan-free?"

"I think we can deal with that without much problem, too. Sure, the direct effect would be a decline in net tuition revenue, but we can offset by admitting a few more international students, since they wouldn't be covered by the policy, and by offering an early decision option to applicants," the President responded.

"I guess I'd need to see more details of the plan," Alexander responded. "How would early decision help offset the decline in net tuition from going loan-free?" he asked. Alexander thought he knew but wanted to hear what Hansen would say.

"Well, we know from the experiences of other schools that students who apply for early decision generally are full-tuition students. They usually come from families that can comfortably afford to pay full tuition, and the fact that they're willing to forego shopping for the best tuition deal means that we don't need to discount our tuition offers to get them to enroll," Hansen explained.

"So, if I understand, you are proposing a complex

package of need-blind admission with loan free financial aid, and you'd cover the cost of those changes by offering an early-decision option. Do I have that about right?" Alexander summarized.

"Yes, that's right," Hansen responded. "It'd be a bold move and certainly get us a lot of attention."

"I think it might fly with the Board" Alexander contemplated. "Can you put together a proposal for us to consider at our next meeting? You'll need to put some numbers on it to satisfy some members of the Board, but speaking for myself, I think it's an interesting idea and something we should consider."

"It'll be tight," Hansen responded. "The next meeting's only a few weeks away, but I'll get my people working on it and we'll see what we can do."

"Excellent," Alexander concluded, with obviously increasing enthusiasm. "If we can get Board approval at our fall meeting, we maybe could roll this out even in time for the coming academic year.... Now, is there anything else we need to discuss before we wrap this up? I need to get to my other commitment."

"Well, I did want to mention that one of our alums is pledging to endow two new professorships in economics. The donor wants one of them to be in environmental economics and the other to be on the economics of the oil and gas industry. We're still working out a few of the details, but that'll be a nice contribution to our endowment, and it'll be funded this year."

"That's good, Tom... though I think it's unfortunate that this particular donor seems to be fixated on economics instead of the humanities.... But at least it sounds like we could get a couple of people who'd help shed light on the problem of climate change. So I suppose, on net, it's a good outcome. I do hope, however, that you'll convey to your advancement people the strong sentiment of the Board that their efforts need to be directed mainly at securing gifts that can support the arts and humanities."

"Yes, of course, Trevor. This donor, however, is an alumnus of the Economics Department. When I met with him, I was hoping for a somewhat different outcome. I think I got some movement in a helpful direction, as his original focus was on finance and accounting, but this was about as far as I could go."

"I see," responded Alexander, somewhat skeptically. "It's good to see that we're in agreement about the focus of development efforts."

"Yes, I believe we are. Since we expect this gift to be funded this year, I've notified the Chair of Economics that the Department can proceed with its efforts to fill these two positions."

As their meeting wound to a close, the President signed the tab, and called for his driver to meet outside the building.

CHAPTER 13

IN THE OFFICE

President Hansen was back in his office early the next morning, after spending much of the previous evening reflecting on his meeting with the Board Chair. He was upset that Alexander had been so unwilling to refocus school resources away from humanities and the arts but elated that the Chair seemed to be supportive of a comprehensive plan to restructure the admissions criteria in a way that could put a spotlight on his leadership of the School's potential move to need-blind admission, loan-free aid, and early decision... a trifecta. Such a dramatic change, he felt, should put Baird well ahead of its peers and would almost assure his ability to move up to a top-ranked private university.

There were, of course, some important nuances that he had chosen not to share with the Board Chair. For one, even though he could not directly shut down programs that were the pets of Board members, he should be able to put them on a diet... one that would help him with his objectives. Hansen felt he would need the savings from such a move in order to support efforts to grow the more quantitative disciplines that were now in fashion. More importantly, he needed the freed-up resources to support the initiatives that would showcase his leadership. It was true that loan-free aid would probably attract more students who were interested in the liberal arts. However, if those applicants could be identified, Baird did not need to admit them and not doing so would save some money. The School could, in his view, keep the aid commitments down by increasing its emphasis on professional education and admitting more international students and students seeking early decision. He would just need to find a way to accomplish this without attracting the attention of the Board Chair.

Hansen had already put the Provost and the CFO on notice that he needed to meet with them this morning. He had kept the meetings separate because he needed different messaging with each. The Provost would be first to arrive.

***

"Thanks for adjusting your schedule, Jim, and making time to see me," the President said. "I had a somewhat difficult meeting with our effing Board Chair yesterday," he said, with a smiling shrug to diminish the expletive. I'd like to fill you in and see what advice you might have for me." Notwithstanding his claim to be seeking advice, Hansen knew well what he hoped to accomplish. His real purpose was to see how far he could move the Provost in the direction he wanted to proceed.

"I'm sure you recall that during the summer you and I were brainstorming on some things we could do to put the School on a more solid financial footing and to reconfigure our programs to be more responsive to the changing needs and objectives of our students. We'd talked about rationalizing our offerings in the arts and humanities, triaging the Ph.D. programs in some of those areas, and shifting the focus of faculty hiring in a more quantitative direction," Hansen summarized.

"I was hoping we could get the Board to support the idea, even if only to a limited extent. But when I met with Alexander yesterday and proposed such a move, it turned out that the SOB was vehemently opposed. I suppose I should have known... given his family background. With hindsight, I wish I'd not even raised the issue. Oh... and he virtually threatened that there are enough Board members who share his view and would oppose the move that we'd never get Board support."

"So, I guess that about takes care of that idea," the Provost shook his head, wanting to support his boss. "Seems to me that these boards are nothing but a pain in the rear... like a big sea anchor, always keeping us from making any forward progress.... And what do they really know, anyway? Trustees usually get appointed because they give money to a school or have the potential to do so. It's clear that some of the current Trustees have vested interests... like they have a kid in school here and want to grease the path for them... or they want to manage a piece of the school endowment, or just hobnob with each other, like some sort of club that gets pleasure out of flexing its muscle. They don't really know anything.... I think we'd be better off without them."

"Well, you and I can agree on that, Jim, as a general point. But in this particular case it may not be all that bad," replied Hansen. "I think Alexander's reaction just means we'll need to proceed more gradually and circumspectly. We still need to redirect resources away from the arts and humanities, but we need to do so gradually, and in a way that doesn't draw attention. In the short run, I think we can use the current budget shortfall to justify curtailing our hiring in those areas. I don't want to call it a targeted hiring freeze, since doing so would surely draw attention. But I think we can allow most departments in the arts and humanities to shrink by attrition... resignations and retirements, that is. We can avoid countering outside job offers and we can be very judicious about approving any new hiring in those areas.... I hope you can oversee that, Jim, and do it very carefully, without an email or paper trail. If we do that, how much do you think we can save over the next three years or so?"

"It's really just a guess, but maybe we could cut wages and benefits in those areas by about five percent per year," the Provost conjectured.

"Doesn't seem like enough. What else do you think we could do?" asked Hansen.

"I suppose we might be able to reduce support for Ph.D.

programs in the areas."

"Okay, Jim. That sounds good.... Would you mind taking a look at that option, too...? And let's see what we can do to in a round-about way to reduce the number of students seeking to major in the arts and humanities. Those students tend to need quite a bit of financial aid, and I'd like to bring that more under control. I think you can do that by telling David that we're raising the admission standards for applicants with a demonstrated high likelihood of majoring in those disciplines and by cutting back on our course offerings in those areas. Again, none of this should get back to the Board. I think we can do this without drawing attention as long as we continue to admit legacy applicants and applicants who have the support of a Board member."

"I guess we might also think about some more subtle things we could do to shift resources," Provost May mulled over, more to himself than to the President.

"That's an interesting thought," Hansen pounced on the remark as if it had been directed to him. "What kinds of things did you have in mind?"

"A few possibilities, I guess..." intoned the Provost, who had not expected Hansen to pick up on his ruminations. "One thing we might consider is we could move some of our faculty hiring away from control by individual departments. So, just as an example, instead of hiring in the English Department and the History Department, we could specify something like a 'cluster hire' that would be transdisciplinary or interdisciplinary between the two. We could create a search committee comprised of members of both departments and ask them to find someone who could contribute to the teaching needs in both.... Or maybe in the arts, we might ask for a cluster hire that would span both dance and theater, or even dance, theater, and music. Doing something like that would probably sound trendy and forward-looking, and not like a budget-cutting move."

"That's a great idea," Hansen joined in. "We could probably cut down on the number of positions we need to fill in those areas by doing that, and everyone would perceive that they were still getting to hire. Maybe there're even some clusters we could identify between the soft disciplines and the more technical or quantitative ones, where we could emphasize the quantitative side. Like, maybe History and Economics, if they were looking for cliometrics or econometrics. We could hire an econometrician who could cover a cliometrics class for History. Or maybe we could pair up Psychology and Biology, so that we wouldn't need to devote so many in-lab resources to the faculty in psychology.

"Naturally, we can't promote those kinds of consolidations too aggressively without causing some pushback, but let's take a hard look and see what we can do on a limited basis this year. Then maybe we can expand the approach gradually over time," Hansen summarized.

"What else did you have in mind, Jim?" he asked.

"Might be that we could work more directly on the way we budget our resources into departments. For the most part, what we do now is sort of need-based budgeting where next year's budget is generally the same as this year's, plus an adjustment for inflation. So, we make sure the various arts departments have enough to support all of the theaters and other performance venues, and all of the related programs, and we provide enough funds to the humanities Ph.D. programs so that they can maintain the sizes of the programs. Given how small the humanities and arts classes are, and how much they need based on their current sizes and configurations, those departments are providing a disproportionately small fraction of the School's operating budget.... I mean, because of the historical growth of the School, the resource commitments to arts and humanities are large compared to what they generate in net tuition and grant support. So those departments are effectively being subsidized by the more quantitative disciplines where class sizes are larger, Ph.D. programs are smaller, and, in the case of the sciences, grant support is greater."

"Maybe we could move gradually in the direction of what you might call 'every tub on its own bottom'," May continued. "Then it would be up to the arts and humanities to, sort of, pay their own ways, by increasing class sizes, reducing faculty, and shrinking expensive programs."

"That sounds like an excellent idea," Hansen responded. "I'm guessing that the effective subsidies to those departments might be pretty large, but I'm not sure. I'm meeting with Martin next, and I'll ask her to look into it."

"So... I guess we're doing this because we think it's important to increase resources devoted to the sciences and some other quantitative disciplines..." the Provost conjectured, "like economics... even though, technically, it's in the humanities."

"Yes, yes... that's certainly right, but there are also a few other things going on that I don't need to bring you into at this point. Just focus on reducing the resource commitment to the soft stuff and do so in a way that doesn't draw the ire of the Board." Hansen felt it was unlikely that the Provost would support using the freed-up resources to support his admissions and aid initiatives. He concluded. "I really appreciate all of your suggestions, Jim... and remember to keep me posted, but only verbally."

The Provost was a bit puzzled as to what his President was actually trying to accomplish. Why would Hansen want to cut back on the very programs that had such strong support from the Board? There must be more to it than just trying to reallocate into more quantitative areas.... He'd just have to wait and see.... But, in the end, it didn't really matter. He had his marching orders and would follow them.

**

In most respects, Hansen was not looking forward to his meeting with Heather Martin since, based on experience, it seemed that his CFO would push back on almost anything he proposed. On the bright side, it appeared that if he played things right the Board would be prepared to support what he wanted to do... unless the numbers did not work out as he hoped. But Heather might need to be brought in line. He thought he should be able to accomplish that by attributing the initiatives to the Board. He'd soon find out.

"Good morning, Heather," he began as she came into his office. "There are a few things we need to talk about, so have a seat and let me just start right in.... As background, in anticipation of the fall meeting of the Trustees, I met yesterday with Board Chair Alexander. We discussed a variety of things, but the one that seemed most important to him, and came as a bit of a surprise to me, was that he wants us to consider a fairly significant restructuring of our approach to student admissions. Mr. Alexander is aware that a number of top private universities have adopted policies of need-blind admission and loan-free financial aid. He's urging us to follow their lead. I told him we'd take a look and see what we can do."

Martin was shocked at the direction the conversation had so quickly taken. She was expecting that Hansen might want to focus on ways to deal with the budget shortfall she had projected for the current year. But, instead, he indicated that the Board was thinking about making the problem substantially worse. "Really?" exclaimed Heather. "I'm sure you must have explained to him how difficult that would be financially."

"Well, I did start down that path," Hansen obfuscated. "But as he and I discussed it, I began to wonder if it might not be good for Baird to go in that direction. It certainly would get us a lot of attention and could conceivably boost our applicant pool. It seems possible that we might actually be better off by running with the Chair's proposal."

"But... but, currently, a very substantial fraction of our students borrow significant amounts from various sources to cover their tuition and other expenses. That change, by itself, providing non-loan-based aid would mean that in one way or another, we'd have to absorb the cost. If we were to do that, our net tuition would probably drop by several million per year.... And, on top of that, I think we currently do take ability to pay into account when we make admissions decisions. So, need blind admission... especially coupled with loan-free financial aid, would cost us even more."

"Yes, that's true," the President responded, "but maybe we're thinking about this too narrowly. That was the way I was originally thinking about the impacts of such a change, but I can see now that I was ignoring the positives. We could get quite a few more applicants. That would enable us to raise our admissions standards and school ranking. I expect we'd get a big boost in donor support. So I wonder if, maybe not immediately, but in a year or two, we could be financially better off."

"Well... of course, I've not had an opportunity to look at it carefully... but, intuitively, it seems really unlikely that the change could be positive, on net," Martin countered.

"I think you may just be focusing too narrowly on the financial considerations, Heather. But the Board will be looking at the big picture. So they'll also be concerned about the reputational benefits. I need to add that there's more to the proposal the Chair and I discussed. In addition to need-blind, loan-free admission, we talked about initiating a program of early decision admissions. I think early decision could go a long way to alleviating your concerns about the financial impact of the other changes. I'm sure you know that students who apply for early decision forego the opportunity to shop around for offers from other schools that include financial aid awards. So, in general, students who apply early are considerably more likely to be fully able to afford their tuition and other education costs. I suspect that admitting 30 to 40 percent of our students by early decision, and by increasing the number of international students, we might more than offset any costs associated with the shift to loan-free aid."

"I guess that might be possible," hesitated Martin, clearly unconvinced. "But I have trouble seeing how we'd get to such high percentages of early decision admissions. A student who applies for early decision is effectively saying that the school they apply to is their first choice. I don't think very many of our current students would say that Baird was their first choice."

"Of course, I understand your concerns, Heather... and, to an extent, I share them. In any case, Alexander wants us to put something together for the November Board meeting. I think we can get into that with a sort of what-if analysis that considers the effects of all three changes, together... like what if the move to loan-free aid, coupled with the other changes, results in no reduction of net tuition or a $1 million reduction, maybe even, say, $2 million.

"I think the impact could be quite a bit more than $2 million," Heather leaned away.

"I suppose so, if you ignore early decision, but this seems to be something the Board wants, so we don't want to be too negative in our projections of what might happen in a worst case," urged Hansen. And, like I said, it ignores the effect of early decision, maybe we could factor in the positive effects of that change. It seems that the combined change could lead to a substantial net positive, don't you think so?" Hansen continued.

"Actually... no, I don't," she responded. "I'm not sure

why Alexander is pushing these changes... I think his intuition, if that's behind it, is way off. I think it's likely to be a plan that could put Baird in a financial hole it couldn't recover from."

"Look, Heather..." Hansen pressed. "We all need to keep an open mind about this and just put something together that we can show to the Board, and that will show what might be possible on the upside."

"Now, I've got a busy schedule today, so I'm afraid we need to cut this meeting short. I'm going to leave it to you to work out the details, and let's meet again next week to go over your work." The President stood, and escorted Martin to his office door.

As Martin left, the President was reflecting on his accomplishments. He had achieved what he'd hoped in his meetings with the Board Chair, the Provost, and Martin, though not without guile. Clearly, Martin was going to be a problem in pushing forward his initiatives, but the others would go along. He felt a touch of remorse about his dissembling but was convinced that it was necessary. Clearly, Martin did not support what he was doing, but he believed that, by pointing to the Board as driving the proposed changes, he had accomplished what he needed to. Moreover, telling her that it was a Board proposal would discourage Martin from speaking directly to any of the Board members about her concerns, even if they were to contact her.

***

Hansen's preparation for his next meeting was interrupted by his AA, who advised him that David Gomez was holding on the phone and had asked to speak with him urgently.

The President took the call. "What's up David?" he asked as he poured himself a coffee.

"We have a serious problem," Gomez reported. "And I'm not exactly sure how to deal with it."

"I see," said Hansen. "Let's hear it."

"Yeah, okay...." Gomez began. "So you know how some of our older buildings still have asbestos insulation, right?"

"Yes... but I think we have that covered by barriers so that it's okay," Hansen responded.

"Well... normally we do... we have the parts of the buildings where asbestos insulation is present isolated from the habitable spaces like offices, halls, classrooms, and restrooms. That works fine... as long as no one interferes with the barriers between those spaces," Gomez continued. "But earlier today, one of the faculty members in the Statistics Department was having a large wall-mounted video monitor installed in his office, and an outside vendor decided to remove some of the acoustical tiles in the office ceiling so he could run a cable line to the monitor."

"I still don't see the problem," Hansen commented.

"Okay, so the acoustical tiles are part of the barrier that separates the asbestos insulation from the habitable space. No one is supposed to remove those tiles without careful controls to prevent asbestos dust from escaping into the living environment," Gomez explained.

"Well, that can't be a very big deal," responded Hansen. "Just have them put the tiles back in place and have the janitorial staff go in and fully clean the office."

"I'm afraid we're well beyond that," resumed Gomez. "When the facilities manager responsible for that part of the campus noticed the penetration into habitable space, he triggered the building fire alarm and ordered the immediate evacuation of the entire building."

"So... just clean up the affected office quickly and move everyone back in."

"That's the problem...." Gomez responded. "Because of the penetration, the building may be out of compliance with OSHA Guidelines for protecting employees and students from exposure to asbestos. We're going to have to keep the building closed until we can get a hazmat team to do a full cleanup of the entire building and get it recertified as safe for occupancy."

"I see..." reflected Hansen. "So how long do you think that'll take? Are faculty and staff going to need to take a couple days off?"

"I wish.... It's going to be at least a month... maybe two, before we can go back in," Gomez explained.

"Holy shit," exclaimed Hansen, finally realizing the severity of the problem and abandoning his usual presidential demeanor. "What an effing mess.... That means most of the building staff will have to be put on paid leave.... We'll have to find temporary workspace for displaced faculty members.... They won't want to put their research projects or other work on hold for two months and they'll need to be able to prepare for their classes.... We'll need to find temporary space for the classes that were meeting in the building...."

"Yeah, all that, and I'm afraid it's even more involved. Because the supervisor pulled the fire alarm, a lot of people left important things behind. I've already heard that some of the women are complaining that they left purses or other valuables in their offices. Some people left behind important prescriptions, a number of faculty members left behind teaching notes they need for their classes, exams they were grading, or data for research projects they were working on."

Full realization of the extent of the problem had finally hit home. Hansen was stunned. Head in hands, "What can we do?" he asked, sounding a bit panicky.

"I think we need to address the most urgent problems first," Gomez calmly responded. "We can start by asking the people who've been evacuated from the building to let us know if there are important prescriptions or valuables they need urgently. We can send in a small hazmat team to locate those items, clean them, and bring them out. The other personal items, things like laptops, exams, and class notes can wait, I think. Faculty will just need to improvise for a while and students will need to wait a bit longer to get their exams back.... In two or three weeks we might be able to let faculty members back into the building, one or two at a time, in hazmat suits, and accompanied by hazmat technicians who can make sure the items they want to remove are safe.... I never thought I'd say this, but I think we might actually have found a use for the library. We can probably move affected faculty members into temporary space there, where they can have access to the campus computing system and the computer lab. We should be able to carve out some larger spaces that we can use as temporary classrooms."

"That all sounds like a pretty good plan." Hansen was relieved. "I'll approve the things you've laid out and delegate you to deal with any related problems that surface. I'll talk to Heather Martin to make sure you have whatever funds you need to deal with the emergency. Oh, and one other thing, David.... Find a way to fire the SOB who over-reacted and is responsible for this mess."

"That might not be necessary, sir," responded Gomez. "I think he knows he went too far and is probably already looking around for other employment."

"Well, good," Hansen concluded. "Now, I need to end this call. I've put off a meeting that I need to take. Call me anytime if you need my help on anything else that comes up on this."

***

"Come on in, Robert," Hansen said, forgetting that the Economics Department Chair went by Bob. "I'm sorry to have kept you waiting, but we had an emergency to deal with.

Fortunately, it all seems to be under control now. David Gomez is handling it and doing a great job of it.

"I wanted to meet with you today to give you the good news about my meeting with your alumnus.... What was his name...? Jennings, wasn't it? I wanted to let you know that I believe he's on board with funding the two endowed chairs in economics we were talking about. Though I think his campus tour, or, more accurately, his co-ed sightings excursion, probably had as much to do with reeling him in as did anything I said."

"That's great news," responded Hill. "I mean the funding, not the co-ed thing," Hill sought unnecessarily to clarify. "I'll let the Department faculty know that it's full speed ahead on our search."

"Yes... well... I do need to mention that Mr. Jennings has some specific ideas in mind.... I know we'd discussed a few possibilities, like chairs in accounting and finance, but it seems that Jennings has other ideas. He's proposing to fund an endowed professorship in environmental economics and one in the economics of the oil and gas industry. He wants to name the chairs after his parents." The President chose not to mention that it was he who had steered the discussion with Jennings away from accounting and finance and into areas of economics that would be less expensive to fully fund. "So what we'll be sending to the Board for their approval is a Jennings Chair in Environmental Economics and a Jennings Chair in the Economics of the Oil and Gas Industry. I hope you agree that this is a great outcome... two additional high-profile faculty members in economics."

Hill was dismayed and could not conceal his disappointment. "Of course... we'll do our best to respect the donor's intent, but I have to say that I'm disappointed that we'll not be able to use those chairs to address some of our more pressing needs. In most cases, when we undertake a search for a new faculty member, some existing faculty members will be disappointed with the focus of the search and others will be enthusiastic. In this case, however, I suspect that virtually everyone will be disappointed."

"I understand, Robert, but I'm sure you can help persuade them. There's always some flexibility. For example, Jennings says he'd like the environmental econ chair to be filled by someone who can push back against all of the research suggesting that we're headed for catastrophic climate change. But I don't think it would be appropriate or consistent with academic freedom to so limit the chair."

"Okay... well, I guess we can try to take a broad view and do the best we can to use the chairs to meet our needs," Hill concluded. "I'll do what I can to bring the faculty on board."

"Great, Robert, I'll follow up on our conversation with a formal letter authorizing the searches in those areas," the President ended the meeting.

CHAPTER 14

THE ACADEMIC PERSONNEL COMMITTEE

The Academic Personnel Committee of Baird University comprises 10 very senior faculty members drawn from departments throughout the campus. While the specific composition varies from year to year, normally it includes representatives from the humanities and social sciences and the physical sciences. With less regularity, it might include members from the arts. The Committee is one of the busiest on campus, usually meeting weekly or even more often. Its main function is to review departmental recommendations for appointments, promotion, and tenure and to advise the Provost and the President on the final determinations in such matters. All members have full access to each case file. In each action that the Committee considers, one member is assigned to carefully review the full file and to present the case to the others on the Committee. The Committee then votes, and one member prepares a formal recommendation to the Provost. To reduce the potential for litigation, these written recommendations are cryptic and intentionally circumspect as to the reasons for any recommendations the Committee might make.

In its first November meeting, among other cases, the Committee was considering the three promotion and tenure files that had been submitted from the Economics Department. As there was no member of the Economics Department on the Committee, all three cases were scheduled to be presented by a faculty member from Sociology.

Members of the Committee arrived gradually to their meeting room, started up their computers, and conversed casually as they waited for others to arrive. The member from Anthropology, whose surname is Tullock, had been commenting on what he felt were problems associated with the way researchers' names appeared on papers they had written. "Does anyone else here have problems figuring out what to do with author order on papers? In my area, it's normal to list authors alphabetically and, if the order is not alphabetical, that usually implies that the first-listed author contributed more to the project. But sometimes I know authors who work together on more than one project agree to shuffle their names, so that whoever's listed first on one paper might be listed in second or third position on another. That's pretty confusing."

"Yes," agreed the member from Biochemistry. "It's even more confusing because conventions are different in different areas. In mine, for example, it's normal to list the project leader last. I guess we can handle those kinds of issues on a case-by-case basis but what are we supposed to do in an area like High-energy Physics, where a three-page paper can have more than one-hundred authors just because they all share access to the same particle accelerator?"

"And my other complaint about citation," continued Tullock, "is the practice, in citing the work of others, of referring to the authorship of a paper by the name of the first-listed author and then all the rest as 'et al.' Sure they're fully listed in the references, but when the name of the first author is used over and over in the text, I think people almost start thinking of that person as the author, ignoring others, who may have contributed as much or more."

"I'm just guessing, Paul, but could it be that the main reason you're bothered by that is because your last name is Tullock, whereas mine's Baily?" chided the professor from English, lightening the jibe with a grin and a shrug. "Have you considered what the effect might be if you were to change your last name to 'Et al?" she smiled.

"Hmm," Tullock responded in mock seriousness, "I'll have to think about that.... Wonder what would happen."

"Did any of you happen to attend last week's Academic Senate meeting?" asked the committee member from the Gender Studies Department, changing the subject. "I was surprised to learn that Biology is proposing to offer one section of their introductory course in Spanish. What would be the point of doing that?"

"I was there," responded the Committee Chair, who was from History. I suspect that Biology is looking at the campus requirement that a student take three terms of a language and is hoping to boost their own majors by introducing a biology course that could count toward the language general education requirement."

"That's absurd!" exclaimed the member from Sociology. "What next? Will the Theater Department be proposing that performing an opera with an Italian libretto be counted toward meeting the language requirement? We have to hold the line on these incursions or eventually we could end up with a single class meeting a half-dozen of the liberal education requirements."

"Maybe you're right about that, Eva, but fortunately it's not a concern of this committee," the Chair remarked.

"Well," said the member from the Department of Literature. "I can assure you that there's no way the campus faculty would support counting a Biology course toward meeting the language requirement."

"But Spanish Literature would be okay, I suppose?" interjected Tullock with a shrug.

"Okay, we're all here," the Chair diverted. "So let's begin." Whereupon the Committee launched into its agenda for the day. After completing its review of a handful of cases from other areas, and generally supporting the positive recommendations coming from the departments, the Committee turned to the three cases from Economics.

"Moving on, now, who's tasked to present the Phillips case, in Econ?" asked the Chair.

"That would be me," responded the member from Sociology. "But, before I begin with the individual cases, I have a concern I'd like to raise. Did anyone happen to notice the salaries of these assistant professors, especially the ones in accounting and finance? It seems to me that they're much higher than the salaries of most full professors in other departments. Now, I know that we're not supposed to be questioning the appropriateness of the compensation, so I'm not really sure why it's included in the files we see. But I wonder if maybe we should be taking the compensation level into account when we think about the adequacy of research output or the quality of teaching."

"I also have questions on that," the Biochemistry professor on the committee joined in. "Most of us work in areas where our research is important to society. I'm not sure the people who work on business related topics can make such a claim. Moreover, our research is important to the University since it brings in grant funding, whereas very few of the people in the Economics Department bring in much grant money. I can't think of a single grant in accounting or finance. Seems to me that the bar for tenure in those areas needs to be correspondingly higher... equal pay for equal work, you know...."

"I'm not so sure." Tullock picked up the discussion. "We had a member of the Economics Department faculty on the Committee last year, when an issue much like this one came up. She argued, fairly persuasively, in my judgment, that we need to accept that salaries are market driven and that we don't have control over the market. If we were to lower econ and business salaries to match the averages in our other departments, we'd be unable to hire good faculty members in business-related areas... or if we moved all departments to the overall averages, we could have a phenomenal English Department, for example, but many of our other departments would suffer."

"That sounds like a good argument for closing down the Economics Department," the member from Sociology rebutted. "These salary differentials across departments are just too divisive. And it seems to me that most of economics is just common sense."

"Interesting idea, Steve," Tullock responded. "Unfortunately, I don't think it'll get much traction with the Administration since so much of our financial support comes from people who work in economics-related professions or who graduated with degrees in economics."

"Well, we can't really do anything about the salary differentials and fortunately for us it's not our job to do so," the Chair sought to close off the digression. "So I suggest that we just turn to the cases at hand. Please go ahead with your summary of the Phillips case, Professor."

"Yes... well... Phillips works in industrial organization, which, I understand to be a field within Economics. He got his Ph.D. about six years ago from the University of Maryland, which I think has a pretty good economics department, but not a top department. He has seven publications, overall. Some of the faculty members in the Department argue that three top-tier papers are needed for tenure and Phillips has three, but they are all coauthored. I'm relying on their claim as to what constitutes top-tier, but there is some evidence on journal impact scores that seems to support their view. Others in the Department argue that the record is good enough. There's also a concern that his best-placed papers are with senior colleagues and his later work is with juniors and hasn't placed as well. So there's some concern about his independence. The outside letters from academics at other schools are generally supportive but with enough caveats that there is no clear guidance. By the way, that's also true for the other two cases from econ."

"Moving on, his teaching seems to be okay. I've been through all of the comments, and it seems that he is doing what he should be. I should also note that the teaching loads in Econ are on the high side compared to the loads in some of our departments, and he's been teaching a lot of students in introductory classes. On the other hand, maybe the loads are high because grant support is negligible. It's hard to say much about his university and professional service. Normally, we expect university service to be low before tenure but professional service to be solid. I think his service seems okay."

"The Economics Department vote on Phillips was mixed… slightly more votes for tenure than against, but also some abstentions so that he ended up with only a plurality in favor."

"I noticed that some of his research is in journals that focus on diversity issues," observed Tullock, "and that he has a couple papers where he tries to compare the productivity of mixed-race teams with that of single-race teams. Possibly, he's interested in that because of his own race. It seems that the economics journals that publish diversity-related research are not usually the top-tier journals."

"That's an interesting observation," remarked the member from Biochemistry. "I have a couple questions. First, I'm not clear on why there are so many 'No' votes in the department. And second, do you think his race might affect his opportunities to join research teams, or the way students react to him in his classes?"

"I don't know about the race question," Tullock responded, "It's just a concern I have. It seems that the 'No' votes reflect concerns about his independence, publishing his best papers with senior coauthors and the rest in lower-level journals. But, as some of us know, split votes seem to be the norm in the Economics Department, and in some others on campus."

"Well, don't they understand that when they send forward a split vote, they are just making the department opinion irrelevant, and leaving it up to us and others who have less information about the candidate to use in deciding on tenure? Usually, when a candidate has the strong support of the department, we go along with the department recommendation. I can't see why the faculty in economics doesn't work harder to build consensus and come forward with clear recommendations," countered the member from Biochemistry.

"True, but I think there are a several faculty members in the Department with strong personalities and an unwillingness to seek consensus," observed the Chair. "In any case, we have what we have from them, and we'll just have to decide."

After further discussion, the Committee voted unanimously in support of promotion and tenure. There was a strong sentiment on the Committee that, as much as possible, their votes should be unanimous, or nearly so, since split votes made it too easy for the Provost and President to ignore the sentiment of the faculty.

"Now, moving to Lopez, the next case I'm on the hook for, he got his degree from the University of Texas six years ago. He's in the finance area and the Department has put forward another split vote. The main issue for the 'No' votes seems to be that he only has four published papers, which apparently is below the norm. He has two papers in top-tier journals, which some Department members say is too few. But others argue that they're single-authored and that there should be some consideration of the extent of co-authorship.

They also argue that his other two are in a journal that some, but not all, schools consider to be top-tier. So, it seems to me that while his record's shorter than Phillips's, there's more evidence of independence and quality. If we weight each paper by the number of coauthors, so that a paper with two authors counts for half of a paper, Lopez has three weighted paper equivalents, whereas Phillips has only two and one-half."

"But I don't think we have a practice of weighting by co-authorship," commented the member from Biochemistry, who, on his own work often had as many as ten coauthors. "So let's not make up a new standard now."

"Okay, but maybe we should also give some consideration to work in his pipeline," commented Tullock. "He seems to have quite a few projects underway, including a couple that seem close to being accepted by top journals. His pipeline seems to be quite a bit better than Phillips's"

"That's fine, but we also don't look at work in progress," countered the Biochemistry member. "How about his teaching and service?"

"I think, on that score, his record is much like Phillips's," the Sociology member completed his summary of the case. "I should also mention that the outside letters are all positive, whereas those for Phillips were a bit more guarded. But the vote in the Economics Department was slightly negative, apparently because some members of the Department consider three papers in top-tier journals to be a requirement for tenure, whereas others, the minority, are more inclined to consider co-authorship, individual paper impact, and future potential."

"Before we vote," interjected the Committee member from Literature, I want to point out that his surname is Lopez. Is he a person of color that we maybe should be thinking about differently?" she asked.

"To your question," the Chair responded, "I don't think

we're supposed to be influenced by ethnic or racial factors, but in any case, Lopez is Caucasian from Spain and not a protected class member."

After further discussion, the Committee voted unanimously against promotion and tenure.

"Okay, one more case," said the Sociology member, "and then we can all get out of here."

"Lin Chang got her degree from UBC. She works in the accounting area and has four top-tier papers, including one that's single authored, and she also has some other work. Since the Department was in agreement that her research record is good enough, and it appears to me that it is, and because all of the outside letters strongly support the research record, I'll move on to the other considerations. It appears that she has some difficulties with effective teaching. Her numerical evaluations are consistently lower than we're used to seeing, and there's no sign that she's improving over time. There are quite a few complaints that her courses are too difficult, that her lectures are dull, and that she's hard to hear. Some members of the Department argue that low evaluations are to be expected in the courses she's been teaching. But then I wonder why the Department didn't move her into courses where she could do better. In my view, the teaching isn't great, but maybe it's okay."

"Unfortunately, it seems that service is also a problem. While we don't expect much campus service, we do expect to see that our assistant professors are actively engaged in the profession, presenting their papers at conferences, serving as discussant at conferences, and reviewing papers for journals. It seems that Chang does almost none of that. So that's my take on the case," concluded the Sociology member. Here, again, the Economics Department vote was split but slightly negative, I think based on the teaching and service."

"But it seems that some of these issues about teaching

and service may be related to gender and cultural biases," commented the Committee member from English, one of three females on the Committee. I think we need to recognize the extra challenges that gender brings to our profession."

Ultimately, by vote of four to six, the Committee voted against tenure for Chang.

"So, on Chang, our vote is much like the split votes coming from the Department. It seems that we'll be leaving the decision on tenure to the Provost, without much useful advice from either the Department or us," the Chair observed. "It is what it is, I suppose. Once the reports are finalized, on these cases, I'll forward them to the Provost. See you all again next week... same time, same place."

CHAPTER 15

THE DEPARTMENT

Anticipating a long department meeting, Krista Novikova was heading for the third-floor restroom. She found it difficult not to grow angry every time she turned into the room marked by a sign in the hall that read, "Women's Restroom/Kitchen." Wondering how the University Administration could be so tone-deaf, even in this era of political correctness, she also took note of the ancient (and probably empty) machine that promised a tampon for ten cents.

Upon leaving, she averted her eyes when she encountered Larry Faquhir coming in through the door to refresh his coffee in the kitchen.

"It could be worse," she reflected to herself, as she walked past Jamie Noach's office, located across from the women's restroom/kitchen and just next to the men's room.

The Economics Department Chair had called this meeting on short notice, mainly to bring the faculty up to speed on the endowed chair search. But there were also a few lesser items on the agenda that he was planning to address first.

"As we wait for the others to arrive," Hill began, though the room was nearly full, "I was hoping to take care of a couple of minor things. First, the Faculty Senate Executive Committee has decided that it's time to rethink our course evaluation instrument and is asking each department to provide a volunteer to work on the project."

"Really?" Edwards exclaimed. "Are they barmy...? I

thought we just did that two or three years ago. What are they saying is wrong with the evaluation instrument we are using now?"

"It seems that some people who typically get good evaluations are complaining that the five-point scale we use is too limiting since it doesn't give enough range to identify the truly outstanding teachers," the Chair began to explain.

Cory Sarks interjected, "I suppose that by 'outstanding' you mean the ones who are the most entertaining, show a lot of videos in their classes, and grade most forgivingly."

"According to the group that's promoting a review of the instrument there's more to it than that," Hill responded. "They also claim that some of the questions on the evaluation instrument are implicitly racist or misogynistic. I'm not really sure what's driving those concerns, but, in any case, this is an argument we can't win," the Chair said. "I'm afraid we're just going to have to accept the notion that we'll have to review the course evaluation instrument every few years. It's kind of like Arrow's Paradox but without formal voting. Once we decide on an instrument that's supported by one group of faculty, it's always possible to cobble together and energize a few disaffected factions that want to change it. The process never converges and is unending.... Maybe I shouldn't so directly express my cynicism about course evaluations. Nonetheless, I hope we can have a volunteer so I don't need to draft anyone."

Trevor Butler, still seeking to score points that would counterbalance the problems he seemed to be having in publishing his research, raised his hand. "It might be interesting to see what kind of thought goes into designing evaluation instruments," he said. "So I'll do it if no one else wants to."

"Thanks TB," Hill pounced. "I'll forward your name to the Faculty Senate Chair."

"The other item I want to mention is that as we get close

to final exam time, we tend to get a few bomb scares. So far, these have been false alarms. It seems," the Chair noted, "that some students have decided it's a good idea to call them in as a way to disrupt the exam. Nonetheless, campus Administration wants us to take the threats seriously and quickly vacate a building against which a bomb threat has been received."

"Well, that's just great," commented Noach, whose final exams had been disrupted several times by such threats. "It really messes things up, especially when it happens right at the end of a term. I don't think it's fair to the students who've been doing well in the classes that are disrupted."

"I recognize that the threats need to be taken seriously, but I don't see why the University hasn't developed a smarter response plan," Novikova commented. "The false threats are only happening because the threat makers get what they want... to disrupt an exam. I think we could remove, or at least reduce, that incentive if we all were to agree on a backup plan in the event of a threat. For example, we could each put in our course syllabus that in the event of a disruption, the class will be moved to a designated alternative location on campus... a room in another building, or even an outdoor location. I think implementing a program like that would pretty much eliminate the fake threats."

"That's an interesting thought," Hill responded. "I'm not sure about the logistics, but I'll pass the suggestion along to the Provost."

"Okay, so now that we have the housekeeping out of the way and everyone's here let's turn to the reason I felt it was important to call this meeting on short notice," he continued. "I met a few days ago with President Hansen to discuss the status of our endowed chair searches. The good news is that Hansen has met with Mr. Jennings, and Jennings has agreed to fund the two chairs in economics."

"That's great news," interjected Nadir Kaur, who was

looking forward to formally initiating a search in accounting.

"Yes," followed up Niki Stewart. "I think I can speak for everyone in saying that we really appreciate all the effort you've put into securing Jennings's support for the Department." Her remark was accompanied by a scattering of confirmatory head nods from those in the meeting.

"Well, before we celebrate," responded Hill, "I need to point out that there are some conditions that the donor has decided to place on the positions. You'll recall from our last meeting that I'd been talking with Jennings about a few possibilities... chairs in micro or macroeconomics or maybe in finance or accounting. Based on his reaction, at the time, I expected that he'd go for a chair each in accounting and finance. And I think you'll recall that in that meeting we had decided to pursue an open search..."

"Just a minute, Mr. Chair," Sarks interrupted. "I took the minutes at that meeting and the minutes clearly state that we would decide on the focus of the search by faculty vote. The record is clear that micro and macroeconomics got more votes than did either finance or accounting."

"Yes, I've seen your draft of the minutes, Cory," Hill responded. "But the draft hasn't yet been approved and I believe the minutes mischaracterize the discussion we had in that meeting. You all recall that, mainly following suggestions from Larry, we voted several different ways. We never voted to exclude the possibility of hiring in either accounting or finance. As you know, Cory, I've asked that you correct the draft before bringing the minutes to the faculty for approval and you seem to be resisting that change."

"Well, of course I'm resisting," Sarks responded. "You appointed me Department Secretary in that meeting, and as such, I am the person with the authority to prepare the minutes. It is not for you to tell me to change them."

"Look, Cory," Hill countered, as others in the room

remained silent, not wanting to engage in a dispute with Sarks, "We could easily spend the rest of this meeting in a pointless argument over how meeting minutes are prepared and who has the final authority to decide on the accuracy of the draft minutes before bringing them to the faculty for approval. In this case, however, as you'll see, the issue is moot. So, if you don't mind, I'd like to move on."

"Well, I do mind, and furthermore, I insist that we follow Robert's Rules and not proceed with the business of the meeting until the minutes are approved," Sarks argued.

"Okay, Cory," Hill was uncharacteristically losing his temper, "we're just going to have to disagree, I guess. I am ruling your insistence that we waste the day debating the minutes to be out of order. We have some important and pressing business to take up."

"I have to object, Mr. Chair. Proceeding without first approving my minutes is improper. Without approving them, this is not a legitimate meeting of the Department, and I will not participate in the farce. I am leaving and I hope others will join me," Sarks concluded, looking pointedly at the untenured assistant professors in the room. He closed his laptop and left the room. Despite a few uncomfortable glances among the assistant professors, no one followed.

"Okay," Hill exhaled. "Now maybe we can move on.... I was saying that we'd been planning on an open search and that I thought the donor was inclined to support professorships in accounting and finance.... I don't know how it happened, but apparently sometime after I met with the donor, his aspirations for the chaired positions seem to have changed. Maybe something came up during his meeting with President Hansen. In any case, the search that's been authorized is for two endowed professors, one in environmental economics and one in the economics of the oil and gas industry."

The faculty were stunned. "But that's nothing we even

considered," Faquhir rejoined. "In fact, it sounds most like what we explicitly decided not to do… narrowly focused niche professorships."

"That's right," Krista Novikova joined in dismay. "Those lines won't help us at all. We already offer a couple courses in environmental economics, and we have absolutely no need for courses focused narrowly on the oil and gas industry."

"Of course I agree," Hill responded, "but I suppose we'll just have to make the best of it. So I'd like to spend the remaining time in our meeting developing a recruitment plan for these two areas."

"Oh…" Larry Faquhir interrupted. "I just realized that I'm late for another meeting. And aren't you supposed to be in that meeting, too, Jamie?" whereupon Professors Faquhir and Noach left the room.

"I think I need to leave, too," said Dan Edwards. "I'm heading for a conference tomorrow and my paper session still needs some organizational work."

After Edwards departed, Krista Novikova spoke up. "It seems clear that we're not going to be able to accomplish anything more in this meeting, Bob. How about if we adjourn and try to reschedule after everyone has had a chance to settle down and come to terms with the new directive from the President."

"Yes, it does seem that we'll have to postpone," responded Hill. "I suppose I could have handled this better, but I'm not sure how. Maybe I'll try to take it offline and find a small group that will agree to serve on the search committee."

CHAPTER 16

HAPPY HOURS

When Krista arrived at the Tilted Kilt after the abrupt conclusion of the Department meeting, Larry Faquhir and Jamie Noach were already there and well into their first pitcher of draft. "Somehow, I suspected that this was the meeting you were referring to when you left the Department meeting," she said to Faquhir. After she joined them at their table, a few other tenured faculty members of the Economics Department drifted in. The mood was glum.

"What should we do about the faculty searches?" asked Nadir Kaur.

"Can we talk about something else?" Nicole Stewart responded. "This topic's a bit too raw."

"How about if we take it up a notch?" Faquhir responded. "I have no doubt that this change of focus was all engineered by our illustrious President. I know he's feeling some budgetary pressure and he's probably afraid of the cost of hiring in some of the areas we were considering. My guess is that he deliberately steered Jennings in a less expensive direction. Jennings would still donate the same amount, but the remaining cost that would need to be borne by the School would be less."

"That sounds right to me," Noach picked up. "Hansen's no mensch, we all know. So I wouldn't put it beyond him."

"Well, if the School is having budget problems, aren't there some other things they could do besides messing with out faculty hiring?" Nicole asked.

"Sure there are," Rearden Koopman responded. "I

remember when I first came to Baird... quite a few years ago, now... the School was lean and focused. We had all the normal core departments that any good liberal arts college would have, and the sciences. We had a small fine arts program, but the faculty in that area were untenured.... It seems to me that in the last few years... maybe quite a few years... we've added a large number of trendy departments. Instead of the four language department we had when I arrived, we probably now have more than a dozen, including languages like Arabic, Farsi, Mandarin, Russian, Swahili, and even Gaelic. And every department wants to have at least three tenure-track faculty members... and a Ph.D. program.... Do we really need to cover all of the languages? Same sort of thing in the arts, though not necessarily with separate departments. In the Dance Department, students can focus on Modern Dance, Ballet, Jazz, Hip Hop, Tribal, Latin, and a bunch of others. Each one requires at least one faculty expert... and now we even give tenure in the fine arts."

"Yeah, and the same thing seems to be going on in the humanities other than languages," Nicole joined in. "It seems that every time someone identifies a new interest group, the School creates a new department. We have departments of Black Studies, Chicano Studies, Pacific Islander Studies, Gender Studies, LGBTQ Studies, Native American Studies, Indigenous Peoples Studies, and a plethora of religious studies specialties.... Some of them seem to be nearly duplicative.... And can't we cover these out of our traditional department structure? It seems that often when we set up these interest-group-based departments, the departments turn into advocacy programs rather than intellectually driven and balanced programs."

"That's all true, of course," Larry responded. "And now we're spread too thin so that many private schools are seeking to improve their financial conditions by taking hard looks at their menus of humanities and arts majors and degrees. I think this has all been a challenge for Baird, especially because so many members of the Board have very strong commitments to the humanities and the arts. Some Trustees have been on the Board for more than a decade. They fostered the creation of some of these new departments and majors, and they're resistant to any move that diminishes their pet programs.... Ready for a couple more pitchers?"

"Why not, Larry...? And we have no champions on the Board," picked up Novikova. "One thing that I find very upsetting is Hansen's nepotism. I suppose you all know that he somehow convinced the Board to allow him to hire his wife to direct the Campus Speakers Series. I don't know what kind of salary she gets, but she seems to have control of a substantial budget for bringing in guest speakers. So, for the past year or more, all we've had is a steady stream of speakers on topics like salary inequality, the glass ceiling, critical legal theory, critical racial theory, anti-capitalism, and the like... topics Ms. Hansen supports and thinks represent important values Baird students should be encouraged to accept."

"So there's no process for selecting speakers or seeking to present balanced points of view?" Rearden asked.

"No structured process, and I'm concerned both about the expense and about the balance," Novikova explained. "But at least it seems that under pressure from a conservative student group on campus, there'll be one conservative speaker on campus next term... maybe someone like Charles Murray, Richard Dawkins, Vivek Ramaswamy, or Tyler Cowan. That should be interesting.... I still think the whole thing with the President and his wife is a bit too cozy. I don't see that she has any relevant background, and it seems unlikely that her appointment could have been the outcome of an open search. It also seems that the School is putting a lot more resources into that speakers program than it needs to. So our department's faculty search seems to be one of the casualties."

"I'm feeling a bit bad about having walked out of our meeting today," said Faquhir, who still sought to control the search as much as possible. "It's not Bob's fault.... I guess we'll have to go back soon and figure out the best way to proceed... maybe go and see Hansen or refuse to serve on such a narrowly focused a search committee."

***

Edwards and Rebecca were on the same flight to Key West the next day. She had taken the window seat and he the aisle on their small Regional Jet. As Rebecca gazed out the window, she got her first look at Florida and the Keys. He, during the flight, had tried to focus on the papers that would be presented in his session, distracted all the while by the brush of her thigh against his.

Leaving Key West International, they shared an Uber to the conference hotel. On arrival, they went separately to their rooms, where each ordered room service and spent the evening preparing for their professional obligations of the next day.

Edwards's session went about as well as expected. Attendance was light, as usual at these meetings, but at least all of the presenters had shown up, as had the discussants, with Rebecca as a substitute. There were, maybe, a half dozen others in the audience, with some in-and-out flow as people dropped in to hear just the paper or two that were of interest to them.

Becca did okay in her debut, Edwards thought, a bit rough in spots, with some evidence that she didn't entirely understand all of the points he'd been making in the slides he'd prepared for her. But it was good enough for a first-time out.

Edwards was back in his room at the hotel and had just showered in preparation for the conference reception that evening. He was gazing out at the waves on the beach when there was a knock at his door. Answering in a hotel bathrobe, he found Becca waiting in the hall, wearing a pair of body-conforming white shorts and a floral print halter top she had somehow managed to pick-up on Duval Street after their session.

Brandishing a bottle of cabernet, "How about a corkscrew?" she asked. "I couldn't find one in my room, but your room looks much nicer and it's probably better stocked." Whereupon she stepped in and nudged the door closed with her hip.

"Aren't you going to the reception?" Edwards asked.

"Actually, I thought we might have a small reception of our own here," she smiled. "The ocean's so beautiful from your window... and we can enjoy the sunset...."

"Oh... I see..." she demurred, her gaze drifting to below the tie of his hotel robe.... How interesting.... I believe I may have a solution for that." She reached for the robe tie. "Maybe we can look for the corkscrew a bit later."

Later, over glasses of wine, and out on the room's balcony, Edwards mused, "I suppose I'll need to advise the Department Chair of our little relationship."

"Oh, I don't think that's necessary.... We're both adults.... Though you are a bit older, of course," she chided.

"Well, it's not about age, you know," he continued. "You're my student... so technically this is a power relationship. I think I need to disclose it."

"Actually, it's not just 'technically'. It *is* a power relationship.... But I don't think disclosing it would be good for either of us," Rebecca countered. "Think about it. If word got out, people might suspect that you'd pressured me into a relationship. That wouldn't be good for you. And it's becoming public in that way could lead recruiters from other schools to think less of me... and maybe to suspect that you had too big of a hand in my research. I say we just keep it to ourselves. It's all going to be over fairly soon anyway, once I land an academic appointment, so we might as well just enjoy the time we have."

"I suppose you're right," Edwards acquiesced. "But then we just need to be careful, so people don't get the wrong idea when they see us together."

"Why do you think I always bring my laptop and a folder to our meetings in public places?"

"Good point," Edwards nodded.

"There's one other thing we should talk about." Rebecca smiled demurely as she refilled their wine glasses. "I know you haven't been quite up front with me, Professor, as to what you think of my dissertation work so far," Rebecca began. "I know the empirical work we've done can be the core of a good dissertation and a well-placed journal article. But, unfortunately, it's clear to me that I'm not really up to the writing part. I haven't failed to notice your furtive looks and even winces as you read through what I've written so far.... I want a good placement in the job market and I'm sure others will spot the same shortcomings you're noticing. I don't think I can get what I want unless you take over rewriting some of the rough parts."

"Well... yes.... Maybe I should have been more direct with you early on. I have to agree that the writing falls a bit short of what we'd like to see in a dissertation or a job market paper. I can take a look and try to give you some more specific comments on the writing," Edwards responded.

"That's nice of you to offer, but I'm afraid it may not be enough. I think I'm going to need for you to rewrite a fair amount of what I've drafted. Otherwise, I may not achieve what I hope to."

"I see..." Edwards reflected, "I guess it'd be okay if I were to co-author your job market paper with you, but at Baird we don't normally do that, and I think co-authorship of the first paper from your dissertation might not be a good way for you to go."

"No, Professor, I wouldn't want that either... and I see the problem with coauthoring. What I'm asking for is more of a ghostwriting arrangement, so to speak... like we often see of books by politicians and other famous people."

"I'm afraid that would be most unusual for academic research. I'd feel better just commenting."

"I understand that it's unusual, but our personal relationship is a bit unusual, too, don't you think? So I'm sure you can make an exception and help me clear this hurdle."

"This is starting to seem like a bit of a threat, Becca." Edwards was studying her firm but smiling expression as he spoke. Rebecca noticed and quickly softened the hard look in her eyes. She moved closer, and stroking his thigh, suggested that they move off of the subject and back on to something more stimulating.

Edwards dismissed the notion that he was being threatened, or at least tried to do so, as he followed her back inside.

Edwards and Becca slept in the next morning. They missed the association breakfast as well as most of the rest of the conference. Instead, they went on a snorkeling tour, took several strolls along Higgs Beach, and tried out several of the bars on Duvall Street.

CHAPTER 17

EXECUTIVE LEADERSHIP TEAM

The week before the fall meeting of the Board, President Hansen convened another meeting of his ELT. The main purpose of his meeting was to do a dry run-through of the items on the agenda for the Board meeting. Doing so was important, Hansen believed, since members of the ELT would be conferring with Board members in several meetings throughout the day and he needed to make sure they were all saluting the same flag. Today's meeting also provided an opportunity to spot issues that could be problematic if they were to surface during the meeting with the Board.

Hansen's main challenge, he believed, was going to be keeping Martin on message. He felt confident that the Provost would support almost any position he took, and that David Knight would be on board, since the changes he was planning to propose would make the job of the VP for Admissions easier. He suspected that Jack Richardson would be grateful for anything that would take the Board's focus off of Advancement, since the record for this year was not looking very good. Martin, on the other hand, might easily go negative and off message, as she had when he originally raised the ideas with her, and again later when they had met to review her preliminary work. To keep her from deviating too far from what she'd been pressed to agree to, Hansen had required that Martin structure her remarks around a PowerPoint presentation. One part of today's meeting was to have her do a run-through of the draft presentation.

"Welcome, again, everyone. I think you've all seen the agenda for the Board meeting next week. I'd like to use our time today to go over some parts of that agenda so that we all know what we're trying to accomplish. Each of you will be giving a brief report, and we'll have a more extended discussion of the proposal for need-blind, loan-free admission, coupled with adoption of an early decision program. Since that discussion could take a while, I'd like to begin with it today, and then we can go back and touch on the other matters.... Sound good?" he asked the group.

"Heather, can we start with your draft presentation, please?" he commanded.

"Yes, of course," Martin complied. "Usually, my role in these meetings is to take the Board through the details of some lengthy financial statement. For that, since it involves a lot of numbers, it works best if I provide paper copies of the financial statements.... So that's a round-about way of confessing that I don't use PowerPoint very often. Because I don't, I thought it'd be good to invite Bill from IT in to help me set up the equipment. So, if you'll give me a minute, I'll get everything arranged." She handed a DVD to Bill from IT and stood aside as he powered up a small computer that had been placed in the room.

He looked briefly at the computer and found that it was lacking a disk drive. I'm going to have to find another way to load this presentation, he told Martin. "Do you have it in an email or in a directory I can access with this computer?"

"I only have the disk," Martin responded. "I thought the project was too sensitive to work on in my office, so I prepared the presentation at home and only copied it to this disk."

"Okay," Bill deliberated. "I guess I can run back to IT and copy the file to a flash drive."

"Could you do that," the President instructed, "and hurry back here as quickly as possible."

"While we're waiting," he continued, "we can take up

some of the lesser issues."

"One quick one... we'll need Board approval for the two endowed professorships in the Economics Department. I can take the lead on that, and let the Board know about the donor's commitment. Then I plan to turn it over to Jim to describe the intended focus of each of the two chairs.... I think the Board will be enthusiastic about the gift, so I don't anticipate any major issues with getting their approval," he concluded.

"Now, on the broader subject of Advancement, I think I'll need to turn that over to you, Jack, to tell the Board where we stand on our targets for the year and to field questions. That might be a bit challenging, since we seem to be falling behind our targets for alumni giving and for major gifts.... So I'll be sure to mention that you're new to the position of VP for Advancement, which should give you an entrée to discuss some of the challenges you've had to face with the transition. I think our overall message needs to be that this is just a temporary setback associated with the changes in your office and that you expect the rest of the year to be better and to be back on track by the end of the fiscal year."

"I hear you," Richardson responded, "but I'm concerned that might be painting a bit too rosy of a picture. With all of the turnover and staff departures, most things in our office came almost to a stop.... We lost a lot of momentum in developing some important relationships, and we're going to have to rebuild those relationships before we're likely to see much of a payoff. That'll take longer than the rest of the year."

"That may be, Jack, but this meeting wouldn't be a good time to raise that concern with the Board. If we get to the spring meeting and things are still lagging, we can break that news to them then.... I hope you agree," Hansen conveyed his expectation.

Richardson, who was not used to the pressure Hansen could bring to bear, equivocated. "I suppose we can do that," he conceded.

As they concluded the Advancement discussion, Bill arrived and was waiting in the outer office. When invited back in, he quickly loaded Martin's PowerPoint file onto the computer and started up the projector, only to find a white screen. "Something's not right," he said. Let me try to figure it out. He tried a couple of obvious fixes... shutting down and restarting the computer... restarting the projector. After a few minutes, he discovered that the cable between the computer and the projector was not connected. Once he connected it, the Windows Home Page appeared on the screen. Bill quickly located the flash drive link and clicked on the presentation file. "Okay, I think you're good to go," he said.

"Thanks for your help, Bill," Heather responded. "But before you go, can you show me how to put the file into presentation mode?"

"I can try," he said, "but I'm not really familiar with PowerPoint."

"Just click on the little icon thing in the bottom tray on the right side that looks like a presentation screen," interrupted the Provost, who had become frustrated with the delay. "It's simple, Heather."

"Thanks, Jim," she responded. "This probably seems second nature to anyone who's been teaching.... So here we go with what I'm planning to say...."

"I learned from President Hansen, a couple of weeks ago, that the Board would like to consider a significant change in our admissions policies. Currently, ability to pay is one of the factors in our admissions decisions, and students or their families that can't afford the full cost of a Baird education may get some aid in the form of tuition remission or scholarship or work-study. To the extent that doesn't fully cover their financial needs, they currently turn to third-party lenders for financial support. Quite a few of them end up with fairly substantial debt burdens by the time they graduate."

"I understand that the Board wants to consider a move to need-blind admission with loan-free aid.... Now, it seems fairly obvious that such a change could be costly for the School. To offset that, President Hansen has asked me to examine the effects of counterbalancing the new financial aid policies against a policy of admitting some students by early decision. So, in purely financial terms, I think the question is 'To what extent can the cost of moving to need-blind, loan-free admission be offset by admitting some students through early decision... maybe including more international students?'"

"Now, before I get into the financial analysis, President Hansen has asked me to mention some of the other considerations that could bear on the Board's decision. I have some of those points listed on this next slide.

> Non-financial effects of need-blind admission
>
> - We would extend the opportunity for a Baird education to more students with significant financial need.
> - We are likely to increase the ethnic diversity of our student body.
> - Baird students will have more exposure to students with different financial and ethnic backgrounds.
> - We are likely to increase the ability of students interested in the arts and humanities to afford a Baird education.
> - Moving to need-blind, loan-free admission is likely to enhance Baird's reputation and attract additional donor support.
> - Other benefits...

"So, it seems pretty clear that such a move would have non-financial effects that are mainly positive. The issue at hand is whether Baird can afford to make such a dramatic change.

"The President and I discussed the possible financial impacts and we decided to look at negative impacts of need-blind loan-free admission in the range of $1 to $2 million." Under pressure from Hansen, Martin had been compelled to acquiesce and limit her analysis to this range, even though she thought the actual impact was likely to be substantially greater. "So this next slide shows how we developed the impact ranges we considered. The move would impact our financial condition in two ways. First, we'd need to provide loan-free aid to domestic students that we would admit under a need-blind policy, students we might not have admitted under our current policies. Second, we'd have to provide loan-free aid to students we would otherwise have admitted but with other forms of aid... enough loan-free aid to make up for the amount those students would have had to borrow.

Financial effects of need-blind admission

- Aid required to support students who might not have been admitted under our current policies:
  - $500,000 to $800,000
- Conversion of loan-based to non-loan-based aid for students who would have been admitted under our current policies:
  - $500,000 to $1,200,000
- Total cost of need-blind, loan-free admission
  - $1,000,000 to $2,000,000

"Now, of course these amounts are really just educated guesses as to what might happen. We have pretty clear evidence on how much our current students borrow, but we don't know how the policy changes might affect our applicant pool or the pool of students who are admitted and actually decide to come to Baird. We think the policy changes might substantially increase the quality of the applicant pool so that the impact on our finances might not be too great.... But it could go the other way," Martin veered briefly off-script.

"Now, let me turn to the positive impact of admission by early decision. We know from the experience of other schools that students who apply under early decision are generally wealthier than those who apply for regular admission. So one of the benefits of early decision is that we'd get more full-tuition students and we'd be able to use some of the tuition paid by those students to provide financial aid to needier students."

"So, here again, we decided to consider a range of early decision student body percentages. Based on the evidence of other schools, the early decision percentage could be as high as 40 percent, or even a bit higher. Since it might not be that high at Baird, we decided to consider a range of 20 to 40 percent."

Financial effects of early decision admission

• Aid available to support need-blind, loan-free admission if 40% of Baird students are admitted ED:
  • $2,500,000
• Aid available to support need-blind, loan-free admission if 20% of Baird students are admitted ED:
  • $1,250,000

"As you can see from this slide, we estimate that the range of support for needy students that could be provided by offering early decision to others is one and one-quarter to two and one-half million dollars.

"My final slide combines the information from these two sets of assumptions, so that we can see the net effect of the possible changes. You can see from this what-if table that based on the ranges we have assumed for the individual effects, the combined effect of the policies under consideration is from a net cost of $750 thousand to a net benefit of $1.5 million. The worst case under the assumptions happens if the cost of need blind admission turns out to be high and the benefit of ED is low. The best case is the opposite."

"Thanks, Heather," the President smiled and was pleased to see that Martin had not deviated from the assumptions he has pressed on her. "That was very nicely done. And, of course, we can also consider admitting a slightly higher percentage of international students. Now let's take a few minutes to see if there are any questions from the group here today."

Hansen had coached his Provost to test Martin by asking a few pointed questions that challenged the analysis she had presented. "What if, because of making aid loan-free, we get more applications from students needing financial aid? What if we don't get much response to the early decision option?" Even though she seemed a bit uncomfortable doing so, Martin, in his view, did a reasonable job of defending the ranges she had presented as having been developed after careful analysis and discussion with the President, and that the ranges had already taken those concerns into account.

After a few more polite questions, the presentation concluded.

"I think this presentation should work well with the Board and help them to see clearly the effects of what they are considering." He knew the Board would go along and just needed cover for whatever they decided. He did not notice Martin's grimace.

"Now, I think the only other item we need to get into here today is Admissions. How's it going so far this year, Dave?" the President asked.

"It's a bit early to know for sure, but I believe we're right on target to achieve our enrollment goals for the year," Knight responded.

"How about with the financial aid situation?" Hansen asked.

"That's even harder to pin down, Tom," the VP for Admissions responded, "but I think we're doing okay."

"Oh, there is one other matter we should prepare for, and that's the asbestos penetration event," said Hansen. "I'm going to be able to report that we've been able to handle it with a minimum of disruption. Unfortunately, quite a few staff members have been on paid leave for over a month, and still none of the faculty can get back into their offices, except for one time each to recover a few essential items. But, all things considered, I think we've avoided a crisis, and, happily, the facilities manager who triggered the incident is no longer at Baird. I think David Gomez deserves a lot of credit for getting on the problem quickly and dealing with it so well."

CHAPTER 18

THE FIRST SNOW

The ELT meeting took place on a day when the weather at Baird had grown cold. Overnight the first snow of the season had fallen. Professor Koopman had been looking forward to the first snow because the Baird co-eds had a tradition of running topless through the campus at 1PM on the first afternoon after the first snowfall. But it didn't always work out so well. Last year, for example, the snow had started early in the morning and had continued through the day. The temperature was so cold that most of the runners had opted out and stayed indoors. The few who had taken to the challenge that was posed by the adverse weather were an unusual bunch and looked a bit strange running topless but with scarves, stocking caps, and cold weather camping pants and hiking boots.

This year, Koopman expected, would be different. The snowfall had been brief, the sun was out, and the day had warmed up nicely, to the upper thirties. Perfect weather, he hoped, for the show he was anticipating.

The whole thing was a bit awkward for him. Many students knew him, and on such a nice day he might run the risk of being noticed. How to circumspectly watch while seeming to be focused elsewhere was the challenge. Koopman ultimately decided to grab one of his *AER* issues, and drift across campus around one o'clock, watching for the parade while seeming to be absorbed in the journal. It would look normal, he thought, since he often was seen to be browsing through the journal as he crossed the campus.

But this time, it didn't work out quite as he'd hoped. As

the runners came into his field of view, one of them noticed him, and waved, shouting "Hi, Professor Koopman" as she ran. Others of the group heard her greeting him and joined in, all waving at him, calling his name, and calling his attention to them.

Fortunately, he was not alone in his voyeuristic adventure. As the girls ran on, they came upon a few other recognized members of the faculty and were only too eager to call them out, as well.

Feeling mildly self-conscious, Koopman returned to his office, vowing to be more discreet next year.

CHAPTER 19

THE BOARD OF TRUSTEES

The fall meeting of the Baird Trustees was, as usual, an all-consuming day. Many of the Trustees served on multiple subcommittees, or on the boards of some of the School's research institutes. Many also sought to spend some time with students and with faculty members from whom they had previously taken classes or from whom their children were now taking classes. But the main event of the day was the meeting of the full Board.

The meeting began with the standard reports from members of the ELT. Jack Richardson, the School's new VP for Advancement was meeting with the Board for the first time and was introduced by the President. Richardson acknowledged that new gifts were running behind what they had been last year and attributed this to turnover in the Advancement office and the need to rebuild some important relationships. When asked what the Board should expect to hear in their next meeting, he adopted the President's stance, that the setback should be temporary and that they expected to soon be catching up.

When David Knight reported on the admissions results for the year, members of the Board were, as usual, congratulatory of his continuing ability to meet enrollment targets. One member did ask about the decline in net tuition due to increased financial aid compared to prior years. In response, the VP for Admissions pointed out that the percentage decline in average net tuition per Baird student was fairly small and probably in the range of normal year-to-year variation. Martin, recalling the warning she had given in the first ELT meeting of the academic year was taken aback by the response. Knight had not even mentioned that the entire decline was due to discounting tuition for newly admitted students so that the average over all students was highly misleading. But she remained silent and continued to think about the special report she would soon have to give on the need-blind and early decision initiatives.

David Gomez was invited briefly into the meeting to discuss the asbestos incident and outline how it was being handled. He left beaming at the congratulatory compliments he had received from several of the Trustees over how his quick response had enabled the School to avoid a more serious disruption.

The Provost gave a brief report on faculty hiring and resignations, but, for the most part, Board members seemed more interested to know about how individual faculty members they knew were doing, or whether a certain member of the faculty, who had taught at Baird for many decades and was now over 80, still had not retired.

Finally, Martin presented her standard report on the financial condition of the School. In a presentation that Hansen had insisted be short, she mentioned the cost overruns associated with new dorm project, the apparent uptick in financial aid, and the over-run of operating expenses. One Trustee commented that the School would need to learn to operate more efficiently or else raise more money that could be devoted to covering operating expenses. It was clear to the CFO, however, that most Trustees were uninterested in financial matters, so she kept her comments general and brief.

Following Martin's regular report, President Hansen turned to the two main items of new business. First, he described the Jennings gift, and asked for Board approval the plan to establish two new endowed professorships in economics. Despite an expression of concern by one Trustee about the cost of staffing those positions, and a request by another that the School work harder to secure professorships in the arts instead of in economics, the Board voted unanimously in favor of the new professorships.

Finally, it was time for Martin's special report on the proposed move to need-blind admission with loan-free aid and the early-decision option. For this discussion, the Board Chair, Trevor Alexander took the lead. He explained that he and the President had been discussing this change as a way to "really move Baird forward and into the ranks of the elite private universities." Hansen then joined in with a few comments on how the change could enable the University to strengthen its commitment to the liberal and fine arts, a direction that was supported by most of the Board. He indicated that both he and the Board Chair recognized that the move would need to be on a solid financial footing. He then re-introduced Heather Martin to present the financial analysis. From their opening remarks, it was obvious to all, including the presenter, that the Chair and the President were both enthusiastic about the initiative.

Martin ran through her brief PowerPoint presentation in much the same way that she had in the ELT meeting, though without the IT distractions of that meeting. Following the presentation, there were a number of questions, including some that challenged financial feasibility. One Trustee observed rhetorically, "I wonder, if it is so easy to move into the top tier of private universities, why other schools are not making such moves?"

Heather had been looking forward to the Q and A session, hoping some of the Board members would recognize that the numbers she presented were not really supported by any analysis. She was looking for an opportunity to alert the Board to her concerns. However, Alexander and Hansen adroitly preempted her and answered the questions in ways designed to allay any such concerns. In reality, it may not have been necessary for them to do so, as, given the obvious support by the Chair and the slightly less obvious support of the President, it was unlikely that any Board member would oppose the initiative. Once the discussion was concluded, the Chair introduced a motion to adopt the initiative. The motion was approved by voice vote and, although some Trustees remained silent, no one was willing to go on record opposing the change.

Having completed their agenda, the Chair called for the Board to meet briefly in executive session. The ELT members were excused from the room, and after they had departed, the Chair requested that the Board consider early renewal of the President's contract. In the Chair's view, Hansen had been doing a good job for them and extending his term for another five years would give him the incentive and ability to see through the changes they had just agreed to.

The Board quickly voted in favor of renewing the contract, effective immediately.

The meeting adjourned and the Trustees joined their spouses, the ELT members, a few selected faculty members, and some invited guests on the Faculty Club terrace for a pre-dinner reception.

CHAPTER 20
PRESS RELEASE

Contact Information:

Baird University
Michelle Taylor
mtaylor@baird.edu

Baird University Commits to Need-blind Admission and Loan-free Financial Aid

At their fall meeting, the Board of Trustees of Baird University voted to initiate a policy of need-blind admission of students, coupled with loan-free financial aid. The policy of need-blind admission will apply to all current domestic applicants to the School and to all subsequent domestic applications. The policy of loan-free financial aid will apply to all current domestic students and to all current and future domestic applicants for admission beginning with the forthcoming academic year.

At the same time, the Board voted to approve an option for applicants to apply for early-decision admission. Consistent with the policies at other schools, an applicant for early decision must commit not to apply for early decision at any other university and must commit that, if admitted to Baird University by early decision, the applicant will withdraw applications for admission to all other universities.

Speaking on behalf of the University, its President, Thomas Hansen, said, "We at Baird are very eager to implement these new policies that the Trustees have asked us to pursue. Adoption of the policies will move Baird to the ranks of the most elite private universities. We are pleased that the new policies will enable us to redouble our commitment to liberal and fine arts education and will enable us to strengthen our commitment to make an excellent private school education accessible to all, without regard to ability to pay."

Baird University is one of the county's leading private schools of higher education. The School was established more than a century ago and is a highly recognized research university that now offers undergraduate and graduate degrees, including Ph.D. degrees in over 30 fields of academic endeavor.

CHAPTER 21

HARVARD SQUARE

As the end of the fall semester neared, Krista Novikova and Heather Martin met again for lunch. Over salads, and after the pro forma exchange of small talk about families and updates about things that had happened since their meeting earlier in the fall, Heather began. "Well, it seems to me that something is troubling you, Krista.... Is it something you want to talk about...? Maybe about Hansen?" she prompted. "It seems more and more clear to me that you and I were right in our opposition to his appointment to be Baird's President."

"Of course completely I agree with you about that, Heather," Krista began calmly. "Even at the time, I think we both recognized that, in the search committee we served on, our opposition to the appointment was going to go nowhere. The committee was stacked from the outset to enable the Committee Chair, who, you'll recall, until a couple years ago was our illustrious Board Chair, to essentially hand pick the next President. Over the course of our search efforts, the he obviously became a big fan of Hansen and started to talk down the other applicants for the position. It seems to me, now, that the new Board Chair, Alexander, is a lot like the former one... except even less of a numbers person.... And he's a Hansen fan, too... possibly an even more committed one."

"That doesn't seem too surprising to me," Heather responded. "During the search, Hansen was always telling the former Board Chair everything he wanted to hear, and he's now doing the same with Alexander.... He's assured Alexander that he's able to bring in some major gifts, and he claims that he's working to generate additional resources by supporting faculty efforts to secure important research grants. He talks enthusiastically, but not truthfully, in favor of growing and strengthening the liberal and fine arts.... So, he's hitting on all of Alexander's hot buttons and is articulating a vision that I'm sure Alexander hopes might take the pressure off of the Board to double down on their financial support for the School... all the same things he said back then to sell himself to the search committee."

"I know...! You and I seemed to be the only Search Committee members who saw through that," Krista picked up the theme. "The former Board Chair was looking for a *deus ex machina* that would take the financial pressure off of the Board without moving away from the School's historical focus on the liberal arts. I think he was willing to buy into almost any promise to do that.... It's the same with Alexander.... And what's upsetting to me now is that I think it's starting to become a real problem for our academic programs."

"Oh?" Heather responded. "Is something different going on now? Is that what's on your mind?"

"Long story, so they say.... Let me try to be brief...." Novikova glanced up at Heather as she stabbed with a bit too much force at the cherry tomatoes in her harvest salad. "You remember, at our last lunch how we were talking about the way student interest has been shifting toward more quantitative and professional disciplines and away from so much focus on liberal arts. I'm concerned that Baird's lagging behind in adjusting to that changing dynamic. It's particularly telling in my department."

"How so, Krista? I thought we were increasing our focus on more quantitative disciplines."

"So..." Krista paused to organize her thoughts and reign in her exasperation, "a decade or so ago we seemed to be on the right track. That was when finance and accounting courses were added to Baird's economics curriculum. It was based on the potential for growth in those areas that I decided to join the Baird faculty. But, for the last few years, we've only had two tenure-track faculty members in finance and two in accounting. There's really no one here I can work with on research and it's hard to even put together a coherent program of course offerings.... Our Department Chair, Bob Hill, recognized the need for more hiring in these areas. For a while, he's been working on one of our alums to provide a major gift... enough to support some additional hiring. I know Bob's been on our side and had been working hard to tailor the gift to address these needs."

"Now, to be sure, not everyone in my department is on board with the hiring focus. So, unsurprisingly there was some pushback by certain faculty members who want to use the gift to promote their own interests.... But that's just the usual stuff and Bob was prepared to deal with it. He got the donor to agree to fund two endowed professorships, and I know he was going to the President to seek support for hiring in accounting and finance."

"But then, something happened.... I'm not sure what, exactly..." Krista stabbed even more aggressively at the stubborn tomatoes, "but I suspect that Hansen may have been scared off by the cost of hiring in finance and accounting.... Of course, we'll never know for sure, but I'd be willing to bet that to save money he managed to talk the donor into redirecting his gift in some different ways that won't be helpful at all for meeting the needs of our students.... So, now, instead of hiring where we have the greatest needs, we're being told that we have to use the gift for chairs in environmental economics and the economics of the oil and gas industry. We're being asked to do that even though we already have people on our faculty who are perfectly capable of teaching courses in those areas."

"I'm sorry to hear that, Krista, and I can see why it's bothering you," Heather empathized. "I've known for a while that for the students it's important to strengthen our finance and accounting offerings... but I guess I'm not too surprised that Hansen would interfere. So... like you said... possibly, he's doing it because of the budgetary pressures he's feeling. Finance and accounting faculty are pretty expensive compared to some other areas of economics, even though they more than pay back in the long run through future donations and good student placements.... I think I also see other signs that Hansen's wanting to cut corners.... There are some things he and the Provost have been doing lately that have me wondering what he's up to."

"Yes, but in spite of all that, doesn't it seem that the President of the University would see the need for more staffing, especially in finance, and would be supportive. So, it's really frustrating and it's causing me to have serious doubt about where Baird's headed," Novikova concluded. "I was so optimistic when I decided to come to Baird, thinking that I could really make a difference. But now I think I made a huge mistake coming."

"I suppose maybe your department could sort of try to fly below the radar, Kristin," Martin sought to lift Novikova's spirits. "I know that in some other departments, when an endowed professorship designation didn't fit the needs of the School very well, they've tried to fill the position by finding someone who maybe could offer one course in the designated area but could spend most of their efforts on things of more value to the department and the students. Like, in Religious Studies, someone wanted to fund an endowed professorship in Jainism...."

"Which is exactly what?" asked Novikova.

"Good question, Krista. I don't really know... but apparently, it's some kind of offshoot of Buddhism that originated in India.... In any case, it only has about five million followers, and the Department wasn't eager to commit a full line to Jainism. They approved the endowed chair, but the department faculty were trying to fill it by finding someone willing to offer one course in Jainism and who maybe had done a relevant paper or two in the past. Maybe someone more generally focused on Indian religions.... You probably know that the Convocation speaker from earlier this year was whom they hired."

"I see what you mean, of course, Heather. We're starting to think about something like that in economics, but I'm not sure how successful we can be at it... especially if the main issue is going to be the cost of the faculty lines.... Also, I think the donor's likely to be pretty engaged in making sure he gets what he wants... or what Hansen has persuaded him to want.... But maybe it's worth a try."

"I get it," Heather responded. "I guess I should mention that it didn't work out too well for Religious Studies either.... You probably could tell when you heard their new professor giving the keynote at the convocation at the start of this academic year.... But maybe it's worth trying."

"But enough about me, as they say, Heather. How are things going for you?

Heather grimaced and tried to cover with a brief laugh. "Hmm..., maybe I need another glass of wine, Krista, and maybe I'm just being hyper-sensitive.... I agree with you that what you're going through, seems serious.... But I can't help but feel that my situation is quite a bit worse."

"Oh...? I've been too focused on myself, Heather, and I blathered on way too long about myself.... Tell me what's going on," Krista encouraged.

"Well... it's about the recently announced changes to our admissions policies."

"I saw the announcement, and was really surprised by it," Krista remarked. "Can the School actually afford to be need-blind and loan-free?"

"Not if you ask me," Heather responded, shaking her head. "But, of course, no one's asking me... and now I even feel that I've been made complicit in getting the Board to approve the policy change."

"In what way would you be complicit?" Krista asked.

"Well, a couple weeks before the meeting I met with Hansen. He told me that Alexander really wanted the change, and he asked me to put some numbers together to show to the Board at the meeting earlier this month. Hansen urged me into some assumptions that I think are ridiculously optimistic, and then asked me also to put everything into a PowerPoint presentation."

"Since I didn't feel I had a choice, I went ahead and did that, but I was sort of hoping there would be enough questions from the Board that I'd have an opportunity to lay out my concerns."

"Unfortunately, it didn't work out that way. I went through the formal presentation of the optimistic numbers, but when it was time for questions, Alexander had already sent a clear message that he wanted the Board to support the policy change. He and the President fielded all of the potentially useful questions and always went back to the phony numbers they'd asked me to prepare. So I never got a chance to tell the Board how concerned I am about the initiative."

"Of course, Hansen knows I'm not a supporter. So he really boxed me in on this."

"That does sound serious, Heather. Way more so than my little problem. It sounds like you think the change could be really bad for the whole University."

"I do!" Heather exclaimed. "But don't get me wrong.... Maybe it's not catastrophic.... I just don't think it's going to be sustainable. Not, that is, unless something really major and very positive happens on the financial front to offset it."

"What I can't really understand," Krista resumed, "is why Hansen is promoting such an extreme change, especially when the outcome could be quite bad for Baird."

"I've been asking myself that same question, Krista. And the only thing I can come up with is that maybe he's more focused on himself than on what's good for the School. He may think that getting the School to adopt those changes will bring enough notoriety to Baird that it could put him in play for a more prestigious position... president of a more highly ranked school or something."

"That sort of sounds right to me, Heather.... Well, in any case, I hope it turns out okay. If not, I'm not sure what I'll do. It's already a challenge to keep up with my research and at the same time try to manage the finance offerings so that all the courses are offered when needed and are competently staffed."

The two had been so focused on their conversation that neither one noticed that they'd made little progress on their salads. They tried to move on to more pleasant topics, but quickly concluded that they couldn't. They wrapped up their lunch quickly and headed out to return to campus.

CHAPTER 22

THE SEARCH

Later that week, Professors Novikova and Kaur met afterhours with their Department Chair for a drink at the Cambridge Inn.

"Thanks for agreeing to see us after work today, Bob" Novikova began. "Nadir and I had trouble finding a time during the day when we both could meet, and we think getting the faculty search started in earnest is fairly pressing. So we have a suggestion of what we think may be a reasonable way to proceed, even if it ruffles a few feathers of some fairly vocal members of our Department faculty."

"It's really fine, Krista," Hill responded. "I'm happy to have the break from work.... So, what did you have in mind for us to discuss? I can tell you that I'm feeling the same urgency as you seem to be and I'm open to any ideas that can get us moving again."

"Well, it seems pretty obvious from the last Department meeting that no one's very happy about having the hiring focus for the two endowed chairs being dictated to us by the Administration. At the same time, we don't want it to seem to them that we're not team players. So Nadir and I've been talking about a possible way to get around the problem and still do what's best for the Department."

"That's right," Kaur joined in. "We've been thinking that we might be able to, sort of, do a work-around. I think we might be able to find a good scholar in the accounting area who could teach a course on the oil and gas industry. The industry has a number of unusual accounting challenges, like accounting for crude oil reserves, as well as some special tax treatments, like the ways firms can claim depreciation expenses on their reserves. So the industry could be an interesting case study. Maybe we could find someone with enough interest in the subject to offer a course, and enough exposure to the industry to be able to discuss it credibly. If we can do that, we can devote the rest of the person's teaching responsibilities to our mainstream accounting courses.... So, that might be okay."

The idea for this proposal had originated with Novikova after her lunch with Heather Martin. She'd thought about it a bit and concluded that it might work. She also felt some urgency because it might not be long before others in the Department came up with similar ideas but would look for candidates who would focus on their own areas of interest. She had spoken with Kaur and explained the idea. He was easily convinced, and so they had scheduled the meeting with Hill.

"Now, in the finance area," Novikova picked up on the pitch, "I think we might be able to find someone able to fill the environmental economics chair... maybe working on the investments side on something to do with avoiding investments in fossil fuels companies, or on the corporate finance side, like valuing corporate clean-tech projects. A few venture capital funds have sprung up recently to search for high-risk investments in clean technology and other ESG-type projects. So maybe we could use a finance line to find someone who could deliver a course in that area, and who has some relevant research. And, like Nadir said, the person we hire could devote the balance of their time to more general teaching and research in finance."

"So, I guess where we are..." Novikova continued, "is that Nadir and I would be willing to co-chair a search committee that would seek candidates in accounting and finance whom we could present to the Administration as sufficiently qualified to address the concerns of the donor."

"It's an interesting idea," the Department Chair responded. "I'm not sure it'll be enough to win the day, but it does seem to be worth trying. I know it won't sit well with some members of the faculty, but I've yet to hear from anyone else who has a better suggestion. So I'm not too sympathetic toward them. Since we're almost at the end of the term, and we need to get moving on the searches or end up not hiring anyone, I'll deal with the pushback and authorize the formation of a search committee with the two of you serving as co-chairs. I'll leave it to you to draft a few other committee members and to get the word out that we're hiring, possibly in those areas but still with an open search. I assume you'll want to include the other members of the finance and accounting groups on the committee, and I'd encourage you to also find a couple of members from micro and macroeconomics to make sure everyone feels represented. That would sure help me out."

"I'll send out a note to Department faculty tomorrow to let them know that the search for new endowed chair holders is going forward and to give them a heads-up that you may be asking a few of them to join the committee."

"Now, unless there's something else, I need to run. Today's my son's sixth birthday, and I have to get home for the celebration."

"No, Bob, that's everything," Novikova said. "Nadir and I will cover the tab. You go ahead and take off... and be sure to wish your son a happy birthday from us."

Their main task out of the way, Kaur and Novikova stayed behind at the Inn to discuss the composition of the search committee they had agreed to co-chair. Kaur replaced his coffee with a draft IPA and Novikova ordered a pinot noir. After that brief discussion, with only a handful of desirable candidates for the committee, they set work aside in favor of small talk.

PART 2

***

SPRING TERM

***

CHAPTER 23

THE SEARCH

Over the winter break, Novikova and Kaur had filled out the membership of their search committee. In addition to Sean Lopez from finance and Lin Chang from accounting, they'd added Kyle Phillips, as well as Nicole Stewart and Rearden Koopman from the economics areas.

Hill had announced formation of the search committee via email to the Department faculty at the very end of the fall term and, as expected, had received immediate hostile responses from Professors Faquhir and Sarks, both messages broadcast to the full Department faculty. Faquhir complained that others had not had an opportunity to organize an alternative committee. Hill responded, without copying the faculty, that through their own initiative the co-chairs had proposed the committee and that, given the urgency of beginning the search, he had supported their proposal. He assured Faquhir that he'd support macro as the focus of the next search. Sarks argued that the process by which the search committee chairs were selected was illegal, a violation of shared governance, and that the Department Chair was exceeding his authority. Hill elected not to respond.

Once the committee composition was announced by the co-chairs, in a message seeking assistance from others in the Department to help identify prospective candidates, Faquhir complained that the committee composition seemed skewed toward finance and accounting. Hill responded that if Faquhir wanted to propose candidates from micro or macroeconomics to the search committee, he was free to do so, and that the essential consideration for each professorship was that a candidate needed to present as being at least minimally interested in the criterion specified by the donor.

All of that occurred over the winter break, during which time, the search committee had been busily placing advertisements of the positions in the important channels, including advertising on the Social Science Research Network (SSRN), placing an announcement in Job Openings for Economists (JOE), and contacting prospective candidates. In deference to University Policy, the committee also advertised the position in the Chronicle of Higher Education and in a couple of outlets that specifically targeted diversity candidates. Both of these were quite expensive and, since everyone with a relevant Ph.D. would know to look on SSRN or in JOE, the Committee had no expectation that these other ads would yield any qualified applicants who would not have learned of the positions through the more standard channels.

In the first Department meeting of the spring term, the search committee co-chairs reported to the faculty on the efforts they had made and the status of responses to their efforts.

At the first opportunity to do so in that meeting, Prof. Sarks reasserted his claim that the search committee had no authority to recruit on behalf of the Department. Rather than to argue the point, the Department Chair agreed to an advisory vote of the Department to endorse the committee. Sarks complained that because those appointed were to be endowed professors, untenured faculty members should not be allowed to vote on the composition of the search committee, and that because they could not actually vote on hiring with tenure, they should not even be allowed to serve on the committee. Hill responded that committee composition was within the realm of Departmental decisions on which all tenure track faculty members are eligible to vote. He acknowledged that assistant professors could not vote on whether to tenure a new hire but pointed out that such a limitation did not preclude their service on a search committee or their participation in selecting the short list of candidates the Department would consider for the appointments.

In the vote that followed, most faculty members seemed to recognize the urgency of moving forward. The committee composition was overwhelmingly endorsed by the faculty, with only two no votes.

CHAPTER 24

A HATE CRIME ON CAMPUS

The first few weeks of the spring term were cold and snowy at Baird, enough so that most students stuck to their class schedules and otherwise stayed in their dorms. Just as it appeared that the term would proceed without incident, the campus was jarred by what was quickly labeled a hate crime. President Hansen learned of the incident from Campus Security. The head of Security reported to him that after attending a campus forum on racial intolerance where she had spoken, a visiting professor of criminal justice, had returned to her car to find that it had been spray painted with racial slurs, several swastikas, and the phrase "white power." Both headlights and the windshield had been smashed and her tires had been slashed. The officer reported that the faculty member appeared to have been deeply shaken by the incident and that she had filed a police report.

As word of the incident spread, several faculty members deemed it to be so distressing for their students that they decided to cancel classes for the day. A small group of students of color and other sympathizers organized a non-violent protest against racism on campus.

When he learned of the incident, Hansen called in the Dean of Students, Bronwyn Warren, and the Provost. The Dean of Students had already requested that the FBI investigate a possible civil rights violation.

"Thanks for clearing your schedules so quickly so we could meet and figure out how to get ahead of this mess," he gestured toward his conference table. "As soon as I heard, I ordered cancellation of all classes for the rest of the day.

But things are already very tense on campus and I'm already getting messages from parents and even a couple trustees who have kids in school here, for God's sake."

"I agree," Warren responded. "There are already some small non-violent demonstrations going on. It won't be long before some non-student organizers get here and start to stir things up even more. But I'm not sure we should have cancelled classes so quickly since taking them out of classes makes it easier for students to engage."

"I've already condemned the incident and identified it as a hate crime," Hansen continued. "I have to say that I'm very disappointed in our students. I thought they were better than this, but I guess maybe we can hope that it's just a few troglodyte troublemakers who think they're still fighting the Civil War. Once this is over, we'll need to take a hard look at our admissions criteria and see if we can come up with a better way to keep these morons from being admitted here."

"Let's keep in mind that we don't actually know who's responsible yet," the Provost cautioned, "or how widespread the problem is."

"I suppose not," Hansen responded. He was concerned that news of the incident would overshadow the attention Baird was getting about its shift to need-blind admission. "But we need to do something.... Even if what we do has little or no effect.... We can't be seen to appear as if we're ignoring the problem or trying to down-play it. I'm going to call on you and others in the Administration to organize a "Day of Reflection and Introspection". We'll cancel all of the classes again that day and we'll sponsor a broad menu of cultural and ethnicity-sensitive programs and speeches. In the meantime, I'll prepare a statement to the campus community and circulate it later today."

***

To the Baird University community,

I write with dismay and a heavy heart to the Baird community concerning the recent hate crime that was committed on our campus. I have always taken pride in the respect Baird students have shown for each other and for our faculty and administrative staff. I am sincerely disappointed that our culture of mutual respect and appreciation of our differences seems to have broken down.

I cannot help but feel that we, at Baird, have somehow fallen short in our efforts to instill sound moral and ethical values in our students. While we have done much to address racial and ethnic prejudice on our campus, we, like too many other universities, still have more to do. Let me say, without equivocation, that there is no place at Baird for the hateful behavior that transpired earlier today on our beautiful campus.

I recognize that some on campus may feel that I have been too cautious in my public comments about hate speech and discrimination at Baird and I apologize for that. While we have done much to address these concerns on our campus, we still have more to do.

I am joining with the Associated Students of Baird University leadership team to push harder for reform on campus. We are taking immediate action to address the matter. Most immediately, we are organizing a "Day of Reflection and Introspection" that will take place later this month. On that day, all Baird classes will be cancelled so that our students can participate in a number of forums and experiential events on campus. I have also asked Campus Security for a full investigation of today's incident. Consistent with our policy of zero tolerance toward hate crimes, we are committed to finding and disciplining the perpetrators.

Every person who steps foot on the Baird campus is entitled to expect an environment free from hate speech and racial or ethnic discrimination. I will be working with student leaders *throughout the spring to deal with this important issue and to provide other universities around the country a model of best practices.*

Sincerely,

Thomas Hansen, President

***

College leaders condemned the hate crime and called in the Federal Bureau of Investigation to investigate a possible civil rights violation. A $10,000 reward was offered for identification of the perpetrators.

That evening, the Baird hate attack was all over the news. Professor Novikova, who was attending a conference in Mexico City, watched hourly reports of the incident on CNN International as she prepared her talk for the next day. The report featured a clip of President Hansen, who mentioned some of the actions the University would be taking to prevent hate crimes and hate speech on campus.

Novikova's immediate reaction was that it seemed likely that the visiting professor had probably vandalized her own car for attention and to advance a cause she believed in and about which she felt any action was justified. In an email message to Heather Martin, Krista wrote, "I am afraid that Hansen may be out in front of his skis on this. My guess is that the actual perpetrators are not Baird students at all. What do you think?"

Many Baird students were offended by the President's letter and by other actions of the Administration. An independent newspaper, the *Baird Free Press*, edited by Baird students, criticized the President's obvious presumption that the perpetrators were Baird students, and the Administration's pandering response to those who sought to characterize Baird students as racist.

A week after the incident, a member of the campus

maintenance staff reported to David Gomez that he had seen the professor spray painting and damaging her own car. Gomez immediately passed along the information to campus security. A few days later, the visiting professor was arrested and charged with filing a false police report alleging a hate crime.

When a reporter at the *Baird Free Press* learned of the arrest, she dug into the professor's background and learned that several years prior, after being arrested for shoplifting, she had filed a report claiming that she had been roughed up by police. As it turned out, her claim was contradicted by a witness who saw the professor bruising her own neck and shoulder and tearing her clothes. The reporter also discovered that the professor had previously been convicted of theft and of impersonating a nurse while calling in a prescription for Xanax. Provocatively, the reporter asked, "What does it take for someone to land a faculty position at Baird? Apparently, not much."

Board Chair, Alexander, when he learned of these details, called Hansen at home, and demanded to know how a person like the visiting professor could have been hired to teach at Baird.

"Well, for regularly hired faculty members," Hansen demurred, "we normally have quite a bit of information, including letters of reference, previous work experience, and the like. But, as you know, Trevor, we also use some lecturers and visiting faculty members. And since those are temporary positions, the decisions are mainly just made at the department level. The departments probably differ in how they do that. Some may hire people they know well. Others may feel more pressing needs to staff classes and may have trouble finding people willing to teach...."

"So, in other words," Alexander interrupted, "you don't do jack."

"It's not like that," Hansen defended. "We normally get quite a bit of information about teaching ability, and if an instructor doesn't do well in the classroom, we don't bring them back."

"I don't see how that would help you spot problem people like this visiting professor," Alexander rejoined. "We can't afford to have embarrassing things like this one happening at Baird. It's going to cost us applications... and donor support. I'm going to ask the Board at our next meeting to direct the Administration to implement mandatory background checks for all faculty and staff."

"I see," Hansen responded. "That's probably going to be pretty expensive. It'll probably also make it harder to staff some classes on time and may discourage some good applicants who, for whatever reason, don't want to be subject to a background check."

"You'll just have to deal with it," Alexander concluded. "I'd suggest that you devote some time before the next Board meeting to developing a background check policy that the Board can accept. If it makes it harder to staff classes, you're just going to have to ask your current faculty to step up and help solve the short-run problems. That shouldn't be too hard for you... since most of them only work a couple days per week and sometimes have whole semesters off, not to mention summers."

"Now, I've got to get back to my family," Alexander said. "But I needed to deal with this quickly. If you're asked by anyone... parents, journalists, whatever... I think you can say that the University is putting a comprehensive background check policy in place."

Hansen thought about trying to explain that the faculty at schools like Baird did much more than just teach their students, but decided against doing so, since such explanations never seemed to carry much weight with people who didn't have university-level experience. Moreover, it wasn't really the focus of the conversation they'd been having, and besides, Alexander had hung up before Hansen had an opportunity to say anything.

CHAPTER 25
THE SEARCH

As the campus was dealing with the alleged hate crime incident, the Economics Department was moving ahead quickly with its search for new faculty. The search committee had identified four candidates for faculty visits and all four had been to campus. One each was from finance and accounting and two were from narrow fields in economics related to the donor's criteria. Other members of the faculty seemed to have expended little effort and had failed to identify any prospects from micro or macroeconomics whom they wanted the search committee to consider. A faculty meeting had been called so that the search committee could recap the short list to the faculty after their visits and the faculty could vote on whether to recommend any of them for faculty appointment.

Professor Kaur spoke on behalf of the committee. "You've all seen the application files for our shortlist candidates, most of you have attended their seminar presentations, and you've all had the opportunity to meet with each candidate one-on-one or over a meal. Let's go through them each in order. Gordon is a professor of accounting, she's currently at Ohio State, which has a top accounting group. She's got almost a dozen papers in top accounting journals and has one of the highest citation counts in accounting. Our committee thinks she can qualify for an endowed professorship because she's indicated she's willing to offer a graduate course on oil and gas industry accounting and she has a paper on the use of special purpose vehicles to promote clean technology."

"That's true, Nadir, as far as it goes… but her seminar was a disaster," Professor Faquhir interjected. "The methodology she used in her empirical work would never fly in a respectable economics journal."

"Maybe not," Kaur responded. "But the methodology is commonly used in accounting research. So maybe it's just a difference in approach between the areas. And, for a senior position, I don't think it would be a good idea to base our recommendation on the methodology she used in a single paper. We need to look at the full file. Based on that, she's clearly a very solid researcher."

"Maybe it's not important to resolve this," said Professor Koopman. "I don't think she'll come, anyway."

"And why not, Reardon?" Kaur asked.

"Well, I asked her what her husband thought about the prospect of moving here…." Koopman responded.

"You can't do that," Novikova jumped in.

"Why not?" Koopman asked. "It's something we need to know and need to consider."

"That may well be, Reardon," Novikova responded, "but we're not permitted to consider a person's marital status and we're not even supposed to ask about it."

"Whatever…" Koopman responded. "All these new rules don't make any sense to me. I think we should just be looking for the best candidate and we need to consider whether they're likely to accept our offer or we're just wasting everybody's time."

"Let's move on," said Kaur. "Fabre is our second candidate. He's currently at the University of Michigan. He's got a great research record and edits one of the top finance journals. I think the paper he presented here was very solid. The committee thinks he can qualify for one of the endowed chair positions because he's taught a class on the financial aspects of socially responsible investing, and he has a paper on how capital structure affects the survival probability of oil and gas firms."

"But I think his best research was from quite a while ago," commented Nikolaidis. "I think he's in decline... a bit too old."

"You can't consider age, Mark, any more than you can consider marital status," Novikova interjected. "Besides, the paper he presented is new and seems to be very timely. I expect that it'll place well."

"Maybe," responded Nikolaidis, "but I think he may be relying on his junior co-authors on that paper."

"I want to keep us moving on," Kaur cut in. "I'm afraid our other two candidates are less impressive. Granville is on the Oklahoma University faculty. He has quite a long list of published papers on the oil and gas industry, but most are in journals that are well below top-tier. Recently, he has several white papers on fracking that seem to have been prepared under consulting arrangements with firms in the petroleum industry. In fact, he appears to be spending a large fraction of his time on consulting, and not so much on real academic work. The committee is concerned that he may be overly committed to consulting and not seriously focused on academic research. His teaching at OU seems to be entirely in courses related to oil and gas and petroleum. The committee doesn't see much potential that he could do a good job in core economics, finance, or accounting classes. That said, his focus is clearly in line with the donor's intent. So, while the committee is bringing him forward to the faculty for vote, it's not endorsing the candidate."

"Nor should it be," Prof. Sarks interjected. "We all... or most of us... saw his paper presentation. The paper is seriously flawed, and not much better than an undergraduate thesis."

"We'll have to see how the Department vote goes on

this, but let me turn now to the last candidate, Barron," Kaur resumed. "He's on the faculty of Cal State LA. Early in his career, he's had a few papers in top journals. More recently, the publications have been lower tier, and most recently, he seems to be focusing on things like op-ed pieces and similar writings for public consumption. In these, Barron takes advocacy positions on topics related to climate change. He seems to get quite a bit of attention because his views emphasize the risks and threats of not taking actions to mitigate climate change. His seminar, as you all probably recall seemed more like a rallying cry. He, like Granville, is narrowly focused in his teaching, and currently only teaches courses related to climate change, though in the past, he has taught some more general microeconomics courses. Again, it seems he'd fit the donor's intent, but the committee is concerned that if he were to join the Baird faculty, he'd seek to act more like a public scholar advocating on the threat of climate change, would not be actively engaged in serious research, and might not be willing to share the kinds of administrative responsibilities that senior faculty members here are expected to undertake."

"Much as I would like to support a candidate who could teach some of our econ courses, I'm afraid I can't do so in this case," Prof. Faquhir admitted. "I think we all need to recognize that neither of these last two candidates fits the parameters of the open-field search we had voted to pursue. Moreover, we've all seen these types at other schools, with their out-of-control egos. I remember one guy who got a Ph.D. from a top school and did some good early research. Then he got into something he calls neuroeconomics and started claiming that some kind of molecule... oxy something or other... caused people to trust others more. He started coming to campus wearing a white lab coat, like some kind of MD, going on talk shows and giving TED talks. After some initial positive reaction, he started getting a lot of negative press. Some others who have replicated this guy's experiments have been unable to support his findings.

He's become an embarrassment to the school where he now works. I'd be afraid of the same thing happening here."

"I think the committee shares some of your concerns, Larry," Prof. Kaur picked up. "So that's a quick summary of where we are. How about we move ahead to voting?"

In the vote that followed, the tenured members of the faculty supported recommending appointments of Gordon and Fabre, with solid majorities. They split on Granville and Barron with modest majorities opposing their appointments. Those voting in favor appeared to do so based on either their opposition to hiring finance and accounting candidates or their belief that those candidates would not accept offers from Baird. It seemed that, even if the candidates were weak, no one wanted the search to fail, and they were afraid of losing the opportunity to hire if they were not successful in this effort.

Subsequently, the search committee prepared a draft recommendation of appointment for the two candidates who had received majority support. The Department Chair forwarded the recommendation to the Provost without change.

Krista felt good about how the meeting had gone. In spite of all the early pushback from Faquhir and Sarks, and the confusing set of votes that had been taken in the earlier meeting, it now appeared that if the hiring was successful and the tenure cases of junior faculty were supported by the Administration, the Department was prepared to do the right thing for its students, and that the finance and accounting areas would gain the critical mass needed to offer a comprehensive set of courses.

***

Shortly after receiving the Economics Department's recommendation, Provost May met with President Hansen to determine how to respond.

"I think you've seen that the Economics Department is recommending professors of finance and accounting to fill the two endowed professorships. I know we were hoping to keep the cost of these appointments down, but these recommendations seem like good candidates. They're likely to be quite expensive, maybe more than we should take on in our current tight budget situation," May began.

"I completely agree," Hansen responded. "This is not what we'd hoped, and not what I was trying to achieve in my meeting with Jennings, when I steered him away from finance and accounting."

"Well, in their recommendation report, the Department faculty is making the case that the two people they're recommending have enough of a record in oil and gas and environment that they can satisfy Jennings's intent," May continued.

"My guess," said Hansen, "is that if either of them were to meet with the donor, he might respond positively to the idea that he can get both the specified focuses of the professorships and his original intent to provide professorships in finance and accounting."

"We need to stop this from moving forward," the President continued. "I think we can do that by notifying the Department that the candidates they're proposing are not sufficiently well focused on oil and gas and environment, so we can't support their appointment.... We need to ask the Department to redouble its efforts to find appropriately qualified candidates who are more solidly in line with the donor's stated intent."

"Can you get back to the Department, Jim, and let them know that they need to keep looking?"

***

When word got back to the Department, the faculty

reconvened, and after discussion, concluded that they were unlikely to find any better candidates than those they had already identified. The faculty then decided that it was better to fill the positions with weak candidates than to leave them vacant and risk losing the opportunity to hire. Accordingly, they voted again on the candidacies of Granville and Barron, and this time, instead of being negative, the results came out slightly positively for both. Novikova, of course, was deeply dismayed by the outcome and the Administration's heavy hand, but was not entirely surprised. It seemed that the Administration just had too many ways of assuring that the outcomes went the way they hoped and not necessarily in ways that were best for the School.

CHAPTER 26

NOT AT MY SCHOOL

In keeping with President Hansen's commitment to promote a climate of openness, the Administration, and the Associated Students of Baird University, had arranged for a surfeit of guest speakers to come to campus. The Associated Students, in developing their speakers program, had solicited recommendations from various student organizations on campus. In response, a group of conservative students had recommended that Ben Shapiro be invited to speak.

When they received the recommendation to invite Shapiro, the ASBU officers debated the appropriateness of inviting a speaker whose remarks might seem threatening to some students.

Shapiro had referred to himself as a radical conservative. He had previously argued that conservative values like small government and self-reliance are superior to liberal ones. He was particularly well known for his criticism of universities for what he described as indoctrination of students and the intolerance of faculty toward conservative speech.

The ASBU group was divided on whether to invite Shapiro. Some members argued that his appearance on campus would be too threatening to the more liberal students, and would, in itself, be a form of hate speech. A few others countered that the program had already featured several speakers who were likely to be threatening to conservative students. Ultimately, the group decided to proceed with an invitation.

When Hansen learned from his Dean of Students that Shapiro had been invited, he expressed deep concern. "Why, when we are struggling to put the incident from earlier this term behind us, does the ASBU decide to fan the flames by inviting such a controversial speaker?" he asked the Dean.

"Well, you know... the idealism of youth..." Warren responded. "The ASBU leaders are striving to be fair and balanced. They've recognized that our speakers, so far, have all been of pretty much the same view, and they felt compelled to bring in someone with a different perspective."

"Yes, yes, of course..." Hansen responded, "but don't they also recognize how potentially explosive it could be, especially in light of what happened earlier this term?"

"I'm sure the group understands that having Shapiro will be controversial," Warren responded, "but they still feel that some gesture toward balance is important."

"I know,' said Hansen, "but it's going to be a problem. Most times, conservative students are fairly civil in their protests of liberal speakers, but, as we've seen at other schools, when a conservative speaker comes to campus, outside agitators follow and stir everyone up... so things can become volatile. We're going to have to beef up campus security during the visit and work hard to keep things under control."

In an effort to downplay the event, Shapiro was invited to appear on campus during the week before Spring Break.

A few days prior, a Facebook post from a group describing itself as "the students of color at Baird" proclaimed, "we will not allow fascism to have a platform on the Baird campus. We stand against all forms of oppression and refuse to permit Ben Shapiro to speak." The Facebook post called upon all Baird students to protest the event because of what they alleged to be, "Shapiro's opposition to the Black Lives Matter movement and his support of racist police officers and fascist law and order." The post, which was directed to Baird students, as well as students at nearby campuses, called upon Baird students and others to, "show up wearing black and bring your comrades because we're shutting this down."

When President Hansen learned of the planned attempt to disrupt the Shapiro talk, he ordered additional security forces and that temporary barricades be put in place to protect the speaker and those who wanted to attend the talk. "We need to make sure this event goes smoothly and that the safety of all of our students is protected," he told Warren and the head of campus security.

Hansen did not attend the talk, but his Dean of Students tried to. She reported that although his instructions were followed, protesters seemed to be undeterred. Several hundred students, organizers, and other demonstrators arrived early at the venue, dressed mainly in black, and in some cases, with faces concealed by masks or partially covered by hoods. The protesters surrounded all entrances to the venue several rows deep. With linked arms, they denied entrance to anyone. Using bull horns, they sought to drown out any expression of views contrary to their own. Campus security forces had been directed not to act by force except for the purpose of protecting students from physical harm.

A number of Baird faculty members also sought to attend the talk, including Professors Noach and Phillips from Economics. They were turned away by the protesters, who refused to allow them entrance. Ultimately, to the dismay of its organizers from ASBU and the cheers of protesters, the event was closed down.

***

Days later, the *Baird Free Press* reported on the incident.

Last Thursday evening, 400 to 500 protesters and demonstrators stormed the Baird campus, chanting "Black Lives Matter" and other, more choice phrases, at the entrance to the auditorium where conservative speaker and author

Ben Shapiro was slated to speak. The speech had been arranged by Baird students as part of their effort to promote open dialogue on campus. Ultimately, through the protesters' efforts to prevent others from entering the auditorium and to otherwise disrupt, Shapiro's speech was cancelled.

Economics professor James Noach was one of several faculty members who grappled with the crowd of protesters in an unsuccessful attempt to gain entrance. One student who sought to support the presenter, brought a large speaker to the patio, blasting "The Stars and Stripes Forever". An unidentified woman wearing a mask ran up and, after a brief scuffle, managed to steal his audio cable, cutting off the music and garnering cheers from the protesters. Campus security took no action in response.

The BFP co-editor-in-chief, who was present at the demonstration, attempted to livestream the protest but was swarmed by protesters who blocked his phone.

Several administrators attended the protest and stood to the side. They later told the BFP that they viewed their role as ensuring student safety.

Noting that campus security guards were present but were not intervening, the BFP asked University President, Thomas Hansen, why no action was taken by campus security. "The head of campus security, the Dean of Students, and I had concluded that forced interventions or arrests had the potential to create unsafe conditions for Baird students, faculty, staff, and guests. Of course, I take full responsibility for the decision to err on the side of these overriding safety considerations," Hansen responded.

We, at BFP note that the protest at Baird illustrates a potent challenge for college administrators who seek to expose their students to a wide variety of opinions but must take the blame when those efforts fail.

President Hansen, speaking on this challenge, remarked, "The *breach of our freedoms to listen to views that challenge us and to engage in dialogue about such matters is a serious ongoing concern that we must strive to address effectively."*

***

The disrupted event was the second time during the term that Baird University found itself the focus of national news coverage. When he saw the news reports, Board Chair Alexander again called President Hansen and demanded to know why the Baird Administration could not seem to keep the school out of the news.

"Two of our trustees resigned from the Board after the hate crime debacle," he said. "Both of them were important supporters of the School and previously we could count on them for significant and regular financial support. They both told me that they felt it was too risky for them to be involved with a university that was getting so much negative press. They also told me that they've been contacted by certain faculty members who wanted to be assured that no disciplinary action would be taken against student protesters. Are those faculty members nuts...?"

"So, I suspect that after this fiasco, we can expect a couple more resignations, and I'm guessing that your Admissions office is also fielding some concerned calls from parents of applicants for fall admission."

"Yes, that's true," Hansen felt compelled to respond, "but it seems not to be widespread, so I think we can absorb the setback."

"I understand that, Tom," Alexander continued, "but you and I aren't just talking about absorbing the impact of a negative event that's in the past. I, and others on the Board, are concerned about the future. We're going to need some assurance that things like this are not going to keep happening."

"I understand," Hansen responded. "We're going to be taking a tough stance against disruptions like the one that just happened. We have some videos from the evening and are reviewing them to see if we can identify the instigators."

***

BFP has learned that Baird University is bringing criminal charges against eight students who orchestrated and led the demonstrations and protests that prevented Ben Shapiro from speaking on campus earlier this month. Explaining the disciplinary actions, University President Hansen commented that, "Blockading the venue breached institutional values of freedom of expression and students' rights of peaceful assembly."

Bronwyn Warren, Baird's Dean of Students, commented, "Students had every right to protest the Shapiro talk, but they did not have the right to prevent those who wanted to hear him from doing so."

When word of the planned disciplinary actions leaked out, some supporters of the students accused the college of treating the students unfairly. Dean Warren responded that students were provided an opportunity to be heard, and to raise objections throughout the process.

In an official statement on behalf of the University, President Hansen stated that Baird "must continue to invite the broadest array of speakers on the pressing issues of the day. One responsibility of our faculty is to help us all understand how to mitigate the forces that divide our society. Baird students must master the skills of respectful dialogue across all barriers. The Baird community must protect our right to learn from others, especially those with whom we disagree."

A lawyer for the students facing disciplinary action called the college's actions "Completely outrageous." She said that the protest was "warranted" because of Shapiro's intolerable and racist views. The lawyer further claimed that Shapiro's freedom of speech had not been limited in any way, in that he was free to give his talk online. When asked about the students who wanted to hear Shapiro, the lawyer asserted, "There is a constitutional right to speak but there is no such right to hear someone speak."

CHAPTER 27
THE SHOOTOUT

At Jennifer Morris's house again, Morris and Mark Nikolaidis were in flagrante when their passion was sidelined by what sounded to be a gunshot coming from the street directly in front. They had, long since their first encounter last fall, foregone meeting at the Cambridge Inn. Instead, Nikolaidis had begun to simply walk to Jennifer's house for an occasional visit.

"Was that a gun?" Mark exclaimed.

Before Jennifer could answer, he heard from the street, "I know you're in there Nikolaidis!!! I know you're there fucking my wife, you SOB! Come out, asshole!" And then another gunshot.

"That's Joseph," Jennifer apologetically stated. "He must have come back from his conference earlier than I expected. Apparently, he's onto our little evenings together." She rose and began to pull on a robe that was lying on the floor beside the bed.

"Well, yes!!!" Mark exclaimed.... "But more importantly, he has a gun!"

"A pistol, you mean," Jennifer said.

"I don't care if it's a pistol or an assault rifle... it's still a gun! Why in God's name does he have a gun?"

"Calm down," Jennifer retorted. "It's not a real gun.... It only shoots blanks. Joey sometimes uses it in his introductory physics classes."

"For what possible purpose would he need to have a gun

in class...? Is he threatening students?"

"Of course not, Mark..." Jennifer laughed. There's a nice long stretch of almost level ground near the stream that runs by the athletic fields. He takes his class of about 50 students out to that area, and lines them up, each about 100 feet apart, so nearly a mile. Then he stands at one end and fires the pistol. The students are supposed to look away from him and raise both hands as soon as they hear the shot. So he ends up doing something that looks sort of like the wave cheer you see at sporting events. It takes almost five seconds for sound to travel a mile, so it turns out to be a very useful way to help students visualize the speed of sound."

"That's actually kind of clever...." Mark was starting to calm down and began to pull on his clothes. "But it doesn't change the fact that we're discovered... and he seems pretty pissed about what we've been doing."

"Don't worry about that, Mark. I'll go out there and take care of it.... I suppose we should say our goodbyes now, Mark.... You've been my salvation these last few months."

**

Jennifer strolled placidly to the street. "Put that silly gun away, Joey, and stop yelling. You're waking the whole neighborhood. Now, let's go inside. I'll put on some tea, and we can talk about what just happened."

Professor Gardner hung his head with a sheepish grin and followed his wife into their house. Nikolaidis was no longer there.

On the same sofa where Jennifer and Mark had started their tryst, Joseph and Jennifer now sat, balancing teacups and saucers on their knees.

"Why did you start up with Mark?" Joseph asked. "He seems like such a doofus."

"Actually, he's a very sweet person, and he's helped me

through a difficult time that I hope is now ended.... But to answer your question, in the last few years, you've been away so much, Joey, that I've felt very much alone and concerned. I've never understood why you're drawn to attend so many conferences, leaving me at home and by myself."

"I'll be direct, Joey.... Are you having an affair with someone? I can't think of another reason for your being so often gone."

"How could you think such a thing of me, Jenn...? I just go to conferences for the normal reasons that people do.... I like the academic milieu with a focus on physics, and I don't get much of that kind of stimulus from my aging colleagues here at Baird."

"I find it hard to believe that's the only reason. I feel that you no longer find me attractive," she said.

"Nothing could be further from the truth," Joseph responded. "In fact, maybe my attraction to you is part of the reason I go away so often. A few years ago, I felt that you were losing interest in me.... I feel old, bald, and kind of... you know... flabby.... How attractive can that be...? But I'm still intensely drawn to you... and to avoid seeming like a pest, I thought it might be better for me to just stay away more."

"Wherever would you get that idea...? I've never suggested that I'm not drawn to you, but I do need to also feel that you're attracted to me... and lately, I haven't seen much evidence of that."

"Don't you still have male urges, Joey?"

"Sure, I do, and that's part of the tension. I don't want to force myself on you."

"But that comes across to me as you're not being attracted.... It still seems like there must be someone else."

"No one else.... It does pose some difficulties.... What you said, I mean." Joseph reddened and stared into the fire that was burning low on the hearth.

"But don't you see that turning away from me because you feel self-conscious is contributing to my own feelings that you don't find me attractive?"

"Now that we're talking about it, I'm beginning to see your point of view. I suppose we need to talk more about our feelings... not the kind of thing you might expect between a mathematician and a physicist, Jenn."

"No, it's not Joey, but perhaps we should learn.... Now, you must be tired.... I know I am... so let's try to get some sleep."

"Well, I was tired, but this conversation has me imagining some other things."

"I see," said Jennifer. "In any case, let's go upstairs. We can just see what happens."

CHAPTER 28

THE PROVOST AND THE PRESIDENT

After receiving the revised hiring recommendation from the Department of Economics, the President and the Provost met again.

"So... it looks like all of this nonsense about Shapiro is behind us and things are settling down again," the Provost began.

"I certainly hope so..." Hansen responded. "Armstrong had predicted we'd lose a couple Trustees because of it. Turns out, he underestimated.... We've lost three... and I've been fielding a lot of calls from concerned parents.... Maybe that's the worst of it."

"I do think we've turned the corner, however," Hansen continued. "Next week we'll be bringing in a former U.N. Ambassador to speak. She was appointed by a Democrat, so probably that'll calm the more liberal students down."

"Good to hear..." May responded. "I have to say that I'm glad extracurricular stuff is not in my wheelhouse."

"Yes, it's in Warren's..." President Hansen responded. "But I'm starting to wonder if she's up to it."

"Well, in any case," the Provost transitioned. "I'm really here to update you on the latest recommendations from the Economics Department for their two endowed chairs."

"I'm surprised they could get back to you so quickly with new names," said the President, signaling his astonishment. "I thought we might be looking at some time next year."

"Yeah... well, I guess they had identified a couple backups in case their initial recommendations didn't fly," May explained. "So I think they just called a quick meeting and re-voted on their fallback nominees. The good news is that I think these two are more in line with what we were hoping. They clearly fit the donor's stated intent, and they work in some splinter areas of economics, not in finance or accounting."

"So, maybe we can save some money," Hansen inferred.

"I think so," said May, "especially since one is currently at the University of Oklahoma and the others at Cal State LA."

"Oh, that's good," Hansen picked up. "So the guy from Cal State is probably not highly paid and who wouldn't be willing to take a pay cut to get out of Oklahoma?"

"That's my thinking, too," the Provost responded.

"Okay," the President responded. "I suppose we're going to have to go ahead and try to hire them this year. Can you work with the Department Chair to try to come up with hiring packages that won't cost us too much?"

"Of course," said May, "and I think the latest recommendations from the Academic Personnel Committee might give us some more latitude on funding. It turns out that Econ has three faculty members up for tenure this year. The votes from the Department Personnel Committee meeting were not very encouraging. One candidate for tenure got a plurality of positive votes, but there were several abstentions. Both of the other two got slight majorities of negative votes. When the files went to Academic Personnel, the Committee largely ignored the Department recommendations. They voted overwhelmingly in favor of one of the candidates, who happens to be black. They were strongly negative on one of the others and were split but slightly positive on the third."

"I see," said Hansen. "Seems like we'll need to go along with the strong positive and strong negative recommendations. What do you think about the third?

May responded that with such weak support from the Department and lukewarm support from Academic Personnel, there wasn't much of a case for granting tenure.

"Okay, so we'll be adding two endowed professorships, but in a year we'll be cutting out the two junior lines."

"Right, and the two we'll be cutting are relatively expensive since they're in finance and accounting," added May. So overall, we may come out at about breakeven in the Economics Department."

"Well, thanks, Jim," said the President. "It's good to see that you're so clearly focused on the cost cutting strategy we discussed a while ago."

"Let me know how it goes with the Department in trying to fill those two positions... and let's hold off for a bit in letting the Department know about the results on those three tenure cases. I'd rather not have them connect the hirings to the terminations."

CHAPTER 29
THE FACULTY

For security reasons, the campus visit of former U.N. Ambassador, Marcia Atwood was only announced a few days before the scheduled event. Atwood was planning to come to campus to promote her new book, "Women in the Lead."

To the surprise of both the Dean of Students and the President, the announcement was met almost immediately by a negative response from a number of Baird's female faculty members. Stating publicly, "We are outraged at the invitation to Marcia Atwood to speak on the Baird campus," and that they planned to protest the Atwood speech. The faculty members cited Atwood's foreign policy role at the U.N. in imposing U.S.-led sanctions that they claimed were responsible for the deaths of thousands of Iraqi children. They also faulted Atwood for supporting the U.N.'s unwillingness to intervene in an African genocide. The professors concluded their public statement by demanding that they be included in the campus speaker selection process rather than leaving that decision up to students and administrators. "

Later that week, the protesting faculty members attended the speech. They took highly visible seats throughout the auditorium, but stood during the entire talk, showing their backs to the speaker.

The incident was picked up by the *Chronicle of Higher Education* in an article supporting the role of university faculty in setting the tone for selecting speakers and presenting a model to students of how to engage in peaceful protest.

Following the story in the *Chronicle*, Hansen emailed his

Dean of Students:

Bronwyn,

I see that we are in the press again. I'm very disappointed. This is going to have to stop.

Tom

Dean Warren, when she received the President's message, fumed. In authorizing the Atwood visit she had merely followed the guidance from Hansen to avoid right-leaning speakers until things on campus had calmed down. She'd been blindsided by the faculty-led protest.

CHAPTER 30
THE EXECUTIVE LEADERSHIP TEAM

A few weeks after Spring Break, President Hansen convened a meeting of his ELT to assess the status of advancement and admissions efforts and to gauge the impacts of the various events that had transpired during the term.

"Thanks for coming, everyone," the President intoned. "Let's all take a seat and get started. I think it's good that the Board has asked us to transition to need-blind admission and loan-free financial aid. Those changes have the potential to move us into the status of an elite university, but they also entail some risks. And I'm concerned that some of the things that have happened recently could elevate the risks. So, I'd like to hear from each of you as to where we stand and what you expect."

"Heather, as we usually do, can we start with you?"

"Of course...." the CFO responded professionally. "You'll recall from our meetings early in the fall term that we were anticipating a moderate budget overrun this year. Except for a few surprises, we've been on track with those projections. But, unfortunately, we haven't made any headway on closing the deficit."

"Can you elaborate a bit, Heather?" Hansen encouraged.

"I'll just mention a few points that seem important," she countered. "First, we had the asbestos problem. With all the disruption, and the need to bring in a hazmat team and find offices for displaced faculty to work and places for classes to meet. That all proved to be quite expensive. I don't have an exact number but somewhere between several hundred thousand dollars and a bit over one million."

"That much?" Hansen exclaimed.

"Unfortunately, yes," Martin continued. "And then there was the hate crime. In the aftermath, we had to retain outside counsel to pursue legal action against the visiting faculty member. It wasn't a huge expense, but it was unanticipated and not within the normal budget.

"And after that, we had the Shapiro talk. You'll recall that we had to make a number of special arrangements... we had to rent security barriers and add a lot of temporary security. Again, the cost wasn't that great, but the things we had to do went beyond what we normally do when we bring speakers to campus."

"My guess, at this point is that because of these kinds of unexpected and unbudgeted occurrences we'll run over our projections by something in the one point five to two million dollar range. That's fairly serious, but since these are just a series of negative surprises, I think they're transitory, so they don't have implications for budgeting in future years."

"So, it's bad, but apparently not too bad," Hansen interpreted.

"I guess that's true," Martin responded. "But remember we were already dealing with some persistent budget shortfalls, and we don't know what will happen with early decision and the other related changes.... And we still have a lot of deferred maintenance to deal with."

"Okay, so, let's move on to Admissions," Hansen continued. "Can you fill us in on that, Dave? I hope you'll be able to assure us that you can work your usual magic and bring in the targeted number of good students this year, as you've been able to do so well in the past."

"So, the short answer is 'yes, I believe we can'," David Knight responded, "but, with all the changes the Board is asking for, the situation this year is quite a bit different from what it has been in prior years."

"When word got out that we're moving to need-blind admission and loan-free aid, our applications ramped up some. My expectation, at this point, is that the increase in applications will more than offset the negative impacts of the press we've been getting this term about things like hate crimes and student protests."

"Good to hear," the President affirmed. "Thanks for all of your efforts, Dave."

"Well, before we move on, Tom," Heather Martin interjected. "Would it be okay for me to ask David a couple of follow-up questions?"

"Of course," he replied. "That's why we're meeting as a group. Please go ahead with your questions."

"Okay...." Martin proceeded. "David, for the purpose of budgeting for next year, can you give me an idea of how next year's financial aid will compare to that in the current year."

"Well... I can try," responded the VP for Admissions, resenting the question he had hoped to avoid. "But, at this point, we don't have much data.... I can tell you all that much of the uplift we've seen in our applications to date seems to be coming from students who are likely to need fairly significant financial aid support. So, while I think we can meet our enrollment targets, it does seem likely that the financial aid to students who are admitted for next year could go up.... But keep in mind that the loan-free aid policy doesn't apply to our current students. It's just the newly admitted students who'll be eligible for loan-free aid."

"I see," said Martin. "So the amount that we'll need to provide in financial aid is probably going to keep going up after next year, and for the next four years or so."

"That could be true..." Knight conceded, with a nod.

"But also keep in mind that after the current round of admissions we'll be able implement the early-decision option that the Board has also requested.... Obviously, we don't yet know what the impact of that will be, but possibly it'll be enough to offset any increase in aid due to the loan-free policy.... And we can also mitigate the impact by admitting more international students, since that policy doesn't apply to them."

"Thanks, David," Martin concluded. "That's very helpful," she remarked without emphasis, feeling that this was all the help she was likely to get from Knight for preparing the next budget."

"So, if there are no more questions for Dave," Hansen directed, "let's move on to Advancement. Now that you've settled into your position as VP for Advancement, Jack, and filled your staff vacancies, what can you tell us about the results for this year?"

"Well... I was hoping to be able to say that last Fall was a period of restructuring and re-staffing the Advancement Office, and that in Spring we'd be catching up and getting back on track with our giving targets.... Actually, we were beginning to do that, but then all the bad press seems to have given prospective donors an excuse to wait-and-see or to redirect their gifts to other schools or other philanthropic pursuits."

"The Board resignations we've had this year were all important donors to the School," Richardson continued. "Some other members of the Board have also expressed concerns about their possible legal exposure. Prospective supporters of Baird that we've been trying to develop for a long time have cooled off substantially. On top of that, our small gifts are down quite a bit compared to last year. The small gifts are probably the clearest indicator of how our constituencies are thinking about the School."

"On the up-side, we did have the Jennings gift, which you all know about," he continued. "But aside from that I think we'll be off by a couple million in donor financial support for the School."

"I do want to say that we, in Advancement, are all working very hard to restore confidence in the School and to re-engage our donors. I think, once things quiet down, we can get back on track for donor financial support."

"Thanks, Jack," Hansen responded. "I knew the events this term were going to be a challenge for our advancement efforts, but it seems, possibly that it's worse than I'd expected.... I hope you'll let me know what I can do to help on this, and I believe that Jim may be able to help track down faculty members who might be helpful.... I'm already working to find some candidates to fill the vacancies on the Board, and I'd like to coordinate with you to fill those positions in the best way."

The meeting continued for another half-hour with a report from the Provost and a general discussion of plans for addressing the mounting financial concerns.

CHAPTER 31
CULTURAL APPROPRIATION

On May 5, a group of Baird students organized a Cinco de Mayo party where they served tacos and margaritas. Several of the students attended in costumes that seemed to stereotype Mexican culture. Days later, a Mexican student complained in the official student newspaper that, as a Latina student at Baird, she felt uncomfortable about the cultural appropriation. Her op-ed included a photo of one of the partying students who was dressed in a costume resembling Pancho Villa. The article precipitated a groundswell of support, including complaints about Caucasian students wearing large hoop earrings and clothing featuring tribal fabric patterns

The problem landed, again, on the desk of the Dean of Students. Dean Warren decided to respond personally to the student who had penned the op-ed. Offering to speak with the students, she emailed that she would welcome the opportunity to engage in a conversation of "how to better serve the needs of students of all backgrounds."

Upon receiving the message from Dean Warren, the Latina student circulated it to several organizations on campus for students of color. The email, through this channel, triggered a new round of student protests. Shortly thereafter, Dean Warren appeared before a group of students who had organized to call for specific change.

The *Baird Free Press* had learned of the planned meeting and sent a reporter to cover it, reporting, in part, as follows:

***

The event began calmly with, sometimes tear-filled, testimonials of students who felt marginalized by the Baird culture and pointing out what they considered to be institutionalized racism. As the event progressed, a bullhorn was passed from one student to another, and even to an occasional outsider who had come to fuel the controversy. The group of students gradually morphed into something more like a mob.

Ironically, in the context of a complaint about students of color being marginalized, the group turned on itself. At one point, an Asian female recounted her experience of having been admonished by an African-American to "Go back to her home." She argued to the crowd that "Black people can be racist, too." The mob quickly commandeered the bullhorn from her and purged her for her insolence.

After hearing a sycophantic apology from Dean Warren and a promise to work on the problems of cultural appropriation and institutionalized racism, someone in the group spotted President Hansen and the Chair of the Board of Trustees standing on the edge of the crowd and called upon them to speak to the assembled group. Turning to Hansen, the Board Chair was heard by this reporter to decree, "I'll handle this." Then, in a pathetic display of self-flagellation, the Chair stepped into the center of the storm, expecting to calm the situation by his silence. Instead, he was confronted with angry chants that were led by one of the organizers using a bullhorn. When Board Chair, Alexander, sought access to the bullhorn so he could respond, someone in the crowd called out, "He's full of bull on his own and doesn't need a bullhorn to help out." Following that lead, the crowd demanded that the organizers not give it to him. Unable to be heard, the Board Chair stood powerless to respond to the protesters. He, nonetheless, did his best to speak over the chants.

After more or less hearing from the Chair that the Trustees were behind the School's efforts to address their concerns about being marginalized, one of the organizers argued, "We need to hit them where it hurts – go after their funding sources." As the Board Chair was engaging with the students, one spectator called out, "Where is the Dean of Students – bring her out." Another asserted that Dean Warren was clearly disinterested in the problem and was actually falling asleep on the sideline. Warren's attempt to respond was greeted by calls of "Fire her." Neither President Hansen nor the Board Chair said anything in her defense.

***

The story was quickly picked up by other news organizations. So, for the third time that semester, Baird made the national news.

Shortly thereafter, Alexander phoned the President. "I just saw the video, Tom. I think I made quite a mess of it. Sorry to say that it never occurred to me that it might be a good idea to keep my mouth shut. I'm sure you'd have handled it better. I should never have assumed that I could control a mob."

"But my involvement aside, Tom, that's three strikes in one semester. I wonder how many you think you're entitled to before someone calls you out."

Even though Alexander had inserted himself and had probably stirred the flame, his call and the warning were not unexpected. Hansen executed on his plan to deflect. He pointed to Dean Warren as the key to fixing the problem. "As you witnessed," he said, "Dean Warren has been in the middle of all or these incidents. She's clearly tone deaf to the needs of the students and continues to handle them poorly. I'll take care of it."

"We'll see," Alexander responded. "I'll pass your remarks along to the Board, but I'm not so sure they'll accept your argument that replacing the Dean of Students will fix the problem…. And, once again, I think we can anticipate some damage to our fund-raising efforts."

"I know we just recommitted to extend your contract," Alexander concluded, "and I'm sure the Trustees won't have the will to try to reverse that decision, but I can also assure you that many on the Board are beginning to regret the decision."

Approximately one week after his call with Alexander, President Hansen accepted the resignation of his Dean of Students.

CHAPTER 32
FACULTY HIRING UPDATE

From: **Bob Hill** <roberth@baird.edu>
Subject: Our Endowed Professorship Search
To: <econfaculty@baird.edu>

Hi, Everyone,

I wanted to let you all know that it appears that our search for faculty has concluded, and the outcome is positive.

Shortly after our last meeting, the Provost approved our recommendations to hire Professor Barron to the position of The Abigale Jennings Professor of Environmental Economics and Professor Granville to the Bernard Jennings Professor of Oil and Gas Economics.

Both Barron and Granville will be joining our faculty in July.

In keeping with their titles as holders of endowed chairs and to keep their salaries more in line, the Provost and I decided to negotiate more on other dimensions. Both of our new endowed professors will be assigned to corner offices on our floor, along with research and travel accounts that are more generous than what we normally provide to full professors. To accommodate these aspects of the negotiation, I will need to ask two of you to relinquish your corner offices and we will all need to accept some belt-tightening in our research and travel accounts.

I look forward to the arrivals of Professors Barron and Granville on campus after the end of the spring term, and I encourage each of you to reach out to them and welcome them to Baird.

Robert Hill

Hill's email message was not well received by some members of the Economics faculty. In a message broadcast to Department Faculty, Professor Sarks objected.

*From: **Professor Cory Sarks** <corys@baird.edu>*
Subject: Re: Our Endowed Professorship Search
*To: **Bob Hill** <roberth@baird.edu>*
CC: <econfaculty@baird.edu>

Mr. Chair,

I read with dismay your message about the recent appointments to endowed professorships.

As you well know, neither of these individuals fits the profile the Department voted on for the purpose of identifying appropriately qualified candidates. Instead, we are doing exactly what we most feared. We are hiring two very narrowly focused individuals whose areas of expertise we do not need and who cannot complement the research interests of others on the faculty. It is a shame that we are now apparently losing the opportunity to hire two truly deserving professors of economics.

It's apparent to me, and probably to others, that University Administration interfered improperly in our searches, a function that is supposed to be specifically the prerogative of the faculty.

Moreover, the impact on our research and travel budgets is exactly what our faculty were concerned about. In fact, it's even worse. While we anticipated that adding faculty would tax our research resources, I don't believe anyone contemplated that there would be actual explicit cuts so that the University could sweeten the deals to these new hires.

The office space negotiation is particularly troubling because it clearly targets two faculty members. As we all know, there are only four corner offices on our floor. One is occupied by the

Department Chair (you), one has been converted to serve as a faculty lounge, and the other two are occupied by Professor Koopman and me. It's quite clear that you're deliberately targeting the two of us. Moreover, since all of the offices on our floor are occupied, one cannot help but wonder what you have in mind for us... a closet somewhere in the basement, perhaps?

I strenuously object to your malfeasance during this entire recruitment process.

Professor Cory Sarks

Professor Faquhir responded to the Chair's announcement with a short message to a selected list of faculty members in the Department:

*From: **Larry Faquhir** <larryh@baird.edu>*
Subject: Re: Our Endowed Professorship Search
To: reardon.koopman@baird.edu;
mark.nikolaidis@baird.edu;____daniel.edwards@baird.edu;
james.noach@baird.edu;____kristina.Novikova@baird.edu;
nicole.stewart@baird.edu; nadir.kaur@baird.edu
CC:

Time for a happy hour ☹ anyone? Usual place. Hope to see you all there.

Larry

CHAPTER 33

HAPPY HOUR

Professor Faquhir arrived early to the Tilted Kilt and ordered two pitchers and ten glasses. When the others began to arrive, he was well into his second pint.

"What a fucking mess," he launched in when the others had taken seats and filled their glasses. "I think we had an opportunity to accomplish something good for the School, something that could benefit our students... especially those in our Ph.D. program. Instead, I believe, that, thanks to meddling in our search by the Provost and the President, we're going to be much worse off than we are now."

"For once, I completely agree with you, Larry," responded Krista. "While you and I disagree about the desired focus of our search efforts, either one of our approaches would have been better than what actually has happened."

Others nodded their agreement. "Well... mazel tov," Jamie Noach interjected acerbically, raising his glass. "We got played.... But what else is new? There are so many different interests involved in faculty searches that I think we're kidding ourselves if we believe we can control the outcome."

"If you ask me," Noach continued, "this whole idea of shared governance between the faculty and the Administration is a cleaver illusion that serves mainly to placate faculty so administrators can do whatever they want.... Remember the last Provost search...? The search committee at the time included student representatives, representatives of the Administration, a board member, and a few faculty members. Even though the committee had a slight majority of faculty, several of those members were hand-picked by the Administration, ostensibly to assure diversity... and all of the non-faculty members were picked by the Administration. So it was likely that the recommendation from that committee would be to hire a candidate whom the Administration supported.... On top of that, the Administration assured itself of a good outcome by charging the committee to provide recommendations of three un-ranked candidates. I served on that committee, and it was a complete waste of faculty time. The outcome had been hard-wired by the Administration."

"I wholeheartedly agree," Edwards picked up. "Much the same thing happens in our tenure and promotion decisions.... We, as a department, spend many, many hours examining the records of candidates for promotion or tenure. Then we prepare a recommendation that goes to the Academic Personnel Committee, but the department chair gets to provide a separate recommendation that we never see and that probably carries as much weight as ours, or even more.... And then the Academic Personnel Committee gets those recommendations, does its own review, and votes again. That whole package goes to the Provost, and he, in consultation with the President makes the final decision."

"I know you all know the process... and, on its face, it does sound like a good and fair process, with a bushel of faculty input. But when you dig down, it's a bloody sham," he continued. "Most of the cases are obvious... clearly tenurable/promotable or clearly not. There's very little chance that the administration would disagree with the faculty on those cases. And then there are some cases where the faculty vote is split. In those cases, the faculty is essentially silent and the ultimate decision is really effectively to the administration.... I suspect that there are very few instances where the administration disagrees with the consensus of the faculty. So maybe campus-wide, we might consider around 100 promotion or tenure cases per year, and there are probably only one or two where the administration and the faculty would clearly disagree.... So much for shared governance..."

"While I'm not pleased with how our hiring efforts worked out," Professor Kaur commented, "I thought I'd try to make the best of it by following up on the Chair's suggestion that we send the new hires a welcome message.... So... I did that.... And I heard back from Barron almost immediately. But his reply was pretty bizarre. He didn't really acknowledge my message. Instead, he just sent me a PDF of his latest op-ed piece on the looming dangers of climate change, and he attached a long list of links to other articles in the public press that featured him. I suspect we know what we're getting ourselves in for."

"I'd like to change the subject, if I may," said Nicole Stewart. "It seems to me that it's been quite a while... several months... since we completed the Department review of our three tenure cases. I can't understand why it's taking so long to learn the final decision."

"You're right about that, Nicole," said Faquhir. "It does seem odd. I wonder if something nefarious is going on."

"That's kind of the same thing I was just talking about," Edwards commented. "Our Departmental votes on those cases were mixed. So it's going to seem to the Administration that we're defaulting the decisions to them. I suspect that the delays in hearing anything are not positive."

"Well, I hope you're wrong about that, Dan," Novikova responded. "We just failed in our efforts to hire in finance and accounting. If the tenure cases in those areas turn out negative, we'll have a very serious problem staffing our classes."

The group sat silent for a while as Prof. Faquhir refilled their glasses.

"This has been one of the strangest academic years I can recall," said Koopman, teeing up a new topic of discussion. "I've been here a long time and I've never seen so much student hostility.... The closest thing I can remember is back when I was an undergraduate, and students were protesting the Vietnam War and taking over campus buildings. It seemed that back then, with war hanging over their heads, almost anything could stir up the students. But I can't really understand what's going on now. There doesn't seem to me to be anything major driving it, and yet student protests seem to be an almost daily occurrence.... And for some reason, Baird seems to be getting much more than its share of negative press about what's been going on. We've been in the news over and over again this term."

"I suspect that there are a number of factors," responded Stewart. "With their access to social media, students these days can organize much more quickly than they could in the past. On top of that, since the word gets out so quickly, it's easier for outside agitators to incite the students and it's easier for those in the media to pick up on campus unrest. Students know that if they're vocal enough, they can get media coverage, which is probably one motivator. And Hansen never does anything proactively to calm things down. He almost never meets with students, and I don't think he goes to any student sports events.... I also think that the faculty bear some responsibility... like what just happened here when faculty members protested the Atwood talk."

"Yes, of course," Koopman responded, "but don't you think Baird is getting more than its share?"

"If you ask me," Faquhir commented. "I think the Baird Administration has to bear much of the responsibility, like Nicole was suggesting.... And they didn't handle the Shapiro talk well... the Dean of Students and the Board Chair made a mess of responding to concerns about student marginalization... and then they drew in the faculty into protesting by not carefully vetting how the appearance of Atwood on campus was likely to be received."

"That sounds about right to me," commented Edwards as he stood. "I'm going to have to get back to campus for a meeting I have in a few minutes. Can you cover my share of the tab, Nadir, and I'll settle up with you tomorrow?"

After Edwards left, Prof. Kaur commented, "I wonder what's going on with Dan, lately. He seems to be a bit distracted and always in sort of a rush."

"You don't know?" Nicole Stewart responded. "Haven't you noticed that when you walk past his office, he's almost always in there working with the same graduate student...? Rebecca something, I think? They seem to be a bit cozier than the normal faculty/student interaction."

"Really?" Kaur countered. "I guess I'll have to pay more attention. Do you think it's all okay?"

"Not our problem," Krista Novikova commented. "It's probably just Dan being Dan."

"Well, I hope the schmuck knows to keep his mind off the shikse," Jamie Noach mused.

"We'll just have to wait and see," Krista said, as they settled up with the pub and headed out.

CHAPTER 34

THE BAIRD FREE PRESS

Not long after the resignation of Baird's Dean of Students, the University was challenged by a scandal of a different type.

The Baird Free Press has learned that the Admissions Office of Baird University has been materially falsifying admissions statistics, perhaps for years. Based on documented information received from an anonymous whistleblower working in the Admissions Office, BFP has been able to establish that average SAT scores reported to such organizations as US News and Peterson's have been overstated by as much as 50 points, and average GPAs have been overstated by as much as one-half of a letter grade. SAT and GPA statistics are used by services, including US News and Petersons in their rankings of colleges and universities. These rankings and the statistics, themselves, are relied upon by individuals in making their decisions about which schools they will apply to, and about which offer of admission they will accept.

Organizations such as US News have well-defined rubrics that schools are expected to follow in preparing and reporting their admissions statistics. It is well-known that many schools manage their admissions practices in order to conform to this rubric while still showing their admissions in a favorable light. For example, US News specifies that the average SAT scores submitted to it by a school are to be based on "all enrolled first-time, first-year students entering in fall." Thus, a school may be able to improve its reported average SAT score by deferring low scoring applicants to spring admission or wait-listing them. It can also avoid reporting low scores by admitting students as transfers, such as from community colleges. Baird's practices, however, go well beyond these common practices.

When our reporter confronted Baird's Vice President for Admissions and Admissions Director, he stated that a few years ago his office had developed a special program that it applied to certain targeted students and student athletes. He indicated that this was a common practice among universities. The Director admitted that since the policy was put in place, these students had not been included in the university's calculated admissions statistics. Baird refers to these as "special admissions" students. When BFP included all students in the calculation for this year's freshman class, Baird's SAT average dropped by 47 points.

The Director further stated that Baird did not report score averages based on including special admission students because the School does not rely on SAT scores of special admission students. He further claimed that excluding some groups from SAT averages was "not unusual" and expressed a concern that including statistics for special admit students could conflict with the School's other policies, such as its efforts to recruit a well-diversified cohort of students.

When the University's President, Thomas Hansen, was confronted with evidence of the biased SAT reporting, he indicated that he was not aware of any problems with the School's reporting of admissions statistics and commented that, "The Vice President for Admissions has a long tenure at Baird and is highly regarded for his ability to bring in excellent and diverse entering classes of students." The Director of Admissions, however, reported to BFP that he had been under severe pressure to meet enrollment and diversity targets and indicated that, since Hansen assumed the Presidency of Baird, he had wanted to see SAT averages

rising over time.
• •

***

When President Hansen learned of the forthcoming *BFP* expose, he contacted Board Chair Alexander and University General Counsel, Gloria Moreno. The three met later that evening with David Knight.

Hansen took the lead. "I guess I should have known, David…. Some things are just too good to be true. It seemed miraculous that year-after-year you were able to bring in entering classes that met our admissions targets, while, at the same time, increasing the test scores of the entering classes and adding to student diversity. But you had such a great track record of being able to deliver the numbers that I think we all just trusted you."

Alexander picked up. "I can't tell you how personally disappointed I am, David…. You and I have been friends for a long time. We've had dinner at each other's homes. We've gone to Baird sports events together. My daughter even babysat for your children…. But now, here we are. I think you know that this story is going to be immensely damaging to the University and I don't see how you could have done this to us. You've put our admissions plans at risk, done immeasurable damage to our ability to raise funds from donors, and you've probably even put the School's credit rating at risk."

"I can see where this conversation is heading," Knight responded. "You're making the case for terminating me and rehearsing your lines for the press and for our various constituencies. But, let me just say that I'm not going without a fight."

"What is there to fight about, David?" Alexander asked.

"Let's not try to kid each other, Treavor. Both you and Tom knew what was going on. In fact, you both pressured me into it. You demanded the impossible. You demanded that my office deliver a steady number of new students each year, while, at the same time raising our rankings in *US News* through SAT averages, and increasingly diversifying our student body. Clearly, we can't distort our diversity statistics since doing so would be obvious... and we can't claim to have enrolled more students than we actually have... and we can only get so far with increasingly generous financial aid awards. So the only margin we can work on is the test scores.... You both know that."

"Now hold on a minute, David," Hansen bristled. "I think you're deluded about what we knew or didn't know. I'm afraid your efforts to deflect are not going to work.... This is all on you, David."

"I don't think so, Tom. I'm far too young to give up my position without a fight, especially because if I take the fall for this, I'll be virtually unemployable in higher education. There was always a risk to me that a day like this would come, so I've held on to quite a bit of correspondence with you, Tom, and even some with you Trevor.... I can easily show that in your quest for University rankings and diversity you both pressured me into admitting larger and larger groups of special admit students. I raised my concerns about declining SAT scores with both of you on several occasions, and you both demanded that I find a way to make the admissions numbers work. I told you more than once that your goals were unachievable, and you demanded that I go ahead anyway.... The message was clear to me, and it will be clear to a jury... if we get to that."

"I'm very disappointed in the way this conversation is going, David," Alexander started to back-peddle. Of course we recognize that you were trying to do what you thought was best for the School. And we fully understand that leaving your position at Baird will be costly for you and your family. The reason we're here now and talking is that we want to find a solution that works for you."

"That's right, David," Hansen joined in. "While there's no question that we're going to have to part ways, I think we can craft a severance package that will work for you."

"Actually, David, I want it to do more than just work for you," Alexander picked up. "I'm confident that the Board will agree to a severance package you'll find very attractive. We can allow you to keep your pension and provide an earn-out package that will maintain your current salary for the next ten years, as long as you refrain from future statements that could be harmful to Baird. That would take you beyond likely retirement age. We can also provide for your children to attend Baird tuition free."

"I think it's a pretty good deal for you, David, and I suspect you agree. But why don't you take a day or two to consider it and then let us know…? In any case, we're going to need a letter of resignation from you, effective no later than this Friday."

"Now, difficult as this conversation has been," Alexander continued, "I'd like for us all to part as friends. Will you join Tom and me for a drink, David? And let's get our minds off this unpleasantness."

"Thanks, but I don't think I can do that, Trevor," Alexander shunned the peace offering. "I'll just head out now, and I'll let you know my decision by the day after tomorrow."

After Knight left, Alexander and Hansen shared a drink.

"Under the circumstances," Hansen said, "I think that went well."

"I suppose so, Tom," Alexander responded. We'll have to wait and see… but no matter what, I think we're in for a difficult time for a while. Frankly, I'm surprised you weren't more on top of this, Tom. I know you're not a numbers guy, so let's bring Heather Martin into the loop and make sure she reviews and signs off on any future data we report to folks like the *US News*."

Hansen flinched at the proposal but decided to remain silent. He'd have to find some way to deal with Martin.

***

In a follow up to its prior expose, one week later, *BFP* reported the following:

> In an e-mail to the BFP, Baird's President, Thomas Hansen, stated that the University had completed a review of the admissions statistics for the past five years and had concluded that the SAT scores for each fall's freshman class "were generally inflated by an average of 20-40 points."

> Following a recent update of the Baird University website, David Knight, the School's Vice President for Admission for more than a decade, is no longer listed as a member of the University's admissions staff. A spokesman for the University confirmed that Mr. Knight is no longer employed by the University.

> President Hansen has told BFP that Mr. Knight had been solely responsible for the misreported numbers, stating, "At this time, we have no reason to believe that other individuals were involved. The University has hired a major law firm to review how the School processes and reports admissions data.

> The University spokesperson told BFP that the inaccurate SAT scores had been provided to all outlets that collect data from colleges, including the Department of Education and U.S. News. Test score data are also used by bond-rating agencies, which require sworn certification.

CHAPTER 35
TENURE NOTIFICATIONS

*From: **James May, Provost** <provost@baird.edu>*
Subject: Re: Economics Department tenure decisions
To: Robert Hill <roberth@baird.edu>
CC:

I write to give you advance notice of the final promotion and tenure decisions on the three cases from the Department of Economics.

Kyle Phillips: Promotion to Associate Professor of Economics with Tenure: Approved

Sean Lopez: Promotion to Associate Professor of Economics with Tenure: Denied

Lin Chang: Promotion to Associate Professor of Economics with Tenure: Denied

Notice of these decisions will be distributed to the above named candidates tomorrow. Please meet with each of them to make sure they understand the implications of these decisions.

The Department Chair was shocked by the decisions. In his separate letters to the Provost, he had supported the promotions of all three, but had argued that the promotions of Lopez and Chang, because of their focuses on finance and accounting, were most critical to meeting the teaching needs of the Department. Instead, the University had approved the one candidate who would have been easiest to replace.

In light of the recent decisions to hire endowed chair holder, neither of whom was in finance or accounting, Hill had no idea of how his department would be able to deliver its curriculum.

Hill knew that when the individual candidates received the news on their tenure cases from the Provost, those notices would disclose the vote of the Academic Personnel Committee, provide a very brief explanation of that committee's vote, and indicate the final determination with a one-sentence statement of the reason for the Provost's decision.

The absence of meaningful explanation, either positive or negative, would be frustrating to the candidates. But in the current litigious human resources environment, that was just how it was done. Nothing was provided in writing that a candidate could use to argue that the decision was unfair. By asking him to speak with the candidates, the University was preserving plausible deniability.

***

When the three candidates received their letters from the Provost, each was reticent to mention the outcome to others. Phillips did not want to mention his positive result out of concern that theirs might not be positive. Neither Lopez nor Chang wanted to mention theirs, because each feared being singled out as undeserving when the others had positive outcomes.

Nonetheless, word did leak out and faculty members in the Economics Department scurried to each other's offices to discuss the outcomes behind closed doors. When they learned of the decisions, Novikova and Kaur were particularly dismayed. Neither saw a credible way to sustain the degree programs offered in their area.

CHAPTER 36

CAMBRIDGE INN

"Thanks for coming, Krista." Heather Martin and Kristina Novikova exchanged hugs as they took seats in the bar after Heather had finished work for the day. "I'm afraid I just need a shoulder to cry on... and you understand me better than anyone here."

"Is this about the reports in the *Free Press*," Krista asked.

"Partly, it is," Heather responded, "but I think it's bigger than that. It's really about everything that's been going on in the last year or so.... It's such a mess, Krista. I can't believe the Board would have approved such important changes to our admissions policies.... And then being hit with the news that Baird... that David Knight... had been faking everything..."

"I feel responsible," she continued. "I'm the CFO, after all.... I should never have let Hansen and May pressure me into making the presentation I gave at the last Board meeting... and I should have picked up on there being something fishy about the stats coming from Admissions."

"But what could you have done, Heather...?" Krista consoled. "You couldn't really oppose what Hansen wanted to do. I've seen plenty of times in the corporate world and at other universities, where the CFO is at odds with the President.... Trust me, Heather, the President always wins those battles.... I think you had no choice but to go along."

"I guess..." Heather continued. "But, even in that case, I should have seen what was going on with the SAT scores."

"But how could you have?" Krista challenged. "We've all heard about how David's a genius at managing the enrollments.... I'm sure there never seemed to be a reason to question him."

"Well, that's all true. It seemed like the one area where things were going right.... But I feel that it's my job to be suspicious. I should have insisted on seeing the records.... Whenever something seems too good to be true, it probably isn't true... but then Hansen never wanted to question the record and was always praising David for meeting enrollment targets."

"It seems to be a flaw of human nature that people want to ascribe what's basically just luck or deception to skill. Those kinds of mistakes are a common theme in one of the finance classes I teach. Do you remember hearing about the Orange County California bankruptcy in the mid-1990s?" Krista asked?

"Not really," Heather said. "It's a bit before my time."

"Well, it's a good illustration even if it is quite a bit dated. Back then the Treasurer for the County... his name was Robert Citron... was convinced that interest rates on debt securities were in secular decline. So he bet on continuing declining interest rates by investing the County's money in some high-risk securities that would gain value if interest rates fell. He did great with that strategy for quite a few years. Interest rates were declining, and his bets were paying off big-time. Orange County was earning rates of return much higher than were normal in the market at the time. The County Board of Supervisors saw the performance and inferred that Citron was some kind of investment genius. They never questioned whether the high returns were due to Citron's skill or just to luck... and they never thought seriously about the risk."

"Then, for a period of only about a month in 1994, Citron was wrong.... He kept betting on interest rate declines, but, instead, interest rates rose... and because the securities he invested in were so highly leveraged, the reversal, even for just one month, was enough to bankrupt Orange County, as well as some others, like San Bernardino and Stockton that had decided Citron was so skilled that they, too, delegated their investment decisions to him."

"You're kind of going all professorial on me now, Krista," Heather joked.

"I suppose... professional hazard, as they say," Krista responded.

"In any case... the irony is that Citron was actually right about the continuing decline in interest rates. After the short spike up, they continued to fall... but by then it was too late for Orange County.... So, my point, Heather, is that no one in leadership positions at Orange County ever saw fit to question Citron's investment strategy. They just patted themselves on the back for having picked such a smart Treasurer. It seems to me that the same thing was going on with Knight. He seemed to be producing amazing results, so no one wanted to question how he did it."

"Is that supposed to make me feel good about not checking?" Heather joked. "I know I'm not responsible for admissions reporting, but I still feel that I should have seen it.... I can see that something like that was going on here, at Baird. But pointing out that people sometimes fail to see the obvious doesn't make me feel much better."

"Well, my broader point is that it seems to be human nature for people to ascribe their good outcomes to some kind of skill but attribute their bad ones to bad luck. It's everywhere. Look at all the smart people who bought into Bernie Madoff's pitch and never asked where the money was coming from that provided the initial appearance of good investment returns."

"I still think I should have seen through it," Heather responded.

"But then, even if you did, you'd have had to go against

Hansen...."

"True, but there's nothing new about that," Heather laughed. "But let's get off this topic. How are things in Econ?"

"Not good there either, I'm sorry to say.... We just made two senior hires that I'm confident are going to be terrible, and, on top of that, we just found out that our junior faculty member in finance is being denied tenure in spite of being a great teacher and having a solid research record and a really good pipeline of work in progress.... Given all of that, I don't see any way for us to sustain our degree programs in finance."

"I'm so sorry to hear that, Krista. I know you've been working really hard to build an excellent finance program."

"Yes, that's true," Krista responded. "I have to say that it's been really frustrating.... I've been trying for a long time just to get us up to three tenure track faculty members in finance, but I've never been able to accomplish that. With three, we'd have what it takes to at least consistently staff our courses with appropriately qualified faculty and keep our reliance on adjuncts and lecturers to a reasonable level."

"But," Krista continued, "I've come to the conclusion that my problems in finance are just a symptom of something much deeper and more concerning, something related to all the problems you're dealing with.... I'm worried about the future of the University...."

"The reason I wanted to meet you here today, Heather, is that in light of all that's going on, I just can't take it anymore. I wanted to let you know that I've decided to leave Baird. I haven't told anyone yet, and I wanted to tell you personally before the word gets out."

"Please tell me this is just something you're thinking about, Krista.... At least you haven't told anyone else yet, so maybe I can still convince you to stay."

"I'm sorry, Heather, but especially after the failure our

latest hiring efforts I'm firmly committed to leaving.... I don't think I really have a choice.... I'll be especially sorry to leave you here to fight the good fight on your own, and I'm sorry to leave Baird after so many years, but there's just no compelling reason for me to stay."

"But, why, Krista?" Heather asked, still searching for the prospect of a reversal.

"How can I say this, Heather...? It's apparent to me that Baird's problems are much deeper than just my area.... The ship is listing badly. I don't think it has enough ballast to right itself."

"I guess I have to admit," Heather responded, "that I have some of the same concerns, but I thought I was alone in them.... How did you come to that conclusion?"

"Baird's not so unusual," Krista responded. "We see it from time to time in the corporate world. Look at Kodak, for example. The company was built on its film and photography products. When digital images began to replace photographic film, Kodak made a half-hearted effort to adapt... but it never gave up on its obsolescing technology. It just couldn't change course fast enough to survive. The company was effectively destroyed by what are sometimes called its 'legacy assets'. Most of its management was tied to old technologies, as were most of its facilities. You might think that the management team could just change its focus, and they did try... but with no expertise in the new technologies, what they needed to do was to really clean house, or just close down the company, sell off the assets, and distribute the proceeds to Kodak's shareholders."

"I know I'm lecturing again," Krista continued, noticing that Heather seemed to be gearing up for another interruption. "But let me finish the point I'm trying to make."

"Liquidating and distributing the proceeds would have been the right thing for Kodak to do for its shareholders, but clearly it would not have been good for the top-level managers who would lose their jobs. And the managers were in control, so to protect themselves, they tried to hang on and reinvent themselves... move toward the new technology in baby steps."

"Now, in fairness, Kodak's not actually dead... but it's a shell of what it used to be. It went through a bankruptcy and after that, it tried to adapt, but not with much success. Under the circumstances, I don't imagine there are many people who would aspire to go to work for Kodak. Even if management does somehow turn the company around, the shareholders would have been much better off if they'd just liquidated and freed up the capital to be invested elsewhere."

"It's a common story in business. Look at Borders Books and its resistance to the internet or Barnes and Nobel and its attempt to straddle brick-and-mortar and on-line distribution. Look at the dairy companies and their failure to adapt to milk substitutes. They all fail because the organizations are unable to adapt to a changing environment."

"I can see that happening in the business world, with its emphasis on profit, but it's not very clear what that has to do with private non-profit colleges and universities."

"I know you don't really mean what you're saying now, Heather.... We both know that competition can be just as intense in the non-profit world, and that even a non-profit enterprise needs to earn a profit to survive and grow... even if they don't call it profit... and even if they don't have shareholders."

"Of course, you're right, Krista," Heather conceded.

"Universities can fail," Krista continued, "just like businesses can.... It usually just takes longer and can be harder to recognize.... But that's where I'm afraid Baird's heading."

"I know we're having some significant problems right now, Krista, but why don't you think the ship can right itself?"

"I think you know the answer to that, too, Heather. Sure, schools deal with setbacks all the time, and with their endowment's many schools have enough of a buffer that they can weather most storms. But this storm... the one that Baird is experiencing... seems likely to be too much... and the unfortunate thing is that it's largely self-inflicted."

"I don't see a realistic way out of the problem," she went on. "It's obvious that there's going to be more fallout from the admissions thing. The School's going to lose good applicants for admission, and some current students are going to transfer away. I'm sure donor support's going to take a major hit, even some gifts that already have been promised might be clawed back.... I know that some former members of the Board have already resigned, and others may, too."

"But don't you think we can come back?" Heather probed.

"In theory, yes, the facilities are good, the location is good, and most of the faculty are solid in their areas. But I don't see the will to turn things around. The best way to get through this would be for the School to abandon its foolish moves to need-blind admission and loan-free aid, and then to rationalize its programs... close down some of the niche departments that have been created in the arts and humanities in recent years, suspend many of its expensive Ph.D. programs, and concentrate its resources on the areas where student demand is high."

"But, as I said, Heather, I don't see the will to make such changes. The faculty will resist any efforts to close departments or Ph.D. programs... and they'll be supported by some members of the Board, who came on so they could champion their pet liberal arts programs. I think Hansen's really the one who wanted the admissions policy changes, probably because he thought they would help provide a stepping stone for him to a more prestigious university.... And he's too far down that road now, to give up on it. Moreover, even if the School were to make such changes, this wouldn't be a good place for faculty to work... with no resources, very limited hiring, and no research support.... I'm sure the people who can leave will be looking around, and the ones who'll remain will be in disciplines where job offers are scarce... or they're among the ranks of those who should never have been tenured in the first place or are overpaid relative to whatever opportunities they could hope to find at other schools."

"That's a pretty grim picture you're painting, Krista.... But I can't say that I disagree with your reasoning, except to say that I'll be here for as long as I can, trying to make things work. Maybe it'll work out."

"I admire your loyalty, Heather, and I hope you're right.... Baird doesn't deserve you."

"Well, I guess the only ray of sunshine in all of this," Heather said, "is that you'll be here for the next year or so, while you carry out your search."

"Actually, Heather, I'll be leaving at the end of this term," Krista responded, apologetically.

"But I was under the impression that academic searches take much longer than that." Heather's eyes teared up at this latest revelation from Krista.

"Yes, in the normal academic search process they do," Krista explained. "But a few schools have been trying to lure me away for a while.... They've offered to put me up as a, so called, 'target of excellence' whenever I'm ready to move. I'm already in touch with a couple schools and I'll go with whichever of them comes up with the most fitting offer."

"So what you're really saying is that this might be our last opportunity to talk," Heather summarized dejectedly.

"No, Heather. I'm sure we'll keep in touch, and we'll have a chance to meet again before I leave. I do hope you're right and that you can at least nudge the School back on course."

After another round of drinks, and a parting round of hugs, Heather and Krista went their separate ways.

CHAPTER 37

THE FALLOUT

After Knight's abrupt departure as VP for Admissions, Hansen surveyed his options for an interim appointment. There was a well-seasoned Associate Director in the office, who had been responsible for leading the recruitment outreach effort to private college prep schools. That person was well-qualified but was on record opposing the need-blind admission policy and also was not optimistic about the School's ability to use early decision and international student admissions to cover the cost of providing loan-free financial aid to admitted students.

Having concluded that appointing the associate director could be problematic for him, President Hansen named his own wife as Interim Director of Admissions. Jacqueline had formerly worked in the admissions office of a private high school while Hansen was launching his academic career as a chemistry professor. When Hansen moved into high-level university administration, Jacqueline gave up her career in admissions, and took on the duties expected of a wife in support of her husband's ambitions. President Hansen had concluded that her prior time in admissions work was enough to qualify her as Interim Director of Admissions at Baird. While he knew his appointing her would not sit well with the Admissions staff, and especially the Associate Director, it was more important, he believed, that the Interim Director be fully supportive of the recent changes in admissions policies.

Upon learning of the appointment, the staff of the *Baird Free Press* penned an editorial attacking nepotism at Baird University. Shortly after the appointment, the Associate

Director's resignation was announced.

***

Rating Action:

S&P downgrades Baird University to bb- from bbb; outlook revised to negative

New York – S&P Global Ratings has downgraded the rating on Baird University's revenue bonds to bb- from bbb. The action impacts $60 million of outstanding bonds. The ratings outlook has been revised to negative from stable.

RATINGS RATIONALE

The downgrade to bb- follows a reduction from aa three years ago and is driven by ongoing enrollment and net tuition revenue pressures that are contributing to weakening operating performance. The weaker operating performance will limit growth potential.

The bb- rating is supported by Baird's market role and prospects for philanthropic support. The rating also considers the university's recent changes in admissions and financial aid policies, as well as the disclosure of significant misreporting of the University's enrollment statistics. Baird is highly reliant on student tuition and other tuition-related charges in a very competitive student market and has thin spendable cash and investments relative to its debt and operations expenses. Weaker cash flow in recent years has contributed to a decline of financial reserves relative to similarly-rated peers even as the pace of capital investment has fallen.

RATING OUTLOOK

The negative outlook at the lower rating reflects our

expectation that operating performance will continue to suffer for the foreseeable future. The outlook also incorporates our expectation of modest continuing declining reserves.

FACTORS THAT COULD LEAD TO AN UPGRADE

- Substantial increase in financial resources relative to debt and operating expenses

FACTORS THAT COULD LEAD TO A DOWNGRADE

- Further material decline in liquidity

- Weakening of operating performance including debt service coverage

***

One week after its editorial criticism of nepotism at Baird, and shortly after the S&P press release, the *BFP* reported on the S&P downgrade of its credit rating for the University. In a front-page article entitled, "S&P downgrades Baird University and revises its outlook to 'negative'," the *Free Press* reported on the downgrade.

Citing "weaker operational results during the past two years and a negative outlook for future financial performance," S&P downgraded its rating of bonds issued by Baird University and is changing its outlook to "negative". The outlook for Baird University's bond rating from S&P Global Ratings has shifted to "negative" from "stable" in light of significant financial pressures weighing on the University, the rating service announced.

S&P stated that the revision of its outlook reflects the university's weaker operational results during the past two years compared with historical operating results, and also its projections that this will continue into future fiscal years.

S&P, noting the likely negative impacts of recent developments including Baird's changes in admissions policies and the SAT reporting scandal, indicated that the outlook for Baird bondholders was being revised down.

Baird's President, Thomas Hansen, responding to the ratings downgrade, said, "I want to assure investors in our debt instruments, that there is no cause for concern. The University expects a significant positive impact coming from its recent admissions policy changes. We expect a significant improvement in our enrollment statistics next year under the leadership of our interim admissions director."

President Hansen acknowledged the ongoing financial stress to our BFP reporter. "After we reported a year ago on how improvements to our physical plant had led to a budget deficit, we established new systems to support more rigorous financial analysis that would enable us to better project revenues and control discretionary expenses." Downplaying the School's recent problems, Hansen said "We still expect to have an operating deficit for the next year or two. But our endowment is strong, and we'll see a significant turnaround after that."

S&Ps rival, Moody's Investors Service, has also noted the financial concerns and indicated that it is in the process of reviewing it credit rating for Baird University debt.

CHAPTER 38

PROPOSALS

As news of the ratings downgrade was circulating around the campus, Professor Edwards and his graduate student, Rebecca, were continuing their relationship over dinner at the Cambridge Inn. Daniel had put hundreds of hours into turning Rebecca's dissertation into something worthy of high-level journal publication. He also had written dozens of letters in support of her aspiration for faculty appointment at a leading university. Resulting from his efforts, Rebecca had presented her research at several top-ranked schools, but for the most part, the academic market for new hires in economics had cleared without her having received a job offer. A few schools, including some top schools, were still seeking to fill their remaining open positions. So maybe there was still time.

Dan and Becca had continued their personal liaison. But as the relationship continued, Daniel began to feel increasingly conflicted. For weeks he had been asking himself, "Should I have pushed so hard for Becca to achieve the goal she sought? Especially when so much of the work is actually mine? Is she really deserving of appointment at a top-level school?" Recently, he had begun to acknowledge, "Maybe it'd be better for her to aim a bit lower." A number of respectable schools were located fairly close to Baird. If he could place her in one of those, then maybe they could continue their relationship. "But is my personal interest in her clouding my own judgement? Am I just rationalizing in an effort to achieve my own objective rather than hers?"

He had thought about this a lot, of late. Eventually, he

had been able to convince himself that what seemed right for him would also be right for her. And he had resolved to broach the matter tonight.

He had ordered a bottle of her favorite cabernet, and, over drinks, he started in.

"You know, Becca, I've been thinking about you a lot... actually, about us," he began. "We've been at this for a while, and quite a few schools have completed their searches for the year. I'm wondering if we should broaden the search strategy a bit. There're quite a few good private and public colleges located not too far from here, and I wonder if getting a position at one of those might actually be more appealing to you.... I know it would be to me. Some of these schools still have openings and they're less tied to the annual hiring cycle."

Rebecca sipped her wine in silence, encouraging Dan to continue.

"Think about it, Becca.... If you were close by, we could continue to see each other... and we could even work on some joint research...."

"So, you're saying I should aim a bit lower, right...?" Becca coaxed. "I should think about working at a school with a higher teaching load and less of a focus on research...?" She continued. "And if I did that, we could spend more time together."

"Yes... well I have to say that the appeal for me is that we could keep our relationship going.... But I think this also could be good for you professionally.... Sure, the teaching load would be a bit higher... but I think we could be a great research team, and you could really build your research track record.... Then, if you still wanted to do so, you could move into one of the top-ranked schools as a seasoned assistant professor with an established research record and a good pipeline."

"But, to tell you the truth," he continued, "I'm sort of

hoping that you'll decide to stay. I'd really like to continue seeing you, and maybe we'd decide to make it more permanent, you know...."

"Well, that almost sounds like a proposal, Dan... or sort of a pre-proposal proposal."

"I have to say that I've imagined a number of ways I might be proposed to, but this one was not on my list."

Dan grinned foolishly and shrugged.

"So let me see if I've got this right..."

"You're suggesting that I look for a faculty appointment that's close by so we can keep our little romance going... and that, if it all works out, at some point we might consider marriage.... Is that it, Dan?"

"Yes, that's part of it... but also, if you don't like the job and if we don't work out as a couple, then you'd be in a great position to move to a top school."

"In other words, Dan, what you're actually proposing is that I give up on my professional ambitions and take a job at some Podunk school with an all-consuming teaching load.... You're proposing that I follow the same course that so many co-eds have followed... marry my professor and give up on my own career?"

"No, Becca...! That's not right...." Dan was stunned by the reversal. He'd thought she felt the same way he did. "You're not understanding me," he stammered. "I'm saying that we might find that we both want to stay together... but if not, you'd be in a great position to move up." Somehow, his polished British accent seemed to have disappeared.

"We both know that's bullshit, Dan..." Rebecca flashed. "In academics, you can only move one way... and that way is down."

"That's not true, Becca. Look at Krista... Professor

Novikova, that is.... We just heard that she'll be leaving. She's going to a great university.... She's clearly moving up."

"You know that's different, Dan. She's very seasoned... I'm not.... So my first academic appointment is critical."

"In any case, I'm not really interested in your proposal, Professor.... I'm not going to abandon my professional aspirations just because we've been fucking for the last few months.... I told you back in Key West that this was temporary. I guess somewhere along the way, you must have forgotten about that... but I haven't."

"Also, I had some good news today.... I got a call from one of the schools I visited recently. They're putting together an offer, and I'm planning to accept."

"Oh, I see...." Professor Edwards was taken aback and struggled to recover. "Well, that's great news, Becca. Had I known, I'd never have suggested what we just talked about."

"Well, let's put it behind us and order dinner," Rebecca said, reaching for his hand. "I'm still going to need your help... and I'll be here for the next couple of months to defend my thesis. We can continue to enjoy each other's company."

Edwards refilled their glasses and raised his, offering a half well-meant toast to Rebecca's job market success.

CHAPTER 39

MORE FALLOUT

US News Suspends Rankings of Baird University

In a largely unprecedented move, US News announced on Friday that, pending a full review, it is suspending its rankings of Baird University and all of Baird's degree programs.

In announcing this action, US News expressed concern that the University had failed to adhere to clearly stated guidelines for reporting enrollment statistics, particularly those related to the reporting of standardized test scores. Acknowledging that the statistics from Baird for undergraduate admission had been misreported by an undetermined amount for an undetermined number of years, the rating service indicated its concern that statistics for its graduate programs may also have been misreported. A spokesperson for US News indicated to our reporter that they anticipate completing their review of the University in time for their next release of school and program rankings.

The University's President, Thomas Hansen, could not be reached by BFP for comment. However, his wife, Jacqueline Hansen, who, in an astounding display of arrogance, had been appointed Interim Director of Admissions, labeled the US News suspension, "A gross overreaction to the missteps of a single rogue individual. US News should not be faulting Baird University for the misguided actions of a former VP for Admissions," she continued. "Moreover," she said, "what the former Director had done, was probably not different from what is going on at other schools that are doing their best to balance their diversity recruiting efforts and commitments to admission based on merit."

In subsequent comment, a spokesperson for the University indicated to BFP that the Interim Director "was merely seeking to explain the failures of the previous VP for Admissions," and that her remarks "did not reflect the official policy of Baird University." The spokesperson stated, "The University understands the desire of US News to review its rankings of Baird and looks forward to a quick resumption of its rankings. The University does not expect that the review will materially alter its ranking by US News."

***

In the face of the Baird's downgraded debt rating and the *US News* suspension of the School's academic rating, President Hansen called an emergency meeting for his ELT. Following David Knight's resignation, Jacqueline Hansen attended representing Admissions.

"Good morning, everyone, and thanks, once again, for coming on short notice. I just felt that, with all that's gone on recently, we should all touch base and see if there are any adjustments we need to make.... My own view," he coached, "is that this is all temporary... just a temporary setback... and that we'll get through it in the next year or so."

This opening remark was greeted by silence and furtive glances among the group, each hoping that someone else might take the lead in responding.

Provost May, dutifully, supported Hansen's position. "I think you're right, Tom.... Of course, we've had a handful of faculty resignations since this all started, and we'll probably have a few more, but we can use the resignations to bring in some new blood."

"Yes," Hansen concurred. "The resignations now could actually be helpful in the short run on the financial side. We can fill the vacancies with temporary lecturers at much lower cost."

"But won't that just add to our rankings problem?" Martin asked. "I thought places like *US News*, looked at reliance on lecturers as a negative factor in their rankings."

"Yes, yes.... Of course they do, Heather," Hansen bristled. "But, as I said, this is going to be just a temporary adjustment. So, I think we're going to be okay on the academic side.... Isn't that right Jim?"

"Yes, I think we will be," the Provost responded, his demeanor evincing his discomfort.

"Hold on for a second." Martin had reached the limit of her patience. "What are we doing here, now...? It sounds like we're just trying to reassure ourselves that the situation's not serious... that we're trying to sweep it all under the rug.... I don't think that's a good idea, Tom. We need to take this seriously... and figure out what to do about it.... I think it's going to require some very hard choices."

"I'm not surprised to hear such a negative view from you, Heather.... But why don't you go ahead and tell us what you have to say?" President Hansen responded with obvious disdain.

"Where to begin..." Martin contemplated, ignoring the President's scorn. "Maybe I'll just start with the effect of the School's credit rating. Our downgrade is going to increase our borrowing cost by about 50 basis points... half of one percent, that is.... Now that's about $300 thousand per year on our outstanding $60 million of borrowing."

"Well, that sounds pretty trivial to me, Heather," the Provost interjected, still trying to run interference for Hansen. "No more than the cost of one or two well-paid faculty member, depending on the discipline."

"Well, I agree with you Jim... that, by itself, maybe it's not so important. But it actually takes about $6 million in endowment to support $300 thousand in annual spending. It's not a big number, but it's coming at a time when we're already overspending our endowment and where, because of all that's happened, it looks like we should expect a substantial decline in giving and even rescission of some gifts that already have been promised."

"What do you think, Jack?" Martin asked of the School's VP for Advancement, the only member of the ELT she felt might be somewhat supportive of her view.

"Actually," Richardson responded, "I think Heather may be right to be concerned. We've already taken a pretty big hit to our endowment, and it does look like our donations are going to be down quite a bit compared to last year.... We're beginning to see that some of the donors we've been able to rely on in the past are now saying they need to rethink their philanthropic plans."

"Well, we all know that the impact on our endowment is going to be negative," Hansen deflected. "But I doubt that it'll be as bad as you seem to be making out, Jack. Can you give us some sort of ball-park estimate of the impact?"

"I can try... but please don't hold me to it," Richardson responded. "Maybe you recall from our first meeting of the year that we started with about $650 million in endowment. And our spending rate last year was about eight percent, or $52 million.... While eight percent is unsustainably high, our actual spending this year is likely to be closer to $60 million. And it could be even more next year, once the new admissions policies kick in. So, even if we're able to hold things flat, so that new gifts and rescissions of promised gifts just cancel out, we'll probably still take a ten percent hit to the endowment... so down to about $600 million... or a bit lower...."

"Normally, $600 million should support about $30 million in annual spending," he continued. "So that suggests that we should be looking for a way to cut annual spending by about $25 million."

"You must be kidding, Jack!" the Provost exclaimed. "There's no way we can cut our annual expenditures by $25 million without taking some kind of drastic action."

"But Jack's right," Heather picked up. "If we don't do that, our financial situation is just going to get worse and worse."

"Well, maybe we just need a bit more time to turn things around," the Provost argued.

"But what would be the impetus for its turning around, Jim?" Heather challenged. "Are you just saying that maybe someone will come along and solve our problem for us by making a huge gift to the School?" she asked rhetorically. "I don't see much likelihood of that... especially to a school that's so clearly in trouble."

"Moreover, I wonder if Jack may actually be understating the seriousness of the problem," Martin picked up. "We haven't even talked about enrollment yet. Maybe Jacqueline can update us on how student applications are going.... I'm especially concerned that the change to loan free aid is probably going to add to our financial problems, and I'd like to know if there are enough full-tuition international applicants to offset."

"I see..." the Interim Director struggled for a satisfactory response. "Well... you all know that I'm new to this... and I've barely had time to move into my office, so I can't tell you very much. But I have to say that my staff are telling me that applications from students who would need significant financial aid are up substantially. And it appears that our recent developments have led to a number of well-qualified students withdrawing their applications and to a drop off in applications from international students. My staff seems to think the new admissions policies are not going to work out as well as we all had hoped.... Now, we could get some benefit from the early decision option... but not for next year, since that policy doesn't take effect for the coming academic year. On top of everything, my staff are also saying that they think inquiries about early decision are much lower than what they had projected."

"So," said Martin, "I think we can infer that the financial situation next year is likely to be even worse that what Jack was suggesting. And, next year there'll be about twice as many students on loan-free aid because both first- and second-year students will be covered."

"And I want to say something about the faculty resignations," Martin continued as Hansen glared at her. "I think some of you know Krista Novikova, in Economics. I only mention her because she's a friend and she's one of the faculty members who've announced they'll be leaving. A few days ago, Krista told me she was planning to leave, and while I tried to talk her out of it, she laid out the case that, in her opinion Baird is in serious trouble academically. Frankly, since she's not involved in Baird Administration, I was shocked at her perceptiveness as to what has been going on and where we're headed.... But I think she got most of it right, and my guess is that the other faculty members who are leaving have also figured it out."

"Well, I'm sorry you're losing your friend, Heather," Hansen patronized. "But as I noted earlier, these departures will help us to address the financial concerns that you and Jack have been talking about."

"Actually, I think that's a bit too short-sighted," Heather blurted, recognizing that her retort would not go unpunished. "I think the people who're leaving are the very ones who are responsible for Baird's academic success. In the sciences, they're the ones who are most capable of bringing in grant dollars. In economics, they're the ones responsible for educating the students who become the future business leaders and entrepreneurs who eventually will become important supporters of the School. Lecturers simply can't do what these faculty members do.... Moreover, some of the tenured faculty members who remain behind are going to be the ones who don't have good alternatives... either they're in fields where faculty positions are rare, or they're the ones who should not have been tenured in the first place."

"Let's take your concerns about our use of lecturers offline, Heather," Hansen fumed. "But I'll concede that you're making it sound more serious than I was thinking," Maybe we should spend a bit of time discussing the kinds of things we might consider doing to address your concerns."

"So what do you recommend, Heather?" he asked, putting the spotlight on her directly.

Martin was taken off guard. "I'm not sure I'd call anything I might suggest for consideration a recommendation," she deflected to buy time, "but a few possibilities have occurred to me. Maybe we should either cancel or significantly postpone the admissions and financial aid initiatives... maybe keep the early decision option, but at least delay the rest. I think we might need to postpone any of the capital projects we have on the drawing board. We can probably live for a few more years without asbestos abatement, and with the hit we're going to take to our enrollments, we're probably not going to need more dorms or offices for a while.... I think we might need to take a very hard look at some of our departments from a financial perspective. There seem to be quite a few where classes have very low enrollment... too low to make them economically viable, unless the department has enough grant support to offset."

"We also have a number of what you might call legacy non-academic programs. Our last president had a bug for trying to promote entrepreneurship in the local economy. He built a separate administrative department under his direction to pursue that objective. Nothing really came of those efforts. But, in spite of that, we still have an office and several staff members devoted to an initiative that clearly hasn't worked."

"And I think we may want to triage our Ph.D. programs," she continued. "In some cases, we seem to be paying students to pursue Ph.D. in areas where they can't realistically hope to find employment. I've never understood why we do that.... Maybe it's so the faculty in those areas will have something to do, or a supply of free labor to help them with their research."

"Nice work, Heather... I see that you've managed to step on pretty much everyone's toes with that list..." Hansen observed. "But let's see what others think."

"Well, many of those suggestions relate to the faculty," the Provost picked up. "I think those are all non-starters.... We can't tell the Baird faculty that we're planning to shutter some departments or close down some Ph.D. programs. There'd be absolute rebellion and faculty demands for all of our resignations."

"That's true," the President joined in. "Not only that, but several of those departments have champions on the Board of Trustees. So the Trustees are not going to go for it, either. I think we can forget about those ideas."

"The Board is also not going to agree to go back on the new admissions and financial aid policies they just approved," Hansen asserted, without disclosing that he was really the one behind them and with no intent to propose such a move to them.

"I think just the capital improvements and the legacy initiatives cuts might be worth considering," Richardson picked up. "But those are probably not going to work either, at least not many of them. In some cases, the capital projects are supported by donors, and we can't go back on them, and the local economy entrepreneurship initiative also had a lot of donor support at the start. Even though that support is now gone, abandoning the initiative would be seen as reneging on promises the School made to those donors."

"So, where does that leave us?" the President asked. "Are there other things we should be considering?

As no one responded, Hansen concluded, that the Team should just try to tighten their belts and do the best that they could to curtail spending without doing anything too dramatic or too likely to attract attention. "I'm not sure what I'll report to the Board when we meet next week."

Martin was disappointed in the meeting. Krysta apparently had been right. The School did not have the will to save itself.

CHAPTER 40

THE DEPARTMENT

The mood was somber when the Economics Department faculty gathered for their final meeting of the academic year. The faculty were stunned by Prof. Novikova's announcement of her plans to leave Baird. To avoid having to field awkward well-wishes, she had decided not to attend the meeting. In light of tenure having been denied to Sean Lopez, and the Administration's unwillingness to appoint a finance professor to one of the Jennings endowed professorships, the Department would have no tenure-track faculty members in finance after next year. Ironically, when George Jennings learned of the problems the School was having with its credit rating and *US News* ranking, he had reversed his decision to fund the two chairs in economics. The reversal came too late to stop the appointments of Barron and Granville to the faculty. Both had already resigned their existing appointments at other schools and had accepted the offers from Baird.

"This has been a difficult year," Department Chair Hill began, striking the neutral tone he had always sought to maintain in his administrative role despite his personal frustrations over the events of the past year, "and I'm sure we're all looking forward to some time away to decompress. But we do still have a few things we need to take up."

"First, we need to think about what we should be doing about finance. I know we still have you here next year, Sean, and that we can count on you to do what you can to maintain the finance program.... But you're only one person and it's particularly hard for an assistant professor to deal with all of the staffing issues that have to be addressed if we're going to continue to offer a comprehensive program, with an undergraduate major and a graduate concentration in finance.... Fortunately, Professor Novikova's two Ph.D. students are going to follow her to her next appointment and will finish up their degrees there, so we don't need to worry about maintaining the finance Ph.D. program for a while."

"My question to all of you is how do you think we should handle this? Should we close down the finance Ph.D. program permanently? And the same for the undergraduate major and finance concentration? Alternatively, should we suspend any of those programs? And, if we decide not to suspend, how should we go about staffing the necessary classes?"

"I say we close them all down," said Sarks, seizing the opportunity he perceived to raise interest in his own courses.

"We obviously can't do that, Cory," Noach responded. "I don't think your suggestion is even serious.... I know that at times, some of us are at odds with the finance group... especially like this year, when the Administration effectively pitted us against each other pointlessly over faculty hiring. And sometimes we're all envious of the salaries commanded in the market for finance faculty. But realistically, I think our finance offerings are important to all of us. Many of our undergraduate students become econ majors because of their interest in finance. Even those who decide to major in finance end up taking a lot of other economics courses. So that's good for all of us."

"I'm offended, Noach," Sarks responded arrogantly. "Under no circumstances would I make a non-serious proposal. Moreover, I strongly disagree with your unsubstantiated claim that finance offerings draw students into our economics courses.... So, let me be clear.... I move to permanently close down the undergraduate finance major."

After a pause of several seconds during which no one

spoke, Prof. Noach responded, "In the interest of moving this discussion forward, I'll second Prof. Sarks' motion, though I don't intend to support it."

Annoyed by Sarks' attempt to cut-off and shape discussion around his motion, Hill recognized that the Department was compelled to follow procedure. "A motion to discontinue the undergraduate finance major has been made and seconded," he stated. "Any further discussion?"

"I agree with Jamie," Prof. Stewart joined in. "I think if we were to close down our finance programs, we'd lose majors across the board and we'd end up losing mainstream economics faculty lines. So, I'm opposed to the motion."

"I suppose we might think about cutting back on the finance offerings in the short run," Noach continued, "maybe even letting students count more of our macroeconomics and econometrics courses toward the finance major for a while."

"That comment is out of order, Mr. Chair," objected Sarks. "The motion on the table is to close down the program, not to cut back on finance offerings.

"I don't see how we can offer the finance curriculum without a senior faculty member," Faquhir argued. "We need to demand that the Administration authorize a senior faculty hire immediately so that we can start the search over the summer and fill the position quickly. If they won't provide the faculty line, I agree with Cory that we should shut the program down.... And now is a perfect time to do so, since we won't have any core finance faculty after next year."

"I'm afraid that demanding a new faculty line isn't realistic Larry," Hill responded. "As we all know, this is a very difficult time for the School financially. I don't see any way that they're going to authorize a line."

"Well, they should," Faquhir argued. "After all, it was because of the Administration's interference in our search that we didn't hire in finance and that now we've lost Novikova. If they won't agree, I think we should go to the Academic Senate and call for a vote of no confidence in the Provost."

"I'm sorry to say this, but that's ridiculous, Larry," Stewart interjected. "The Senate's too political to do anything useful, and they won't be sympathetic at all to a demand to hire in finance since they all think finance salaries are too high."

"By that you mean 'higher than theirs," Faquhir responded. "They're just going to have to recognize that the salaries are market driven."

"I think we're getting off the point," Hill preempted, recognizing that Prof. Faquhir was just venting his frustration and that the things he was proposing would not accomplish anything. "I know we're all feeling much the same way. But I don't think we're going to get anywhere trying to blame the Administration... and trying to remove the Provost seems likely to just invite retaliation. I think what we need now is to focus on how to best deal with the difficulties we're facing."

"I agree," Stewart joined in. "We're just wasting time with all this talk of threats and no-confidence votes. We need to focus on what's good for the Department and for our students."

"Yes," Sarks piled on. "We are just wasting our time. We've said that without staffing, we can't sustain the finance program and that we can't get the Administration to agree to further staffing. It seems that the choice is obvious. We need to close down the program. Mr. Chair, I call the question."

In the ensuing vote, Sarks's motion failed overwhelmingly, as most faculty members viewed it as non-serious showboating.

"Well, Mr. Chair," Sarks picked up after the vote count was announced, "if you're not willing to close down the finance programs and you're not willing to take on the Administration about our need to hire in finance, I sincerely believe you should consider foregoing the teaching release you get as Department Chair and taking on direct responsibility for maintaining the integrity of the finance curriculum and offerings. You could use the release to teach one of the finance courses, yourself."

"I know it's not my area, but I'd be willing to help out," offered Trevor Butler, seeking to score points with Hill. The year was nearly over, and he still had not been able to publish his dissertation research.

"That wouldn't be a good idea, TB," interjected Prof. Kaur. "At this point you need to focus on publishing your research. You don't need the distraction of having to prepare and teach a course outside your field."

"I agree with Nadir, TB," the Chair joined in. "And I'm not sure it'd be a good idea for me to teach finance, Cory," Hill responded, seeking to foreclose the direction Sarks was trying to promote. "As you know, finance is not my area, either. If we want to maintain the finance curriculum, I think we're all going to have to pitch in, in some way."

"Well, even if you don't actually teach part of the curriculum," Sarks responded, "It's obvious to us all that you're the person in the Department who's in the best position to find lecturers to cover the classes."

"And, sorry to say this, Sean," continued Sarks, who had a well-established track record of pressuring junior faculty members, "but now that the University has decided to deny your tenure, there's no real justification for the School to keep you on a teaching load that leaves so much time for research. You could easily teach six courses per year, instead of the normal four-course load of someone who's on track for tenure. You'd still have some time for research compared to the normal loads at teaching schools, and your teaching more courses would buy the Department time to work on a permanent solution."

"Hold on just a minute," interjected Stewart, who was used to hearing such proposals from Sarks. "We've had other junior faculty members who've been denied tenure, but I can't recall even one time when those faculty members were asked to take on additional teaching in their terminal year."

"That may be true, Nicole," Faquhir joined in. "And normally I'd agree with you. But this is a unique time. I'm afraid that if we don't want to suspend the undergraduate major, I don't see any solution that doesn't involve Sean teaching a few more sections of finance."

The Department Chair was feeling responsible for the way the meeting was going, how no senior member of the faculty seemed willing to step up and help out, and how some members of the group seemed to have turned on Sean Lopez. "Let me think about this a bit," he requested of the group. "I don't want to impose such a heavy burden on Sean. I'll think about it, and maybe re-evaluate whether I can pick up some of the slack myself, or find someone to join us temporarily."

"The other thing we need to discuss today, is somewhat related," he transitioned. "It seems that campus Administration is concerned that we might experience a decline in enrollments campus-wide."

"For which they deserve full responsibility..." Faquhir interjected.

"Yes... well... in any case, the Provost is asking every department to think about what we can do to attract additional enrollment next year. So, can we give some thought to that?"

"I suppose one thing that might be helpful is if we were to invite prospective applicants to visit our classes when they are on campus to kick the tires. They could see some of us in action, see how the classes go…" Prof. Kaur trailed off.

"No way I'm letting anyone who's not enrolled in my classes to attend," Sarks countered. "It would disrupt the flow too much. It's already hard enough to cover what I need to without something like that going on."

"While I don't agree with everything Cory just said," Faquhir remarked, "I do agree with him that we shouldn't be letting prospective students into our classes. I think it could easily backfire. You need to remember that, no matter how highly we think of ourselves, we're not all the world's best teachers. An applicant might easily have a more positive attitude toward Baird based on the classes he or she imagines rather than the ones that actually happen."

"I suppose you're right, Larry," Kaur joined in. "But maybe we can pick a few of us who are known to be good in the classroom and direct applicants into their classes. Maybe Dan, for example."

Before Edwards could respond, Sarks reacted. "You know it's just his English accent and his GQ styling that draws the students, especially the co-eds. Not all of us are so blessed. I say we either all do it, or none of us does."

"So, I guess that's another thing I'll need to think about," Hill concluded, wanting to depersonalize the discussion. "Larry may be right that it might do more harm than good…. Any other suggestions of how we might be able to help out?"

"Maybe it's time to think about modernizing our curriculum," Noach said. "It seems to me that it's been a long time since we took a hard look at our offerings. Maybe we should set up a committee to go over the offerings and figure out what's obsolete, what needs to be updated, and what needs to be added."

"I support Jamie's proposal," Sarks commented. "I know I've been keeping my own classes up to date, but I'm sure that many of you haven't done so. We probably still teach Phillips Curves in Intermediate Macro. Does anyone actually think that approach works?

"Well, I don't see the need for such a formal process," Kaur commented. "I think we all do what we think we should to keep our courses relevant and timely.... And in accounting, we've added courses to keep up with the changing needs of our students. For example, we just added a course on using blockchain technology for auditing."

"Really... blockchains?" Stewart exclaimed in surprise. "What does that have to do with auditing?"

"We think it's a serious and important new development. Blockchains for cryptocurrencies essentially audit financial records for free. It's not difficult to imagine them taking over most audit functions for businesses and doing so at low cost. So it's something accounting students need to know about when they design their own careers.... But the point I was trying to make is that we don't need a formal review of the curriculum. I think we all try to keep our classes relevant."

Prof. Koopman, who had remained silent throughout this discussion, could no longer hold back. "Why is it that every time we go through an episode of low student demand, we blame the curriculum...? It's nonsense! Even when student interest in majoring in economics drops nationally, our response here seems always to be that we can fix the problem by revising our curriculum. How naïve is that...? I can tell you from decades of experience here that messing with the curriculum does nothing... absolutely nothing... for enrollment. Yet it's always what we, the faculty, turn to."

"I think it's like the old joke about why a professor who lost a quarter while walking on a dark street was searching for it under a streetlight. He said the light was better under the streetlight. I think we're doing the same thing.... The entire school is facing a decline because of administrative blunders. Yet we're looking to address it be reviewing our curriculum. Give me a break!"

"Reardon's right," said Edwards. "It's not going to work... just a big time-suck."

"If we want to seriously consider what attracts students to a private university like ours," he continued, "I think the curriculum in any area of study has very little to do with it. I'm pretty sure that the school social network... the students, the alums, the sports teams, the clubs and other social groups, the employers who regularly hire our students... that has at least as much to do with a student's choice of where to go to school as does our teaching.... And, right now, Baird doesn't look so good on that front.... We've had a steady stream of student protests and unrest, an admissions scandal, the suspension of our US News rankings... It's delusional to believe that we can compensate for all of that by tweaking our curriculum."

The department meeting continued for a while, with further discussion of curriculum review, but no other suggestions to boost enrollments at Baird. The group finally broke up with no commitment to do anything. Uncharacteristically, there was no call for a post-meeting happy hour.

CHAPTER 41

BOARD OF TRUSTEES

In the week following his meeting with the ELT, President Hansen continued to reflect on what he should say to the Board. After meeting with his VP for Advancement and conferring with Jacqueline about the admissions and enrollment concerns, he had come grudgingly to the conclusion that Heather Martin was more-or-less right. Something more than belt tightening was going to be needed. That said, he did not want to become the scapegoat for the School's financial problems. But at the same time, he did not want to give up on the enrollment and financial aid initiatives that he still felt would be his entre to moving to a more highly-ranked school. It was now becoming apparent that the School would need to make serious financial cuts or else face continued worsening of its financial condition. His agenda for the meeting gradually became clear to him... to find a way to preserve the enrollment and aid initiatives and, at the same time, to protect his own position at Baird.

In his final meeting with the Board after the Spring Commencement activities, Hansen felt his best strategy would be to simply lay out the financial problem the School was facing and deflect potential criticism away from himself. He could refer back to David Knight's falsifying of admissions stats and suggest to the Board that Heather Martin had failed to keep him and the Trustees fully apprised of the School's worsening financial situation. Hopefully, the Trustees would be looking to cover their own culpability, see the situation as a challenge, and ask for some serious restructuring, or maybe he could nudge them in that direction. If he could position such a restructuring as something the Board had demanded, perhaps he could deflect responses from faculty and students on to them and protect his own position with both the Board and the faculty.

The Board meeting was to take place in the private dining room of the Faculty Club. After the lunch dishes had been cleared and the room had been reconfigured as a small conference venue, Board Chair Alexander, called the meeting to order. "Thank you all, once again, for attending and participating in this year's Commencement exercises this morning. We all recognize that Commencement is a big deal for the students who are graduating and for their parents. It's important for them all to see us there to congratulate them for their achievements and to show our support for the University."

"Now, turning to our agenda, we're all aware of how difficult this year has been for Baird. In light of all that's happened, I thought it might be a good idea to suspend our regular order and just take some time for an open discussion with President Hansen."

"Perhaps I can pose the first question to you, Tom.... It's about the mess-up with admissions." Conveniently ignoring the fact that he had previously discussed this fully with the President and had even participated in the termination negotiation with the former VP for Admissions, Alexander continued, "I know that some of us on the Board are having trouble understanding how the problem of falsifying admission and enrollment statistics could go unnoticed by your administration for so long.... Maybe you can explain."

Hansen had hoped for more cover from Alexander, but, in the end, was unsurprised by the Board Chair's apparently adversarial tone, which he viewed largely as theater for the benefit of the others in the meeting. His stance would give Hansen an opportunity to explain and then when it appeared that Alexander had accepted his explanation, the rest of the Board would probably follow like sheep. It really was all just theatrics.

"Yes, of course, Trevor.... I'm sure many of you know Dave Knight from some of our previous meetings. David had been here for quite some time and had been our Director of Admissions for at least the last seven or eight years... so, before my time. He's always had an outstanding reputation for doing a great job of managing admissions and enrollment. In fact, that was one area of administration that never raised any concerns with anyone. We also got no red flags about potential problems. The SAT scores that were being reported were generally rising slightly over time, as we all thought they should be doing."

"Now, all that said, I do have to mention that I'm not sure David was doing anything much different from what other schools have been doing for years. They all have tactics for managing the statistics they report to *US News*. They all exclude certain students from the averages they report. And the reporting requirements of *US News* are not entirely clear. It seems that David may just have gotten a bit too aggressive in what he was reporting."

"So, Tom, I think you're telling us that there was no reason to suspect a problem with the reported figures and that maybe Baird was just an unfortunate example for other schools," Alexander summarized for the benefit of the others on the Board.

"Yes, that's true, but I do want to add that we're not going to allow this to happen again. We've put a formal audit process in place to make sure that whatever we report complies with *US News* guidelines.

"I can accept all of that, Tom," interjected a Trustee whose daughter had recently graduated from Baird. "But I'm more concerned with the long-run reputational harm to the

School and its graduates. How long is it going to be before *US News* resumes their rankings of the School, and what do you expect to be the impact on the rankings at that point?"

Although he had no clear answers for the Trustee and no evidence to support his claims, Hansen responded, "We're working hard to satisfy *US News* and get the rankings restored as quickly as possible. Based on what I've seen, the impact on our ranking should be slight."

"Personally, I'm more concerned about future enrollments, Tom," interposed a Trustee who had graduated from Baird with a degree in economics and had risen to the position of Executive Vice President of a major investment bank. "What do you expect will be the impact on future enrollments?"

Seeing the opening he'd been anticipating and had prepared for, Hansen responded. "You're right, of course, that the episode is going to impact future enrollments for a while. We've been tracking, and, compared to last year, our applications are down somewhat, and some applications have been withdrawn."

"And how about applicant quality? Is that holding up okay?" the Trustee asked.

"Well, actually, that also seems to be down somewhat."

"So, in other words, Baird is either going to have to enroll fewer students or enroll weaker students," the Trustee inferred.

"At this point, we're not sure." Hansen responded, though the evidence he'd seen of negative impact was incontrovertible. "Possibly a little of both."

"But isn't it going to be costly for the School to enroll fewer students?" the Trustee pressed.

"In the short run, yes. But it seems better to bend a little on admissions standards for a while and take a smaller hit to matriculations than to try to maintain student quality as we work through this. We'd take a bigger hit to the endowment if we were to do that." Alexander joined in.

"Well, maybe we should revisit the admissions and financial aid policies we approved at our last meeting," the Trustee pressed. "Do we still have time to undo those?"

"Actually," Alexander responded, "I think that could make things worse... more negative press... and it'd be embarrassing for all of us... make us look like we don't know what we're doing."

"Well, maybe you don't, Trevor," the Trustee sniped.

Alexander ignored the barb, but turned to Hansen, already knowing the answer he would receive. "What do you think, Tom? Would it help to reverse our earlier decisions?"

"Not as far as I can see. The policies we have in place are helping keep our applicant pool up. In fact, I wish we could move ahead with the Early Decision option sooner, but that's not possible the way the application cycle works." Hansen sought to avoid telling the Trustees that there had been a shift toward a larger fraction of applicants needing financial aid; that international applications were down; or that inquiries about Early Decision were well below what had been anticipated.

"I'm thinking this problem is deeper than just the drop in enrollments," the Trustee persisted. "We all know about the credit rating downgrade, but I'd like to know how we're doing with our fund-raising efforts."

"It's true," Hansen responded, "that we've had some setbacks on that front. Some of our promised gifts haven't come through yet and alumni giving is off compared to this time last year. We're prospecting for a few major gifts. But we all know that the timing on those is always uncertain."

"So what's the bottom line, Tom...? How big of a hit is

the School going to take?" the Trustee demanded.

"Well, as you know, anything I say now is pretty speculative, but as you've seen in our briefing materials, our CFO is saying she thinks the endowment could be off by about 10 percent next year," Hansen responded, not telling the Trustees about the pressure he'd applied to Martin to be as upbeat as possible.

"Only 10 percent," exclaimed a trustee, who, after completing a degree in literature, had gone on to become a successful novel writer. "If it's so little, we can make it up in a year, can't we?"

"Unfortunately, it doesn't work like that," the investment banker countered. "With enrolments down, the endowment down, and no major gifts on the horizon, I can say from experience with clients in other settings, that the School is headed for the rocks unless some serious corrective actions are taken."

Hansen was pleased that the discussion had come to this without the need for him to try to steer the talk. Based on the discussion, he should be able to go forward with some downsizing of expensive programs and a selective moratorium on hiring. He chose to remain silent.

"We need to cast off the excesses that are going to drag the School down," the Trustee continued.

"Like what," asked the novelist. "What do you consider to be excess?"

"Anything that's a drag on the rest of the School," the I-banker continued. "But I haven't done any analysis, so I don't know what that is. Maybe President Hansen can tell give us some idea."

"Well, if the Board is asking me to do so, I can look into it and come up with some specific suggestions..." Hansen responded. "I should point out that Baird wouldn't be the only

School looking at cutting programs due to budgetary issues. It's true that our setbacks this year have made the issue more pressing, but we're all facing increasingly intense competition from online programs... and the needs of our students are changing faster than our institutions are changing in response."

"Another private university, about the same size as Baird but with a larger endowment recently announced their plan to cut 40 percent of their academic programs. That school's planning to eliminate undergraduate degree programs in areas like philosophy, religion, theater, dance, and languages. They're also planning to drop graduate programs in such areas as fine arts, education, history, math, chemistry, and geosciences."

"You mean they're planning to abandon the liberal arts and core sciences?" the novelist asked. "How can they even think about such a thing and still call themselves a university?" he exclaimed.

"Well, not abandon, exactly," Hansen responded calmly. "They say they plan to keep the foundational courses. They're dropping the degree programs where they only graduate a handful of students each year and they claim that the overwhelming percentage of their students will not be affected by the move.... Perhaps we should consider a similar hard look at our programs."

"That sounds like just what the School needs to do to deal with the current crisis," the I-banker remarked.

"I disagree," the novelist retorted. "I don't see how any self-respecting private university could even think of doing such a thing!" Several other Trustees appeared to nod their support. "I think what this school needs to do is to redouble its efforts to raise funds from donors and to generate more grant support. I'm sure that if they worked harder at it, they could find a solution without cutting the programs that are the lifeblood of this university."

After further discussion with President Hansen, the Board decided to meet in executive session, without the President. Later that evening, the Board Chair contacted Hansen by phone.

"I'm sorry to say, Tom, that the Board is firmly against cutting academic programs in the arts and humanities for budgetary reasons.... As you know, a number of our Trustees have strong ties to the liberal arts and are unwilling to consider cuts in those areas. They're okay with your making some cuts in other areas, such as to the professional programs. Most board members seem to want you to work harder to direct students into liberal arts degrees and away from professional programs."

"But surely they understand that many of our students are concerned with employability after they graduate, and that they don't see liberal arts degrees as likely to be very helpful for that?"

"They do see that," Alexander responded, since he shared the sentiment of the Board, "but in their view... and mine, that misperception just reflects a failure of advising. Most of the Trustees realize that the purpose of undergraduate education is to create well-rounded and thoughtful adults, and that professional education should be reserved for graduate school. Keep in mind that many of the Trustees have liberal arts backgrounds themselves and have moved on to successful careers, often without any graduate training."

"Most of the Trustees are also strongly of the view that you should be able to deal with the budgetary problems with other kinds of cost cutting, and by a more aggressive effort to secure donations and grants.... Some members question whether Richardson is the right person to be leading the School's advancement efforts, and some insist that the Provost should be applying more pressure on faculty to produce and secure grants and to take on additional teaching."

"Of course we can try those things… and I'll think about whether we need to replace Richardson, but I'm not optimistic that we can cover the shortfall that way."

"Well, do what you can, Tom, and let's see how things go this coming year…. If things get worse, maybe the Board's attitude will soften."

"Oh, and Tom," Alexander continued. "One other thing…. There was pressure from some of the Trustees for the Board to begin looking for your replacement. Ultimately, that position didn't gain traction, except with a few. The others seem to want to follow their normal practice of allowing your five-year term to play out and then to consider renewal or replacement…. So, I think you're on safe ground for now, but you probably do need to show some results over the next year or so."

"Anyway, that's about it from today's meeting, Tom. Now, I need to head for the airport, or I'll miss my flight home."

EPILOGUE

Baird University Trustees Consider Radical Restructuring Plan

The Baird Free Press has learned from anonymous source that earlier this summer, in their final meeting of the academic year, the Trustees of Baird University discussed a proposal to close down a number of the School's undergraduate and graduate degree programs. According to a source, the discussion was precipitated by recent events that pose a threat to the financial stability of the University.

In the spring of this year, the campus was rocked by discovery that its Admissions office had been falsely reporting student enrollment data to US News for years. When the fraud was discovered, US News suspended its ranking of Baird University pending a full investigation that has yet to be completed. Anticipating that the suspended rating could adversely affect student enrollment for the coming year, and possibly longer, major credit rating agencies have downgraded the University's debt issues. Our source indicates that the scandal has also negatively impacted donor support for the University.

When the Free Press learned of this discussion, our reporter reached out to several of the School's Trustees for comment. Although responses were guarded, we have been able to confirm that the trustees were considering closing down a number of low-enrollment degree programs, predominantly in the liberal arts.

After initially declining to comment, Baird University President, Thomas Hansen, described the Board's discussion as "purely academic." Hansen stated that "every university must be sensitive to the changing needs of its students," and that "occasionally, it can become necessary for a school to restructure some aspects of its curriculum. However," Hansen said, "after careful review, the Baird Trustees had concluded that no programmatic adjustments are warranted."

***

At the start of the fall term, consistent with its long-standing practice, Baird University held its opening convocation. Interim President May strolled across campus, following the same path that Hansen had followed the year before. In a hastily called mid-summer meeting on Zoom, the Board had appointed May to the position of Interim President following the hasty and unexpected departure of Thomas Hansen. It turned out that Hansen's plan to use Baird as a springboard had worked, but not as well as he had hoped. He'd been offered the presidency of a small liberal arts college that was interested in implementing some of the same kinds of admissions and enrollment initiatives as Baird had done under Hansen's leadership. That college had been willing to overlook the issues with misreporting of SAT scores and campus unrest, ascribing those problems to others in the Baird Administration who had been appointed prior to Hansen's assuming the presidency. Expecting that it would not be long before the full extent of the problems became apparent to the Baird Trustees, Hansen had decided that acting quickly was his best course of action.

Interim President May, who had also retained his position as Provost, gave much the same opening speech as Hansen had given the prior year. There were, however, noticeably fewer faculty members in the procession and on the dais, and there were fewer students and families in the audience. Faced with the unwillingness of most liberal arts faculty to give a keynote speech at the event, the organizers turned to newly hired Economics Professor, Barron, who spoke energetically on the dangers posed by global climate change, ending by urging the new students to use their time at Baird to "make a difference."

In contrast to previous convocations, attendees this time found that they had to make their way past a small group of faculty members and students who were protesting the Administration for threatening to close down degree programs in the liberal arts, a concern that had not resolved with Hansen's departure, despite May's attempts to placate and reassure the faculty.

***

Early in the fall term, Joseph Gardener cancelled one of his classes so that he could attend a Physics conference in Vienna. As he spent the day in academic sessions at the conference, his wife, Jennifer Morris visited the local sites. She spent the morning strolling through the atrium of the Schmetterlinghaus, admiring its many species of butterfly and the atrium garden. After wandering past the churches around Stephansplatz, Jenn stopped for a late lunch at a restaurant near the Danube, and then returned to the conference hotel by wandering through the Wiener Stadtpark. That evening, she joined Joey and some of his physics colleagues for cocktails, and the two of them had dinner for two at the rooftop restaurant of their hotel, before returning to their room. The turmoil at Baird never came up.

***

At its first meeting of the academic year, the Academic Senate entertained a motion for a vote of no confidence in the University Interim President, accusing him of continuing the agenda of the previous president and calling for his resignation or termination. After lengthy discussion, including a pained response by the May, the faculty members voted overwhelmingly that they had lost confidence in both the former President and, by extension, in him.

Upon receiving the vote of the faculty, Trevor Alexander, the Chair of the Board of Trustees responded that the school restructuring discussion had not been initiated by the Interim President, that the discussion was one that would occur in the normal course of business at virtually any university, that the Board was firmly committed to maintaining and supporting all of its existing degree programs, and that in executive session the Board had reaffirmed its earlier decision to appoint the Provost to serve as Interim President.

The faculty fumed at what they considered to be the arrogant and dictatorial tone of the Board Chair's response to their motion and demanded that the Administration and the Board recommit to the long-standing tradition of shared governance, including that no programmatic initiatives would be undertaken without faculty support.

***

As was their practice, the Executive Leadership Team held their first meeting of the academic year at the President's house, now occupied by the Provost acting in his capacity as Interim President. They had waited until a few weeks after the start of the term this year, hoping for a clearer picture of the School's financial situation.

There were no major surprises. Jacqueline Hansen, who was no longer serving as Interim Director of Admissions, had reported before her departure in mid-summer that the total number of enrolled students was expected to be down about twelve percent compared to the prior year. She conceded that it had been necessary to admit some weaker students to avoid an even more negative impact. Further, she reported, the need-blind admissions policy was on track to result in a reduction of net tuition per student, and the loan-free aid policy could be expected to result in an increase in financial aid provided by the School. In response to questions at a meeting just before her departure, she told the group that, based on information available at that time, international student enrollment could be expected to drop off considerably as a result of *US News*'s suspension of the School's ranking, dashing the hope that high enrollment of international students would help off-set the negative financial impact of the other initiatives. When asked about the prospect for some recovery in the next year, she told the ELT members that early decision enrollment was unlikely to exceed eight to ten percent next year, well below what the Board had hoped, further diminishing the School's financial prognosis.

Jack Richardson reported that the School was continuing to experience declining donor support and that it was unlikely that gifts in the next few years would be enough to offset expenses that needed to be covered from endowment.

Acting in his continuing role as Provost, Interim President May told the group that over the summer there had been a few more faculty resignations, mostly in areas where the School would need to search for replacements. Although the faculty had been concerned about the possibility of cuts to liberal arts programs, there had been no significant departures of faculty from those areas. The Interim President suggested that, while the Board had rejected cutting any degree programs, the University might still want to consider trying to downsize the faculties in some areas by offering buyouts to senior faculty and not replacing faculty members who decided to leave or retire.

Finally, May turned to the University CFO. "How do things look from your perspective, Frank?" he asked. In an abbreviated search, just before his own resignation, Hansen had appointed Frank Moore to be Vice President for Finance after Heather Martin's abrupt departure. During the summer, under continuing pressure from Hansen to window-dress the School's financial situation, Martin had ultimately concluded that there was no real hope that Baird could make a full recovery. After leaving Baird, she easily found employment at the investment banking firm where one of Baird's Trustees was a top-ranked partner.

"Well, we all know that we're in for a difficult year," Moore began. "Based on what you each are reporting, our endowment is going to be down by several million this year. It's hard to say how long that problem will persist. It could be just a transitory thing that we'll begin to recover from next year. Possibly it will take longer. I've got some staff working on a model, but we'll just have to see. For now, I'd say we just need to be careful about our expenditures… maybe avoid capital outlays we can defer… try to beef up recruitment of international students… things like that."

"So… no major adjustments, it seems," May summarized, still trying to come to terms with his new responsibilities but pleased that his new CFO was not going to challenge the financial direction of the School. He was glad that Hansen had succeeded in his efforts to pressure Martin into moving on without too much involvement by himself.

After further discussion, the meeting broke up. As was their tradition, the group joined their spouses on the patio for cocktails and a catered dinner.

***

At their first departmental meeting of the fall term, Department Chair Hill called the meeting to order. "We have several important matters to discuss today, and I'd like to begin with…"

"Point of order," Prof. Sarks interrupted. "Following Robert's Rules, we need to begin with approval of the minutes from the last meeting. In fact, I'm afraid you've been a bit careless about this Mr. Chairman. In several of our meetings last year, no minutes were even taken…. So we don't even have a record of our actions…. We do have the minutes from the meeting last fall, because I took them…. We, at least need to approve those minutes before we proceed."

"I was hoping to avoid having to confront the matter of minutes taking, Cory.... As you know, you and I have gone around on this matter several times now.... The problem, for the benefit of the others here, is that your draft minutes of that meeting are just not accurate. Instead, what you have written seems to be merely an attempt to backdoor your own personal preferences as to what happened in that meeting."

"I object to that characterization, Mr. Chair," Sarks responded. "In that meeting, you designated me Departmental Secretary, and, as Secretary, it's my sole responsibility to prepare the minutes."

"That's not accurate, Cory. In that meeting, you volunteered to take minutes, but that is not the same as you're having been appointed to the position of Departmental Secretary. We don't even have such a position in this department. Moreover, your responsibility in that meeting was to prepare a draft of the minutes, and to provide it to me. When you did that, I pointed out several inaccuracies and asked you to revise the draft accordingly, which you refused to do."

"Again, Mr. Chair, I object to your disparaging remarks," Sarks postured. "There are no inaccuracies in the minutes. They should now come before the Department faculty for approval."

"Not true, Cory. Just one example... in your description of our first vote, which was on the acceptability of disciplines for recruiting focus, your draft says that the Department voted to not consider candidates in finance or accounting.... Those of us who were in that meeting all know that is not what we decided. The vote was just on acceptability and all four areas received majority votes on that question."

"Clearly, it was my mistake to agree to your offer to take the minutes in that meeting.... I won't make that mistake again.... Now, since we couldn't even agree on a draft to bring to the Department, I believe it's best just to forego approval of the minutes from that meeting. And that's one reason I didn't bring up the need to take minutes in subsequent meetings last year."

"Mr. Chair, I resent your personal attacks. You need to stop bullying me. We should proceed with approval of the minutes."

"We're not going to do that, Cory. There are so many misstatements in your draft that we would be here for hours just trying to get a correct set of minutes for the Department to approve. In any case, the whole matter is moot now. We've moved ahead with the hiring so whatever we voted doesn't matter anymore."

"I understand that we have different views of what happened and that you don't think we need to resolve them," Sarks challenged. "But that is exactly the purpose of the minutes approval process as the first order of business in a faculty meeting. I insist that we follow proper procedure."

"That's it!" interjected Prof. Noach. "I've heard all I can take of this fakakta bullshit...! Our school is about to go under... and we're wasting our time on whether or not to approve the minutes of a year-old meeting.... Let's move along."

"Thank you, Jamie..." Hill responded. "So, as I was saying before we got onto this digression about the minutes..."

"Point of order," Sarks persisted. "Is the Chair planning to proceed without approval of the minutes, may I ask?"

"I am," Hill responded.

"In that case, the entire meeting is improper. I move to adjourn."

"We can't adjourn," Prof. Stewart protested. "We need to figure out how we're going to deal with the budget cuts and the drop-off in students."

"Mr. Chair, please explain to Prof. Stewart that my motion to adjourn is not debatable. It's time to vote."

"Okay, Cory, if that will satisfy you and we can end this obstruction, we can vote on the question of adjournment."

"Again, you insult, Mr. Chair. Since when is insisting on proper procedure obstructive?"

In the vote that ensued, the motion to adjourn was defeated with only one vote in favor.

"It's unfortunate to see that our Department has come to this, Mr. Chair. I'm afraid I can no longer participate." Whereupon Prof. Sarks closed his laptop and left the meeting.

"Well, it's unfortunate that Prof. Sarks has decided not to participate in today's meeting." The Chair began. "As you all know, we do have some important matters that we need to act on. Most critically, because of the drop-off in enrollments and the overspending of our endowment last year and anticipated this year, the Administration is asking all departments to seriously curtail spending. For that, we're going to need to take a hard look at faculty research and travel support, support for our Ph.D. program, and our teaching commitments."

"Let's start with research support. I'm open to suggestions as to where we should be making cuts… anyone?"

"Maybe we should try to prioritize," Nicole Stewart responded. "It seems to me that it's most important to make sure our untenured faculty members have adequate support. After all, their tenure decisions will ultimately depend on their research productivity and their professional involvement. How could we, in good conscience withhold research and travel support now and deny tenure later based on low research productivity? So I propose that we maintain the research commitments to our untenured faculty members. The rest of us, I believe, can get through this difficult time. I realize our productivity will suffer, but we should be able to make up for it later on."

"But what if there is no 'later on'?" Prof. Noach challenged. "I don't see how the School is going to be better off next year, or the year after that, or maybe ever…. We're all going to need to keep up our research or we'll be trapped here and go down with the School. So I'm not willing to give up my research support just to help the School hang on a bit longer."

"Right you are, Jamie," Prof. Edwards picked up. "We all know about common pool problems where we can see what might be good for the overall but makes each of us worse off. So I'm with Jamie on this…. We need to refuse cuts to our budgets."

"I have a suggestion," Prof. Koopman spoke up softly. "As you all know, I'll be retiring soon. Even as much in trouble as it is in, I think Baird can probably still outlive my time on the faculty. So, I'd be okay with giving up my share, even if others don't. Also, I've been under-spending my research budget for the last few years, so I have a bit of a surplus. I'm okay with giving that up, too. And maybe there are others who have surpluses that the School could claw back."

"Hold on a minute, Reardon, before you go giving away my reserve funds," countered Prof. Faquhir. "I've been accumulating surpluses for a few years now so that I'd have enough to go on a full-circuit roadshow, so to speak, presenting some of my latest research at conferences in a number of different countries. I'm going to need that money this year, so please don't start proposing clawbacks."

After further discussion, Hill summarized, "So what I'm hearing is that we all think it is important to support the research programs of our untenured faculty, but that most of us with tenure… except of Reardon, that is… are unwilling to accept cuts to our own research budgets and most of us would not agree to clawing back any unspent funds from prior years. Is that about right…?"

"Okay, then, hearing no dissent, I'll advise the Provost that, with the exception of Prof. Koopman, department faculty are unwilling to accept voluntary cuts to their research accounts.... There could, of course, still be mandated cuts, but there's nothing we can do about that at this level."

"What about Professors Barron and Granville?" Faquhir challenged. "I know they both got substantial research commitments as part of their appointments. Surly we should be pulling those back and treating them more like the rest of us."

"Why do we always call them Barron and Granville instead of using their given names?" Prof Kaur interjected.

"Who even knows their given names? They're never here." Noach quipped. "Maybe we just call them Thing 1 and Thing 2, like Dr. Seuss," he continued derisively, "or Mutt and Jeff".

"I thought that question might come up today, Larry, and I'm sorry that neither of them could make it to today's meeting. But I did speak with them both separately in anticipation of this discussion. As you might expect, they both turned to their contracts, and each insisted that the University honor its commitment to them. For the rest of us, our research support is just an internal record keeping within the Department. So if we were to agree to a cut of the total Department budget, the internal allocation of that cut would be up to us to manage."

"Then, maybe we should propose separate cuts for Barron and Granville anyway," Prof. Nikolaidis posed.

"Well, I did raise that as a possibility with Interim President May, but he indicated that he'd been advised by campus counsel that the contracts are binding and that there's nothing to do.... And neither of them is willing to agree to voluntary cuts."

"Speaking of them, where are they today?" asked Stewart. "I thought they'd be here for their first faculty meeting."

"Yes... well... I got an email earlier today from Professor Barron that he can't make it to our meeting because he's with a group of undergraduate students who are organizing a protest against investing portions of the University's endowment in companies involved in fossil fuels."

"Really?" exclaimed Edwards. "He's doing that even though his chair was endowed by a crude oil producer? That should go over bloody well."

"I wonder if he even realizes that restricting endowment investments in that way would be imprudent," commented Nadir Kaur. "I'm sure that if Krista were here she'd be telling us that dropping those investments would likely cause investment returns to be lower, not to mention the risks associated with underdiversification of the investment portfolio."

"What can I say?" Hill responded with a shrug.

"Well, speaking for myself, I can't say I'm surprised about Barron's priorities," Faquhir commented. "This is what happens when the administration gets too involved in faculty hiring."

"What about Granville?" Stewart asked. "Where's he?"

"Apparently, away on some consulting project for one of the big oil refiners," Hill responded. "He's been away for almost two weeks now."

"So, who's covering his classes?" Faquhir asked.

"That's just it," replied the Chair. "Apparently no one is. I've been seeing a steady stream of students the last few days, asking where he is, what they're supposed to be doing, even demanding tuition refunds for the course."

"We're screwed," Noach interjected. "If we can't even count on our own faculty to do what's right, how can we ever hope to turn things around?"

"I know," Hill responded. "I'll speak with him when he returns. Maybe it's out of character for him."

"Not what I heard," said Faquhir. "Several of his letter writers mentioned that he's away a lot."

"Well... let's move on," Hill said. "The Interim President and Provost is not going to be happy with our response to his request to cut back on our research and travel budgets, and, as I said, he still may insist on more aggressive cuts."

"Not if he wants to keep his job, he won't," Faquhir asserted. "Can you imagine the rebellion that would occur campus wide if he tried to cut those budgets...? And he can't just single out the Economics Department. He'd have to do it everywhere."

"I'm not so sure," Hill responded. "In any case, he's also asking for cuts to Ph.D. programs and use of lecturers. Maybe if we can offer something on that front, it'll help to smooth things over."

"So what are you thinking about the Ph.D. program?" Stewart asked.

"I think he'd like to see a moratorium on admitting new students to the program, and also for us to keep our existing Ph.D. students to not more than four years of support. He'd also like to see more of that support come in the form of compensated undergraduate teaching, as a way to reduce reliance on lecturers."

"That seems totally unrealistic to me," Edwards commented. "We need a steady stream of new students to assure the integrity and quality of the program."

"Really...?" Stewart objected. "Is it really so important to program integrity that we bring in students every year or is that just something you want to maintain for your own benefit… to support your research… or whatever? I think we should be able to have a moratorium on bringing in new students for a while. I'm less sure about holding the current students to four years of support. Most Ph.D. student in econ take five years to complete the degree. We'd be forcing our students into the job market too early, and they'd be more likely to fail in their first positions, or to not even finish their degrees. And we already use students in their last year as lecturers to give them some teaching experience. I don't think it would be fair to our undergrads for them to be taught by someone who's just in the first few years of the Ph.D. program."

"I agree with Nicole," Noach commented. "We can hold back on admitting new Ph.D. students for a year, but that's it."

"Well, I agree with Dan," said Larry Faquhir, who regularly taught in the Ph.D. program and would need to prepare for and teach other courses if admissions to the program were suspended. "I think we need to maintain the steady follow of students into the Ph.D. So I move that we advise the Provost that it's the intent of the Department to maintain its Ph.D. program without interruption, and that we don't see a way to cut back on or modify our financial support policies for Ph.D. students."

"So, you're saying that the Department should effectively take the position that the current financial problems were not created by the Department and that we're unwilling to help the School work through them. Is that right, Larry?" said Kaur. "That's not going to sit well, so I oppose the motion. I think, at a minimum, we need to suspend admission of students to the program. Otherwise, we don't look like team players."

"That's easy for you to say, Nadir, since we don't have a Ph.D. program in accounting…. In fact, given that we don't, I'm not even sure you should be voting on the question. Maybe you should recuse yourself or abstain."

"Actually, I think you're the one who should recuse yourself, Larry, since so much of your teaching is in Ph.D. seminars... and maybe Dan should, too."

"Can we stop the chest thumping, boys?" Nicole Stewart jumped in, out of character for her, but showing her frustration. "There was no second to Larry's motion, so maybe we can just tell May that we'll take a hard look and do what we can to control the Ph.D. program budget."

"Let's go with that approach," said the Department Chair, who thought it was probably the best he could hope for. "I know the Provost... er Interim President... is seeking a more substantial commitment, but it seems clear that we're not going to get there... and the discussion is too polarizing."

"Let's move on to the final matter, our use of lecturers. The Administration is asking that we each agree to a temporary increase in our teaching load by one course so that we can reduce reliance on lecturers. What are your thoughts about that?"

"Are you kidding?" Faquhir responded. "Lecturers are cheap. Is the University really suggesting that saving a few dollars on lecturers would get the School through its financial crisis...? What a joke! It's like the ship is going down, and May is trying to keep it afloat by asking everyone to hold their breath."

"Every little bit helps," said Koopman.

"Maybe it's okay with you, Reardon, since you're not so research-active anymore," Noach responded. "But, like we said earlier, the rest of us need to commit time to keeping up our research. Taking on extra teaching would cut into that time."

"Noach's right," said Larry Faquhir. "My contract with the University specifies my teaching load, and I see no good reason to allow the University to deviate from that. We do have provisions for overload teaching that we can each consider individually, but the compensation for overload teaching is quite a bit higher than what a lecturer gets paid for a course, so I don't see how that would benefit the University."

"Did you happen to ask Barron or Granville about extra teaching, Bob?" Noach asked the Department Chair.

"I did, and they both insisted on staying with the teaching loads promised in their contracts."

"No surprise there," Noach commented. "If the hand-picked candidates of the Administration aren't willing to take on extra teaching, then neither am I, and neither should the rest of us."

Looking around the room, the Chair summarized, "I don't see much support for the idea of our taking on extra teaching. I'll let May know that we will see if we can reduce our reliance on lecturers by cutting back on the number of course offerings, but that we don't think imposing extra teaching on core faculty would be healthy for the Department or good for our students."

Discussion in the meeting continued for another half hour, but without real substance. The meeting finally adjourned following a proposal from Prof. Stewart for a fence-mending happy hour at the Tilted Kilt.

***

Dan Edwards arrived first to the pub and ordered two pitchers anticipating arrival of the others. He was in a bit of a hurry but did not want to miss out on the postmortem from the earlier meeting.

Next to arrive was Prof. Kaur, and gradually the others drifted in. They all seemed to be holding off on discussing the issue that was top of mind to them. "While we're waiting for the others," Kaur began, "I'd be interested to hear your take on special accommodations and how you're dealing with them."

Larry Faquhir arrived and overheard the query. "Are you talking about things like student requests for extra time on exams, distraction-free environments, or ADA accessible presentation materials?" he asked.

"I am," Kaur responded. "At first there were almost no requests for extra time, and I could handle the few that arose fairly easily by administering the exams separately in my office. But lately, it seems that the numbers have been increasing. Last spring, it seemed like almost half of my class was asking for extra time."

"Mine, too," said Koopman, joining the discussion. "What's going on with that? Are all those students really needing extra time?"

"Well, it's so easy to get approved for it if you know the right people," commented Kaur. "All you need is something from a doctor saying you need it."

"That's right," Faquhir agreed. "And even though we know some of the requests are fraudulent, we can't do anything to challenge them. We just have to accept and accommodate."

"Yeah, but how am I supposed to accommodate such requests from such a large fraction of my students? The University seems to be putting it all on us to find solutions."

"Are you guys kvetching about that mishegas accommodation policy?" Jaime Noach joined the group. "It drives me crazy.... If it gets worse, I think I might plotz."

"I have no idea what you just said, Jamie," Edwards remarked.

"It's all schmegegge!" Noach responded.

"Not helping, Jamie," said Edwards.

"It's all bullshit!" Noach explained

"Oh, codswallop. I agree," Edwards responded.

"Apparently, the hop juice is working."

"Now I'm the one who's confused," laughed Noach.

"Very funny, you guys," Kaur interjected. "But can we get back on topic? What are we supposed to do about all of these fake requests for accommodations? I think it's mainly the rich kids who are able to come up with the unwarranted doctor's excuses."

"So, we're supposed to ignore the requests if they come from wealthy students?" Prof. Stewart chided.

"Well, you can see the problem and you can see that it's getting worse," Faquhir joined in as he refilled his pint. "Once students started getting special accommodation, other students felt they were being disadvantaged. So, if they could find a way, they would get an accommodation, as well."

"And why not do that?" asked Stewart rhetorically. "Other than some inconvenience for them, there's virtually no cost. It doesn't show up in the course grade or on the transcript that they were given an accommodation. So for those who don't really deserve it, it seems to me that it's nothing more than sanctioned cheating."

"Yeah, and we seem to be complicit," Faquhir commented. "We're effectively misrepresenting the student's capabilities to prospective employers…. It makes me very uncomfortable."

"Well, there is an alternative view," Stewart responded. "If the purpose of a college education is to foster a well-educated society and not just to help prepare students for employment, then maybe the accommodations are warranted."

"Are you sure you're in the right department, Nicole?" Faquhir chided. "This is the Economics Department. Maybe you were looking for Sociology."

Stewart ignored the jibe.

"Well, maybe we should just move to the logical conclusion of what's going on," Noach commented. "Eventually everyone finds a way to get an accommodation, so we just give everyone extra time.... We give 40 minute exams in our hour-long classes... everyone gets time-and-a-half."

"Somehow, I suspect that's not going to work," said Faquhir.

"Now that we're all here... except for our two new illustrious endowed chair holders and the assistants, that is, oh, and Cory... can we move on to what's really on all of our minds?" Edwards asked, feeling some time pressure and wanting to move the discussion along.

"What's that?" Kaur asked, facetiously.

"I'll answer that," said Noach. "This School's in deep shit. What are we going to do about it?"

"I don't see that there's much to do," Faquhir responded. "We didn't create the problem and we don't control very much, and I think we established fairly clearly in today's department meeting, that we're not inclined to make the extreme kinds of cuts that would be needed. I'm reasonably sure that similar discussions are taking place in other departments throughout the campus."

"I completely agree," said Noach. "It's like we're on a ship that's taking on water, and there is no way we can bail fast enough to keep it afloat."

"Well, if you think that's true, Jamie, how long do you think the School can hang on?" Stewart asked.

"I don't know," Noach responded. "We've seen other schools fail. Normally, they do so slowly... over decades. They overspend and draw down their endowments each year; they eventually start losing donor support and student quality starts to decline; but the faculty are unwilling to change from what they've always done or to give up on what they have been promised; the trustees are unwilling to make the hard choices required for survival and just hope for some magic donor to materialize and save them, which it almost never does; the presidents are unwilling to give up on their pet projects, and the administrative staff members just continue to perform their assigned tasks, never questioning whether what they're doing adds value."

"That sounds about right to me," Kaur joined in. "It's different for private universities than for corporations. Usually, a private university can survive for decades on its endowment. It takes a long time to bleed to death from a nosebleed. Usually corporations are different. They don't have big cash cushions to keep them going when they fail to respond to the pressures of competition. I think, given all that's happened this past year, Baird may be more like a corporation. The School took a big hit. I can't say whether future years will also be big hits, or just slow decline.... The only one of us who doesn't need to worry about this is you, Reardon. The rest of us need to begin thinking about our next moves."

"Well, on that note, I think it's time to order a couple more pitchers and see if we can ask the bartender to put on some upbeat music," said Faquhir.

"Not for me," Edwards said. "I need to get back to my office for a meeting with one of our Ph.D. students who's asking me to chair her dissertation committee."

As he left the Tilted Kilt, the others followed his departure with knowing gazes.

THE END

The author is currently a Professor of Finance at the University of California Riverside, where he holds the Philip L. Boyd Chair. He has previously taught and served on the faculties of an array of public and private universities, including: Arizona State University (Tempe), Case Western Reserve University (Cleveland), Chapman University (Orange, CA), Claremont Graduate University (Claremont, CA), Kobe University (Kobe, Japan), Universidad de Anahuac (Mexico City), the University of California Irvine (Irvine, CA), the University of California Los Angeles (Los Angeles , CA), and the University of Oregon (Eugene, OR). He is author of four academic books on entrepreneurial finance and over 50 articles in academic journals. *Within the Ivory Tower* is his only work of fiction. He and his spouse reside in Park City and Saint George, Utah. Their two daughters and their families live in Oakland, California and Salt Lake City, Utah.